Novels of the 1740s

Novels
of the 1740s

Jerry C. Beasley

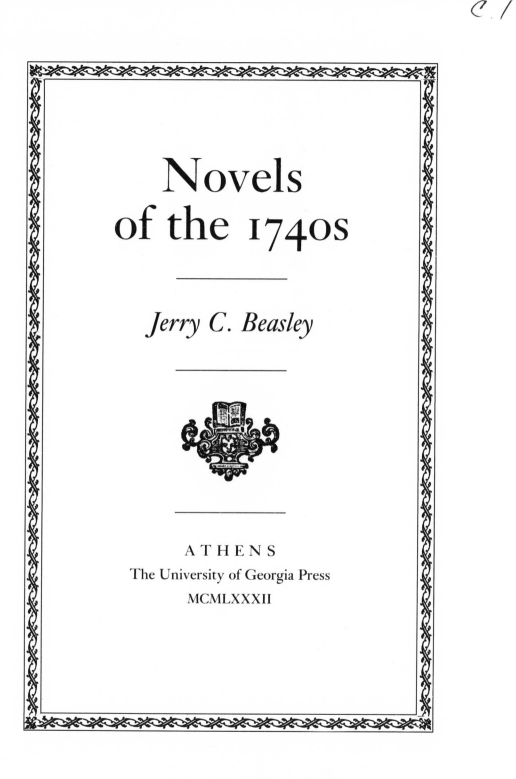

ATHENS
The University of Georgia Press
MCMLXXXII

Copyright © 1982 by the University of Georgia Press
Athens, Georgia 30602

All rights reserved

Set in 10/13 Mergenthaler Janson
Designed by Francisca Vassy
Printed in the United States of America

Library of Congress Cataloging in Publication Data

Beasley, Jerry C.
  Novels of the 1740s.
  Includes index.
  1. English fiction—18th century—History and
criticism. I. Title.
PR851.B4   1982   823'.5'09   81–10390
ISBN 0–8203–0590–1   AACR2

The publication of this work was made possible in
part through a grant from the National Endowment
for the Humanities, a federal agency whose mission is
to award grants to support education, scholarship,
media programming, libraries, and museums in order
to bring the results of cultural activities to the general
public.

to the memory of
Nell

Contents

Acknowledgments

T HIS STUDY HAS BEEN many years in the making. I am
sure it is a better book than it might have been, because the passage of time has allowed it to profit from the thoughtful criticisms
of many of my friends and colleagues. To Robert D. Mayo, who suggested the idea to me while I was still a graduate student at Northwestern
University and who has generously encouraged and advised me during all
the years since, I owe a debt of gratitude that is greater than I know how
to pay except by continually reminding him of it. Martin C. Battestin
read a draft of the manuscript with amazing perceptiveness and care; the
final version is significantly different and significantly better as a result of
his attention to a good many blunders and stylistic lapses. I deeply appreciate his encouragement, his criticism, and his kindness. Edward H. Ro-
senberry and Donald C. Mell, my friends and colleagues at the University
of Delaware, gave of their time to read my work in various stages of completion; their enthusiasm for the subject emboldened me at some crucial
moments. I am especially thankful to Donald Mell, whose thoughtful suggestions saved me from many an embarrassing awkwardness of style. I
also want to mention gratefully two scholars who, as pioneers in fields
closely related to my own, stimulated my interest and determination by
showing me through their example how a study like the one I wanted to
undertake ought to be done, and by helping to convince me that it was
worth doing. That my book was ever written at all is owing in part to the
appearance of William Park's two seminal articles, "Fielding *and* Richardson," *PMLA* 81 (1966): 381–88 and "What Was New about the 'New Species of Writing'?" *Studies in the Novel* 2 (1970): 112–30, and John J. Richetti's fine book-length study, *Popular Fiction before Richardson* (Oxford:

ix

Clarendon Press, 1969). The debts I owe to other scholars are less specific, though great indeed. Many of them are acknowledged in the notes accompanying the text, but another book of mine, a bibliography of scholarship entitled *English Fiction, 1660–1800: A Guide to Information Sources* (Detroit: Gale, 1978), much more completely reflects the various obligations I have incurred while working on the present study. I only wish it were possible to pay each of these debts here, in this preface.

My work on this book has been assisted by a grant from the National Endowment for the Humanities, for whose generosity I am extremely grateful. I am thankful as well to the editors of *Studies in the Novel*, who allowed me to adapt for use an article published in the pages of their number for the summer of 1973. Chapter two originally appeared, in somewhat different form, in *Studies in English Literature: 1500–1900* 16 (1976): 437–50 and is reprinted here by the kind permission of the editors. No study of the sort I have undertaken could ever be completed without the help of those unsung heroes and heroines of scholarly endeavor, the librarians. I have received much kind and patient assistance over the years, and I wish to mention with special gratitude the librarians and staff members of the Newberry Library, the British Library, and the libraries of the University of Illinois, the University of Pennsylvania, the University of Delaware, Harvard University, and Yale University. Lori Henderson cheerfully lent her able hand to assist with the typing of the manuscript, the preparation of which proceeded under the expert guidance of my wife, Rita. I am most grateful of all to my family, for their confidence and their forbearance. I think they probably know by now, even better than I do, what George Orwell meant when he said somewhere that writing a book is like enduring "a long bout of some painful illness."

Preface

D URING THE YEARS between 1740 and 1749 the English
novel as we know it today was born and nurtured through its
infancy. This was the important decade when Samuel Richardson, Henry Fielding, and Tobias Smollett made their sudden appearance
as novelists of the first rank. So great and concentrated a burst of artistic
energy as occurred at this time is rare indeed in literary history, and therefore extremely interesting. One thinks immediately of the few years just
around the turn of the seventeenth century, and the splendid dramatic
triumphs of Shakespeare and his talented contemporaries; of the brief but
brilliant flowering of romantic poetry following the publication of *Lyrical
Ballads* at the very end of the eighteenth century; of the decade of the
1840s, when Dickens reached his maturity and when Thackeray, the
Brontës, and Elizabeth Gaskell stunned the English literary world with
their simultaneous arrival upon the scene as novelists of superb talent and
striking originality. That study of such a period may profit all who are
interested in it has already been demonstrated by Kathleen Tillotson in
her fine book, *Novels of the Eighteen-Forties* (Oxford: Clarendon Press,
1954). I confess that my own book is to a great extent inspired by Profes-
sor Tillotson's. My method and approach are very different from hers, as
indeed they must be, but I have tried to illuminate the 1740s in much the
same manner as *Novels of the Eighteen-Forties* cast new light on the fiction
of the later decade. My immodest hope is that a variety of readers, from
the beginner in the field to the practicing scholar, will find in my study
something of the same kind of value that serious students have been discovering in Mrs. Tillotson's book for the last quarter century.

Nowadays, the six major works of fiction produced in the 1740s by

Richardson, Fielding, and Smollett are generally the only ones remembered, although historians of the novel do occasionally mention the names of Sarah Fielding, Eliza Haywood, and Mary Collyer. Actually, of course, *Pamela, Joseph Andrews, Jonathan Wild, Clarissa, Roderick Random*, and *Tom Jones* came out simultaneously with a great crowd of lesser works, of a remarkable variety. Most of these forgotten books are worthless, and deservedly neglected. Yet studying them can tell us a good deal about how the major novels came to be what they were—about the themes, conventions, and methods exploited by the great novelists of the period, all of whom claimed to be original writers of deliberately innovative kinds of stories. Equally important, we may discover much about the literary climate into which Richardson, Fielding, and Smollett sent their new novels with such high hopes of success as they all three expressed.

Altogether, some three hundred works of fiction were published between 1740 and 1749. This total includes, besides the major novels and other new English fiction, an impressive number of foreign works in translation and a great many native stories reprinted from earlier years. At first glance, the lawless variety of all this fiction may confuse the casual observer. Few works frankly identified themselves as invented tales. Most writers, reacting to contemporary prejudices against fictitious narrative, offered their books as true stories, and doubtless many are only marginal works of the imagination. Of course, these purportedly truthful tales were competing for readers with avowedly invented novels and romances, and on some of the same grounds. That is, they supplied the same satisfactions as "story," only under different names. My approach to the amorphous bulk of narrative literature published in the 1740s may seem a little arbitrary, for I have grouped individual works according to general kinds. It was necessary to reduce the decade's great volume of fiction to intelligible terms. Admittedly, every so-called form or type of fiction included ingredients from other types, and no category can be altogether coherent. The reading audience itself was anything but homogeneous, and most writers had little respect for literary kinds. Therefore the boundaries separating the various modes of storytelling I have identified remain somewhat vague. In the course of my discussions I have tried to take account of the many ambiguities, and my categories are, I believe, flexible enough to accommodate them. All of the prevailing narrative modes were, of course, the result of historical process, and in dealing with them I have naturally given some attention to works published during the several decades prior to the appearance of *Pamela*.

The approach by types, or narrative forms, has many real advantages, for it helps to illuminate the most important contemporary interests reflected in the works of popular fiction writers. The novels of Richardson, Fielding, and Smollett reflect those same interests, and in some of the same ways, though with much greater ingenuity and originality. In the chapters that follow, I have tried to place these major works in the clearest and most intelligible relation to the other narratives published in the 1740s. Chapter One offers a discussion of the broad contexts in which all of the decade's fiction was produced. In these pages I have reviewed the relevant background in politics, social history, and literary criticism. The purpose of this preliminary overview is deliberately limited. I have not tried to break much new ground, nor have I made any effort to enumerate all of the decade's important preoccupations, literary or otherwise. Rather, I have attempted to bring into sharp focus those matters most crucial to our understanding of the novels.

Succeeding chapters take up the various modes of storytelling popular in the decade, culminating in a discussion of the unique contribution of Henry Fielding as the writer who most vigorously and most convincingly affirmed both the newness and the value of the novel as a form of imaginative literature. I have not sought to provide a systematic bibliographical record of the fiction of the 1740s. For that kind of information the reader should consult my *Check List of Prose Fiction Published in England, 1740–1749* (Charlottesville: University Press of Virginia, 1972). Neither have I dealt with all of the novels I know about, although they have all contributed to my understanding of the decade and its fiction. Instead, I have selected representative works of each kind for discussion in some depth.

The first such discussion treats the kinds of romances current in the decade, and demonstrates how the major novelists adapted conventions of these forms. The spirit of the age did not favor romance; "pure" romance had virtually ceased to attract English readers by 1740, and the various types of romantic fiction—heroic, didactic, and oriental—that survived all employed a strategy of topical reference to familiar issues and events. In their general retreat from romance in the 1740s, readers and writers alike displayed an increasing interest in history and biography, and in three related chapters I have studied the several important ways in which fiction served that interest. Secret histories (or *chroniques scandaleuses*) and spy stories deliberately posed as contemporary history. Meanwhile an astonishing variety of memoirs, lives, adventures, and voyages offered themselves as historical or biographical accounts of familiar characters whose experience, whether in the public or private spheres of life, reflected important cultural ideals of the period. All three major novelists thought of themselves as historical writers, or what we might call moral historians. Their work relates importantly, and in some very specific ways, to the decade's lesser achievements in the area of fictionalized history and biography. *Joseph Andrews* and *Tom Jones* are both imaginary histories of quite ordinary people elevated to the status of great Christian heroes; *Jonathan Wild* and *Roderick Random* are ingenious adaptations from the mode of rogue biography; *Pamela* and *Clarissa* are best understood, in contemporary terms at least, as confessional records of spiritual life possessing some of the attractions of devotional literature. I have deliberately placed these novels against the background of the kinds of minor writing whose conventions they most conspicuously exploited so as to demonstrate their contemporaneity and to show how alert and serious their authors were as they went about the business of fashioning daring and original new works from familiar materials.

A sixth chapter takes up a heterogeneous class of admittedly fictitious narratives that may be called novelistic. The stories of Richardson, Fielding, and Smollett, of course, belong to this class. The origins of the contemporary novel lay in venerable Continental forms, but in the 1740s the label *novel* itself really meant only that a work was avowedly invented, that it professed not to be a romance, that it very likely tried to tell a story of common life, and that its focus was probably on a love affair of some kind. A great many works avoided calling themselves novels, possibly to escape the stigma attached to the name, though this could not always have been the only reason. The typical novelistic story is actually a synthesis of conventions from many modes of popular narrative, some of them factual or pseudofactual. Authors themselves tended to be somewhat apologetic about the fictitious nature of what they had written. Most often, while aligning their novelistic tales with one or more of the fashionable modes of history or biographical writing, they justified their own invention on the grounds of some homiletic purpose. Richardson followed this practice in the 1740s, and indeed very nearly excluded himself from the ranks of novelistic writers by posing so seriously and—in *Pamela*, at least—with such conviction as the editor of collections of letters. Smollett was less oblique in *Roderick Random*. And Henry Fielding, in his festive comic fictions, boldly proclaimed the nobility of the storyteller's calling and the artfulness of his own elaborate designs.

The concluding chapter on Fielding is intended to suggest that by 1749 the English novel had progressed past a milestone in the course of its history. Fielding's celebration of prose fiction as a form of art in *Joseph Andrews*, and even more deliberately and conspicuously in *Tom Jones*, was a momentous gesture provoked in part by Richardson's more cautious circumstantial manner, and it represented a great step forward from the surreptitious fiction of *Pamela*, published only a few years before, at the beginning of the decade of the 1740s. This is not to say that the one writer must be ranked over the other in some hierarchy of early English story-tellers. Richardson, Fielding, and Smollett as well were all great novelists of huge talent but different sensibilities, and it is one of those truly lucky accidents of literary history that they all commenced writing at virtually the same time. Their interactions with one another as contemporaries and rivals surely affected the content and form of their own works in many ways, thereby hastening the transformation of the novel itself from the amorphous thing it was when they began their careers into the shape or shapes we now recognize as the foundation of modern English and American fiction.

The interactions of these major novelists with the lesser writers of their day were hardly less important, as the following pages attempt to show. Seen from the vantage point of historical perspective, the major and minor novels of the 1740s may be said to provide each other with a mutual frame of reference. They really constitute a single body of work, but their vast differences in quality separate them into two distinct classes of achievement, the one class helping to illuminate and define the other. With the inescapable fact of this mutuality and reciprocity in mind, I have made it part of my purpose to try to respond to all the novels of the decade, and particularly those by Richardson, Fielding, and Smollett, as many of their first readers would have done—although I have, unlike those readers, enjoyed the benefits of modern scholarship and the distance of more than two hundred years.

It should be said that I have felt no need in this study to supply a comprehensive account of contemporary reactions to the novels of Richardson, Fielding, and Smollett; that work has already been done admirably by biographers and literary historians. And I have deliberately overlooked aspects of the major novels that might be expected to engage the attention of a twentieth-century critic. Such oversights are the price one pays for the indulgence of a particular point of view, and are by no means intended to imply a devaluation of the kinds of things that have interested others who have written on the novelists with whom I am concerned. I have learned from them all. My aim, however, has inevitably led me to observations that may not always square with some of the commonplaces of recent formalist criticism. Such criticism has its own kind of real value, but its criteria for study and judgment do not regularly take into account the contemporaneity of the works and what that can tell us about the nature of, and the reasons for, their excellence. I might say of my own purpose what Kathleen Tillotson said of hers in the preface to *Novels of the Eighteen-Forties:* "I have wished to make clear the main centres of interest" revealed by the major novels, and likewise "the quality of the art which created them."

A Note on Texts

IN QUOTING from the minor novels studied, I have (unless otherwise indicated) always used the first edition. For the major novelists I have used the modern editions best combining the attractions of excellence and availability, as follows. The edition of *Pamela* by T. C. Duncan Eaves and Ben D. Kimpel (Boston: Houghton Mifflin, 1971) is the most reliable we have, while the four-volume Everyman's Library *Clarissa* (London: J. M. Dent, 1962), though not so reliable, is as good as any. References to *Pamela* cite page numbers, and for *Clarissa* I have given both volume and page numbers. The Wesleyan Edition of Fielding (Middletown, Conn.: Wesleyan University Press, 1967–), still in progress, provides the best texts of *Joseph Andrews* and *Tom Jones*, both edited by Martin C. Battestin; of the *Miscellanies*, volume 1, edited by Henry Knight Miller; and of *The Jacobite's Journal and Related Writings*, edited by William B. Coley. Otherwise I have turned to the Henley Edition (London: Heinemann, 1903). References to *Joseph Andrews*, *Tom Jones*, and *Jonathan Wild* cite book and chapter numbers only. Since the new standard edition of *The Works of Tobias Smollett*, edited by O. M. Brack, Jr., et al. (University of Delaware Press) is not yet in print, I have used the excellent recent edition of *Roderick Random* published by Paul-Gabriel Boucé in the series of Oxford English Novels (Oxford: Oxford University Press, 1979). Reference is to chapter numbers.

CHAPTER I

Fiction in the 1740s:
Backgrounds, Topics, Strategies

I am à novelist. And being a novelist, I consider myself superior to the saint, the scientist, the philosopher, and the poet. . . . The novel is the one bright book of life.

D. H. LAWRENCE[1]

BY THE TIME D. H. Lawrence began to write in the early years of the present century, the novel was well established as a dominant form of literary expression. But its beginnings, two hundred years before, were humble indeed. Saints were perhaps suspect among Englishmen in those days long ago, but a majority of people at least publicly regarded the scientist, the philosopher, and most of all the poet, as manifestly superior to the lowly writer of fiction. Among elite readers the literary climate discouraged recognition of imaginative prose narrative as a legitimate form. Among others, a Puritan heritage worked with equal force. Pious Dissenters characteristically viewed the writer of nonallegorical fiction as the purveyor of the untrue and the frivolous; to these readers the very term *fiction* usually meant "lie," in the fullest pejorative sense, and for a work to be publicly described as a romance or a novel typically carried a stigma if not an outright condemnation. Indeed, in this period English fiction had virtually no status at all, popular though it became with contemporary readers. The situation would not improve significantly for many years—not, in fact, until the emergence of Jane Austen and Walter Scott.

During the earlier decades of the eighteenth century, the problem of public acceptance faced by the aspiring writer of fiction was truly a formidable one. In an age still under the powerful influence of Locke, Descartes, Newton, and the seventeenth-century Puritan apologists, an age which placed so much intellectual and moral emphasis on the value of empirically verifiable "truth," fiction was "false."[2] In an atmosphere charged with the presence of the great Augustans Pope and Swift, fiction rested on no solid and respectable foundations of quality, literary tradition, or critical theory. Even quite able works by avowed novelists like Jane Barker, Penelope Aubin, and Mary Davys suffered from lack of recognition of their real though limited worth. Only two years after the publication of *Tom Jones* an important admirer of Fielding, the novelist Francis Coventry, severely blamed the class of literati and certain aristocratic dilettantes for the hollow contempt with which prose fiction was characteristically treated. Coventry sneered at the "pride and pedantry of learned men, who are willing to monopolize reading themselves, and therefore fastidiously decry all books that are on a level with common understandings, as empty, trifling, and impertinent." And he despised as "some of the greatest triflers of the times" those "beaux, rakes, *petit-maîtres*, and fine ladies, whose lives are spent in doing the things which novels record," but whose professed disdain for the fiction they so avidly read was no less forward than that of the puritanical or the genuinely learned.[3] Coventry's burst of anger expresses his very acute sense of the low estate of the novel in his day.

Much of the English fiction published in the first two quarters of the eighteenth century was, it must be said, tenth-rate pulp, artistically depraved and morally shallow. It is the stuff of history's dustbin, and it richly deserved the scorn or contemptuous neglect with which almost all popular fiction was alternately treated. Many contemporary booksellers—Edmund Curll is only the most notorious example—were easily as cynical as the most opportunistic modern publisher of formula romances and shoddy self-help manuals, and they were therefore eager to offer anything that would sell, without regard to quality.[4] Neither they nor the many drudges they hired to scribble for them seem to have been greatly discouraged by the public reputation of prose fiction, although the fact that works of fiction were held in such low esteem surely affected the attitudes of those who invented them, and ultimately the tendencies of the works themselves. Few fiction writers, it is clear, paid much attention to the small community of literary elite. Interested primarily in the marketplace, they were content to exploit what they and their booksellers judged to be the tastes of a heterogeneous popular audience that included, besides a newly leisured and educated group of middle-class readers, a goodly number of barely literate members of the lower classes. Many of these latter were domestics who, like Pamela Andrews, had learned to read in the households they served.

Samuel Richardson, Henry Fielding, and Tobias Smollett, when they arrived almost simultaneously on the scene as the first great novelists in the English language, took their places as writers whose achievement made them stand out from the crowd of their lesser contemporaries. But they addressed in part this same uncultivated audience, and they surely did so quite deliberately. Nothing could be plainer from the phenomenal sale of their novels,[5] and from their purposeful attention to the modes, conventions, and subjects of all kinds of popular fiction. Of course, these three novelists were also serious artists anxious about literary quality, and intent upon establishing prose fiction as a respectable mode of imaginative writing. By the sheer force of their achievement Richardson, Fielding, and Smollett won applause from such eminent readers as Pope, Lyttelton, and Warburton, but they nonetheless contended with prejudices about as strongly opposed to popular prose fiction as they were strongly in favor of entrenched forms in the drama and satiric poetry.

In the 1740s the literary establishment's most characteristic response to contemporary fiction was one of silent neglect. Ralph Griffiths's *Monthly Review* was not founded until 1749, and the *Critical* did not follow until 1756. Serious literary-political organs like the *Universal Spectator* (1728–46), the *Craftsman* (1726–47), and *Common Sense* (1737–43) paid little attention to works of mere entertainment. The *Gentleman's*, *London*, and *Scots* magazines all published monthly registers of new books, it is true, and these often included works of fiction. But such listings were almost always devoid of comment, and the registrars of new books often seemed at a loss as to what to do with fiction. They frequently did not distinguish it from other types of writing, and sometimes even when they did, they carelessly consigned it to categories headed "Entertainment" or "Miscellaneous." Occasionally, for the diversion of their audience, magazines like the *Gentleman's* offered brief tales or extracts from popular works of fiction. One periodical, Eliza Haywood's *Female Spectator*, was almost wholly devoted to fiction. But this practice by no means implied critical acknowledgment or respect, nor was it very widespread at this time. Even as entertainment, the novel had not yet made its big burst into the magazines.[6]

So lightly was the new form considered in contemporary periodicals of all kinds that the major novels of Richardson, Fielding, and Smollett inspired only a small handful of serious critical discussions of any notable length or significance. The remarks of one "Publicus," writing in the January 1743 number of the *London Magazine*, typify the prevailing attitude of journalistic critics to fiction in general and the "novel" in particular. It is interesting that "Publicus's" concern over the artistic depravity of most fiction derives from his awareness of its potential as a didactic instrument. His essay, which is entitled "Some General Advice for the Advantage of the Fair Sex" (12:32–34), begins with an invidious comparison between poetry and fiction, and then proceeds to argue that

> *Novels* are either exceedingly useful or dangerous, according to the Nature of their Composition: For the Reader, under the Notion of Entertainment, comes open and unguarded to them; our good Humor disposes us to be affected; and Love and Pity, the tenderest of all the Passions, being the only ones that are generally addressed to in these Performances, the Impression strikes deeply, and has a lasting good or bad Influence upon the Mind and Temper, in Proportion as the Images are more or less pure and just. So obvious a Consideration as this is, should, I think, have deterr'd these Writers from varying in the least Degree from Probability, human Nature, and moral Tendency, the Standard they ought to propose to themselves; but, so far from this, we find them, on the contrary, abound with the Marvellous and Incredible, . . . with false Conceptions and loose Images, that are fit for nothing but to pervert the Judgment and inflame the Passions. (p. 33)

In addition to the real liabilities mentioned by "Publicus," prose fiction suffered further from its reputation as an upstart genre. Before Fielding wrote his preface to *Joseph Andrews* (1742), no one had seriously attempted to place native fiction in any tradition, much less to defend it with classical associations.[7] Prose fiction, that literary foundling, was also ill-bred and undisciplined. Popular storytellers wrote in lawless variety, with no articulated distinctions among the modes of narrative in which they practiced. Theoretical statements discussing the nature and objectives of prose fiction had always been scarce outside prefaces attached to the works themselves, where, typically, authors of small talent and less critical acumen revealed only their lack of sensitivity to formal principles of literary composition. Most fiction writers, of course, had to pursue the main chance, and so the only thing to do was to write as many books as they could, as fast as possible. The environment of Grub Street did not encourage even gifted technicians like Eliza Haywood to be especially concerned about the quality of what they wrote, much less about such rarified matters as the subtleties of critical theory, or the poetics of prose fiction.[8] It is not surprising, then, that the English fiction writers who were at work in the early years of the eighteenth century showed so little serious interest in the rich possibilities of narrative art. It is obvious from his works that Defoe cared about such things, as did Richardson, Fielding, and Smollett. These novelists are the striking exceptions in the period, and since Richardson alone among them avoided the grime of Grub Street, one wonders how they managed it—through some rare combination of talent, sensibility, and artistic integrity, perhaps.

The comments of "Publicus" notwithstanding, most fiction writers, in composing the obligatory prefaces to their stories, occupied themselves almost solely with hackneyed justification of their work on moral grounds and with simplistic defenses of its fidelity to life and human nature. These preoccupations, which date from the seventeenth century, arose from the need of fiction writers to accommodate a variety of contemporary biases—social, literary, intellectual, and religious. Declarations of truthfulness are as ancient as Greek fiction, and they abound in the old chivalric romances and the Italian novella, but they really began to prevail in English fiction about the time of Bunyan.[9] The pressures exerted by received opinion drove many eighteenth-century writers, like Defoe and Richardson, to declare that their invented narratives were the records of actual persons and events. Others, bold enough to admit that they wrote fiction, protested that their works imitated or accorded with a higher reality and thus were morally and intellectually acceptable. This mimetic posture, insofar

5

as it was literary, developed largely from a reaction to popular romance. In 1702 Tom Brown, in the important preface to his *Lindamira*, set down one of the best early statements of a mimetic theory of fiction writing, in the process sneering at the extravagances of romance:

> If the Histories of Foreign Amours and Scenes laid beyond the Seas, where unknown Customs bear the greatest Figure, have met with the Approbation of English Readers: 'tis presum'd, that Domestick Intrigues, manag'd according to the Humours of the Town, and the natural Temper of the Inhabitants of this our Island, will be at least equally grateful. But above all, the Weight of Truth, and the Importance of real Matter of Fact, ought to overballance the feign'd Adventures of a fabulous Knight-Errantry.

William Congreve had urged much this same attitude toward the virtues of "realistic" narrative in his more famous and influential preface to *Incognita* (1691). The mimetic defense of prose fiction as a mode for rendering the truth about life as it "is actually lived" became a common critical convention in subsequent years, figuring in dozens of succeeding prefaces and dedications by Delarivière Manley, Mary Davys, Eliza Haywood, Penelope Aubin, and a host of other minor fiction writers.

Claims of truth to life were, of course, usually only subterfuges. Works having very little to do with the close rendering of actuality routinely and quite soberly recommended themselves for their fidelity to a mimetic ideal. A little "novel" called *Injur'd Innocence; or, The Lives and Surprizing Adventures of Amicorus and Amicana. A True and Modern Story Wrote by a Friend* (1740) may serve as a case in point. "The Narrative," the anonymous author writes in his preface, "is real Truth, and as near as cou'd be, is literally express'd. . . . As the whole is real Truth, it ought not to be wrote in a Romantick Stile. And as it's a good Moral, it's thought most suitably express'd in a plain Narration of Facts." The work itself, which appeared (in an alleged second edition) almost simultaneously with *Pamela*, is a sentimental love story. Amicana, the heroine, is separated from her beloved hero by her forced marriage to a lecherous, jealous old beast. Amicorus himself, thinking Amicana dead, weds her best friend. At last, when both hero and heroine are freed by the deaths of their respective spouses, they are reunited to live happily ever after. The story, though certainly conventional, is remotely plausible, while the narration is low-keyed and "plain." But the characters are totally unblemished stereotypes, altogether unconvincing, and when they speak or write letters their rhetoric is as extravagant as that in any romance. It is clear from the claims made for *Injur'd Innocence*, and indeed from the comments in most prefaces to works of fiction published in the first four decades of the eighteenth century, that during this period the critical theory governing the relation between fiction and reality did not progress very far after Congreve and Brown.

Among many early mimetic apologies for fiction there actually emerges a double dimension. For some writers, "truth to life" meant only the reproduction of the surface of existence—the straightforward record of "facts," of events that really happened or could have happened. The author of *Lindamira* urges this first dimension. But for many writers, including Defoe and later Richardson, Fielding, and Samuel Johnson, "truth to life" also meant the evocation of a moral reality; that is, the circumstantial re-creation of the inherent structure of life, of which moral law is an essential part. *Robinson Crusoe*, as Defoe described it in the preface to the *Serious Reflections*, was both "allegorical" and "historical," the "beautiful representation of a life of unexampled misfortunes," written for the "common good of mankind."[10] This second dimension is most often only very superficially realized; rare indeed is the work like *Robinson Crusoe* or *Clarissa* that really comes to grips with the moral issues it professes to dramatize. Yet, concerned as they were to declare their fidelity to some kind of empirical reality, fiction writers were usually even more preoccupied in their prefaces with defending the ethical utility of their productions. The author of *Injur'd Innocence*, while arguing the circumstantial "truth" of his narrative, also claimed emphatically that it was written "to shew an excellent Patern, for the Young, and Inexperienc'd, to imitate. . . . And, I hope, we are not, never to be pleas'd with any Thing but gay Toys, airy Flights, and ludicrous Tales, but will sometimes admit of moral Entertainments." Throughout the greater part of the eighteenth century, most of those who pronounced upon the subject of prose narrative made truthfulness of representation the servant of morality. Dr. Johnson, in the famous *Rambler* No. 4 (March 31, 1750), lent his great authority to this emphasis. Most novelists before 1800 clothed themselves in the sober gar-

7

ments of didactic literature, and the claim of moral efficacy became a routine gesture in prefatory comments and final chapters.

Even John Cleland's pornographic *Fanny Hill* (1748–49) pretended to a
didactic purpose, while the anonymous author of *Leonora; or, Characters
Drawn from Real Life. A Novel* (1745) pressed the same moral claims for her
work as the author of *Clarissa* a year or two later, echoing perhaps the
preface to *Pamela* in her first sentence:

> If to convey Delight with Instruction is, or ought to be the
> grand Aim of all who write; 'tis hoped the Author of the fol-
> lowing Sheets has not entirely deviated from so excellent a
> Rule. . . . The chief Point in View has been to regulate the
> Conduct of her [the author's] own Sex, by guarding them
> against the treacherous ensnaring Arts of the other: At the
> same Time giving all such due Encouragement to true Merit
> in the latter, as may convince them she is an Enemy to none
> but the false, the vain, and the superficial.

Many prefaces were far more emphatic than this in their moral pretensions, but their writers all plucked the same strings. In the preface to the
first edition of *Pamela*, Richardson went into much greater detail, the note
of urgency was much more intense, and he adopted the strategy of having
several writers lend their voices in a kind of moral chorus; but the claims
he made for *Pamela* are not essentially different from those made for *Injur'd Innocence* or *Leonora*.

Only two imperatives, then, the ethical and the mimetic, are constants
in most commentary by early eighteenth-century fiction writers on their
own work. Thus lacking any kind of formal tradition or set of critical
foundations, the body of fictional literature that offered itself in 1740 was
a confused assortment of narratives rarely self-conscious as art and not
always even identifiable as fiction. Many works took elaborate steps to be
anything but what they were, disguising themselves as real histories and
biographies, voyages, and confidential reports on actual events in high
places or in foreign lands. There were a few heroic and didactic romances,
oriental tales, and collections of "novels" that frankly offered themselves
as fiction. But the prevailing kinds were scandal chronicles and spy narratives after the manner of Delarivière Manley's *New Atalantis* and Mar-

ana's *The Turkish Spy*, along with fictitious voyages, memoirs, and lives that sometimes may have had a basis in fact, but were really contrived to provide pleasures a later age would associate with imaginative works.

During the decade that followed, the great crowd of lesser novelists were quite content to follow in the footsteps of their predecessors, although the lines of demarcation separating the various kinds of fiction still remained very uncertain. With no formal tradition in prose fiction as an independent art, and no support from neoclassical critics, a general state of lawlessness inevitably prevailed. The buyers of fiction appear to have been as unsure of their tastes as the sellers themselves. Many works, disregarding the logic of established modes, combined the methods of quite different writers, possibly with a view to capturing the widest possible audience. Thus a spy-letter tale like Thomas Lediard's *The German Spy* (1738) borrowed machinery from imaginary voyages and freely employed magical elements from oriental romance in an otherwise circumstantial, pseudohistorical narrative. Similarly, Mrs. Haywood's exotic political satire *The Adventures of Eovaai* (1736) imported motifs from her earlier "novels" of amorous intrigue as aids in her assault on Sir Robert Walpole. The minor novelists of the new decade of the 1740s were similarly eclectic, as were their major contemporaries. But Richardson, Fielding, and Smollett capitalized upon the prevailing lawlessness and made it license for genuine experimentation. The combinations of forms they effected obviously resulted from serious and purposeful artistic choice instead of mere commercial opportunism, and this is one reason why we are justified in calling these writers great innovators.

Among the most important literary influences felt by virtually all fiction writers of the 1730s and 1740s we must count the imposing body of foreign fiction in translation. French and Spanish stories in particular were in great supply during the early years of the eighteenth century. There were no international copyright laws during this period. In the trade, works like *Paradise Lost* and *The Seasons* enjoyed the respect accorded all valuable literary property in the English line of succession. But Cervantes's *Don Quixote*, or Scarron's *Roman Comique*, or LeSage's *Gil Blas* were available to any predator willing to pay for a new translation. Booksellers found a particularly rich quarry in French fiction, translations from which continued to be an extremely important commodity throughout the century. The fact that competing translations were sometimes available at the same time indicates how keen the interest in French fiction actually was. The effect of this foreign competition on native fiction writers was surely portentous, although difficult to define. On the one hand, a ready supply of French novels helped to generate an English taste for fiction, and thus aided all novelists.[11] On the other hand, foreign fiction as a whole was technically more advanced than English; it appealed to a much broader range of cultivated tastes, and its superior sophistication, joined with its very great availability, no doubt discouraged booksellers from paying decent prices to native writers. Before the appearance of Richardson and Fielding, the presence of French fiction in the marketplace appears to have been more a depressant than a stimulant.

Unquestionably, the most important foreign work to be translated during this period was *Don Quixote*, whose fame exceeded that of any other single work of fiction, native or foreign. Between the years 1700 and 1750, Cervantes's masterpiece enjoyed as many as eighteen or nineteen editions, eight of them in the 1740s alone. *Don Quixote* is a crucially important work to any understanding of the age's tastes in fiction, as Henry Fielding must surely have known when he took Cervantes as his avowed model in *Joseph Andrews*. Like the comic work of LeSage and Scarron, Cervantes's great assault on the idealized nonsense of chivalric romance belongs to a large group of very successful works (not all of them translations) that may be described as antiromances, though they do differ from each other. In these fictions, most of them satirical, interest always centers on an antihero— an ordinary man or sometimes a rogue who passes through a real world of foolish, villainous, or otherwise imperfect people on a journey that is typically a parody of the heroic quest. This antihero embodies a reaction to the grand and lofty personages of heroic romance and epic. His own character is usually flawed in some way. He may be a naïf like the amiable gentleman Don Quixote, or a scheming, venal scavenger like the impoverished picaro Gil Blas, or even a consummate fool like Scarron's dilettantish, blustering lawyer Ragotin. He is always interesting in his own right, but the meaning of his comic adventures is characteristically defined through direct clashes between his antiheroic personality and an essentially hostile environment. He functions as a kind of moral barometer registering the folly, hypocrisy, vice, and cruelty he encounters in a world that is anything but remote or idealized. The kind of fantasy life provided by this familiar pattern of antiheroic experience was obviously powerful in its appeal to contemporary readers, if we judge from the number of works, both native and foreign, in which it is repeated.

❦❧❦

The extraordinary contemporary success of works like *Don Quixote* and *Gil Blas* in England is in fact one important demonstration of the character of the age itself. Few Englishmen conceived of themselves or their time as heroic. Accordingly, they came to reject heroic literature in favor of "familiar" narratives or, as we shall see later, in favor of romances that appealed primarily through a strategy of explicit reference to current issues and recognizable people. Apparently, what the average reader of the 1730s and 1740s really enjoyed was an entertaining, ethically authoritative literature that translated heroism into immediate contemporary terms or at least addressed itself to topical concerns—moral, social, political, religious—that were within the scope of his actual knowledge or interest. Readers of the age had, in fact, found new kinds of heroes in ordinary people like Robinson Crusoe and Clarissa Harlowe. By their moral strength and endurance, moreover, such figures fully exemplified the Christian heroism praised earlier in the homiletics of seventeenth-century latitudinarian divines like Isaac Barrow and John Tillotson, and in Sir Richard Steele's popular *The Christian Hero: An Argument Proving That No Principles but Those of Religion Are Sufficient to Make a Great Man* (1701).[12] The idea of the Christian hero was as old as the medieval romances of Chrétien de Troyes, and it had been importantly renewed in the seventeenth-century biblical epics by Milton and a number of popular French writers.[13] But the eighteenth-century conception of the Christian hero more completely rejected pagan warrior virtues and aristocratic values and substituted instead a new code of honor which, as Ian Watt describes it, is "internal, spiritual, and available without distinction of class or sex."[14] Christian heroism, as projected in narratives by Defoe, Richardson, Fielding, Smollett, and such lesser writers as Penelope Aubin and Sarah Fielding, constituted a new delineation of the ideals of the age; this kind of heroism represented an exalted state accessible to anyone, of whatever class or rank, who simply had the courage to embrace the Christian virtues of charity, humility, and chastity and to live a good life in a wicked, vexatious world.

The rewards that accrue to the Christian heroes and heroines of popular fiction are real and substantial, and they are often represented by happy marriage and retirement to a rural environment (sometimes an estate)—to a kind of Golden Age retreat of natural harmony and loving family life, as Fielding characterizes it in *Joseph Andrews*. The country retreat itself stands for a moral ideal which combines neoclassical versions of pastoral tradition, as found in Pope's *Windsor Forest* and Thomson's popular *Seasons*, with the idea of a restored paradise.[15] The Bedfordshire estate to which Pamela and Mr. B. retire after their marriage is clearly delineated as an Edenic paradise, a blissful place where the disharmonies and corruptions of the world of experience no longer threaten, and where peacefulness and contentment reign. In the real world, wrote Richardson to his friend Miss Highmore, a world hostile to goodness, "content is heroism."[16] For characters like Pamela Andrews, Roderick Random, Sir Charles Grandison, and a multitude of minor heroes and heroines, persistence in (or cultivation of) the Christian virtues leads to contentment, and in their stories the almost inevitable rural retirement, in its function as metaphor, defines a triumphant vision of the personal efficacy, the heroism of resolute goodness.

The applause which greeted ordinary characters like Pamela Andrews, Abraham Adams, David Simple, and Tom Jones may be at least partly explained in terms of their exemplary role as Christian heroes, although they are very different creations indeed. Of course, it is impossible to say with absolute precision what the preferences of the early eighteenth-century reading audience actually were; we know so very little about the readers themselves. The price of the typical work of fiction—about 2s. 6d. to 3s. per volume in the 1740s—tells us something about who bought the books, which were beyond the means of poorer laborers and craftsmen. The commonplace assumption that the middle classes made up the bulk of fiction's public is surely correct.[17] At any rate, judging from the works themselves, the members of the audience for fiction obviously wanted to read about people who were, or were fancied to be, rather like themselves: characters from more or less ordinary walks of life who, as Christian heroes, possessed (at least by the end of their stories) the virtues of charity, chastity, industry, and prudence; who were engaged in the business of domestic life, or (to some degree) in the great public events and controversies of the day, or in both.

※✕※

It appears that in the 1740s the surest way for an English fiction writer to win the attention of the public was to make his narrative as explicit in its reflections of familiar life as he could. "The proper study of mankind," said Pope, "is man," and storytellers and their readers seem to have agreed that the proper subject of popular narrative was man in the contemporary scene. The fiction of the 1740s, major and minor works alike, is deeply rooted in the pressing social issues of the decade, in its religious controversies, and, most important of all, in its politics.

Broadly understood, the political issues as projected are an articulation of old antagonisms going back at least to 1714, the date of the Hanoverian Accession and the year the Whigs began their long period of supremacy. The focus falls most often on the mightiest and most controversial Whig of all, Sir Robert Walpole, and on the two most dramatic political events of the decade, the downfall of Walpole himself (in 1742) and the unsuccessful but spectacular Jacobite rebellion of 1745–46. Walpole, surely one of the most capable leaders in the annals of English politics, was also one of the most shameless and corrupt. The self-styled Patriots of the Opposition both hated and distrusted him, as they showed in the pages of the *Craftsman, Common Sense,* and later Fielding's *Champion,* where they heaped mountains of invective upon him throughout the late 1720s and 1730s, and into the 1740s. Fiction writers entered the fray too, and the years of Walpole's reign of power produced literally dozens of stories attacking him, most often ferociously. Popular feeling on the subject of Walpole was intense; as Herbert M. Atherton has observed, he was at the very center of a "folklore" of contemporary politics.[18] The prime minister's long-awaited tumble from power was a momentous event, one in which not only the tireless Opposition but Englishmen of all classes and political persuasions could participate excitedly. Anti-Walpole journalism and early fictionalized attacks like the virulent *History of Benducar the Great* (1731), Mrs. Haywood's *Adventures of Eovaai* (1736), and *The Secret History of Mama Oella, Princess of Peru* (1733), had long since made the "Great

Man" into an almost archetypal figure of evil and corruption, preying on an innocent people.

In *Jonathan Wild*, Fielding put certain finishing touches on the portrait of Walpole as villain, and certainly this is the character drawn in the 1740s by all of the various works of minor fiction dealing with him, from the anonymous little secret history *A True and Impartial History of the Life and Adventures of Some-body* (1740) to George Lyttelton's brutal piece of orientalized invective, *The Court Secret* (1741). In this fiction, Walpole and the issues raised by his career are calculatedly magnified into simplified ethical abstractions embodied in exaggerated stereotypes like Lyttelton's consummately wicked vizier Behemoth. *The Court Secret* marks the rare appearance of a member of the literary establishment among the ranks of popular storytellers, and it is a work at once shrewd and crude. Lyttelton structures his tale around the portrayal of Walpole as a hideously bestial creature who, for his own ends, singlemindedly pursues a virtuous Patriot to the grave. In works like *The Court Secret*, both moral and political judgments are so immediately clear as to be transparent in their ideological appeal to established popular beliefs and prejudices. Simple narrative denunciations typically define a work's attitude toward its targets, and equally simple imperatives reveal a more desirable order. A similar method is usual in most prose fiction dealing with political issues, whether Walpole and his career, or Jacobite daydreams of a return of Stuart rule (there were a good many such works), or later the 'Forty-Five.

The Rebellion itself, with its tense drama and its decisive end on the bloody battlefield at Culloden Moor, was a stunning episode which electrified all England, and inevitably stirred up much activity in London printing houses. A multitude of pamphlets and news sheets exercised themselves over the twin dangers of Stuart rule and Catholic oppression. While Fielding's *True Patriot* (1745–46) and *Jacobite's Journal* (1747–48) successfully agitated readers over the invaders' real threat, a number of works of fiction, most of them vigorously anti-Catholic and anti-Jacobite, capitalized on the aura of romance that lay over the whole affair. Some of these, like M. Mitchell's *The Young Juba* (1748) and an anonymous secret history called *The Amours of Don Carlos* (1749), exploited the mysteries surrounding the glamorous, melancholy figure of Prince Charles Edward himself. Others, like Archibald Arbuthnot's *Memoirs of Jenny Cameron* (1746) and *Life of Simon, Lord Lovat* (1746), were lively but vicious assaults on the prince's Scottish allies, and were apparently devoted to celebrating an end to all the years of tension and anxiety the defeated cause had cost England and her Hanoverian rulers. The lingering excitement over the serious, controversial issues raised by the Rebellion doubtless supplies one explanation of why Fielding chose to synchronize with it Tom Jones's adventures on the road to London.

The third of the great controversial political issues of the 1740s, the long and agonizing War of the Austrian Succession, for some reason received very little notice in the decade's fiction. *Roderick Random*'s extended account of the disastrous expedition to Carthagena was an exception rather than the rule. But the policies of colonial and commercial imperialism that brought on the war found at least indirect expression in the many imaginary voyages that appeared. Probably the most rudimentary appeal of these works was to a taste for exciting "firsthand" tales of exploration, discovery, and bizarre adventures in remote parts of the world. The widespread belief that expansion was good for England's soul and pocketbook surely supported that taste, and helped the many voyage narratives to succeed in the marketplace.

If much of the new fiction published in the 1740s was intensely political, it was singularly unintellectual in character. Except in the area of religious controversy, it largely avoided participation in the important philosophical debates of the decade. It took no direct notice of Hume, for instance. The intellectual temper of the period seems to have exerted on most fiction an influence more general than specific; that is, while it did not stimulate serious philosophical argument in the form of stories, it did encourage narrative literature to take as its province the circumstances of daily life, as Ian Watt has shown in the early chapters of *The Rise of the Novel*. Religious concerns, however, did engage the minds of storytellers, although it would be inaccurate to describe the treatment of religion found in most popular narratives as anything resembling actual theological discourse. Current theological debate, in fact, was far too sophisticated to receive full airing in much of the minor fiction of the day. Few writers were interested in giving formal, cogent expression in story form to the arguments raging among physicotheologians, deists, and Anglican apologists;

probably still fewer would have been able to do so. Nevertheless, it is worth remembering that Matthew Tindal's formidable defense of deism, *Christianity as Old as Creation* (1731), was still very current in 1740, as was William Law's fervent response to Tindal, *The Case for Reason* (1731). Bishop Butler's *Analogy of Religion* (1736), and George Berkeley's *Alciphron* (1732) and *Syris* (1744), were widely praised as eloquent apologies for Anglican orthodoxy. What is interesting is that the debate as it continued seems to have left something of a vacuum. In the minds of many believers, the Church—even the Church as it was defended by the likes of Butler and Berkeley—had become the tool of secular interests and the bastion of rationalist theologians whose speculations had undermined its spiritual function. For large numbers of Christian worshippers, probably including many of those who read the day's fiction, the Church provided an inadequate outlet for religious expression—or no outlet at all. To fill this vacuum, of course, the very controversial Methodist movement arose in the 1730s. It was simply the fact of the void, and the theological hurricane it signaled, that probably engaged the attention of most common men and women.

Considering these eddies and crosscurrents, it is not surprising that fiction of all kinds should have frequently addressed itself to religious questions. The major novelists, of course, and particularly Fielding, approached religious issues on a rather high plane of sophistication, though they did not engage in theological debate. In narratives like John Kirkby's utopian physicotheological fantasy, *The Capacity and Extent of the Human Understanding* (1745), or the antideistic, pseudooriental *Memoirs of the Nutrebian Court* (1747), or Mary Collyer's deistic epistolary novel, *Felicia to Charlotte* (1744–49), most of these same issues received exactly the kind of popularized treatment readers apparently wanted. Surprisingly, the Methodists get very little notice in the fiction of the 1740s, though Fielding, in a number of places in his novels, eagerly attacks George Whitefield's brand of "enthusiastic" Methodism. In *Tom Jones*, Thwackum's perfervid doctrine of grace smacks of Whitefield, although his leanings in this direction are qualified by his equally fanatical allegiance to the Established Church. The most telling of this novel's blows against the Methodists is struck when Blifil, that paradigm of sneaking hypocrisy, turns Methodist at the end of the story. Aside from Fielding's sneers in *Tom Jones*, in *Shamela*, and briefly in *Joseph Andrews* (1.17), this extraordinary religious movement is all but ignored in the decade's novels. But the spirit that actually supported the popularity of John Wesley emerges frequently. Richardson, Sarah Fielding, Charlotte McCarthy, and a large number of other writers produced stories characterized by a conspicuous and fervent piety. Most of these pious works, including Richardson's, show no direct interest in religious controversy. Instead, they concentrate on the more pressing question of future rewards and punishments, and they turn upon what is essentially a social problem, the prevention of the soul's corruption in this life.

Most fiction writers of the 1740s, whether truly pious or not, at least pretended to be serious moralists. There was much in contemporary life to agitate them. The arrogance and promiscuity of fashionable society loomed large as a problem, while crime was rampant in the streets of London and the judiciary and police were incompetent or unwilling to deal with it constructively.[19] The problem of crime was magnified by widespread abject poverty, as M. Dorothy George and J. H. Plumb have shown[20]—Defoe's famous injunction, "Give me not poverty, lest I steal"[21] was no less timely in 1740 than in the earlier years of the century. Corrupt "trading justices," and penal regulations which gave preference to the wealthy while they persecuted the poor, made the legal system discriminatory as well as inept. Meanwhile, the Whig policy of laissez-faire, which failed to provide for adequate government oversight of the internal economic life of the nation, tacitly encouraged all manner of businessmen—shopkeepers, tailors, landlords, shipowners, and merchants—to exploit both laborer and consumer. Lawyers and physicians, their activities ungoverned by laws or professional codes of ethics, were notoriously untrustworthy.[22] The clergy itself, as Fielding was so well aware, often proved guilty of greed, hypocrisy, and other behavior unbecoming to the cloth.

Anyone who has read Smollett or Fielding knows that most of these problems engaged the interest of the major novelists of the 1740s. They are likewise reflected in the lesser fiction of the decade. In most narratives of this general period, the teeming realities of actual daily life were in one way or another accommodated to a moralizing impulse. A majority of storytellers, in other words, joined the mimetic and ethical imperatives they followed in a single didactic purpose. The fictional representation of Christian heroism typically details the experience of an isolated moral agent pitted against the follies and villainies of the contemporary environment. In this kind of context, what Ian Watt has recognized as the age's intense preoccupation with individualism takes on an added dimension. The Christian hero or heroine—Tom Jones, Clarissa, Roderick Random, Charlotte McCarthy's Emelia, the heroines of Penelope Aubin—often stands as an individual rather violently (and sometimes literally) separated from the world and made terribly lonely by the very fact of his or her moral worth. Isolation as a consequence of goodness only underscores the reader's sense of the character's heroism. Such characters may be flawed, in need of self-knowledge or "true wisdom," in Fielding's phrase, but the novelist's most severe judgments are reserved for the world's dark hostilities to their virtue. Sometimes, of course, as instanced in the many stories of criminals and other rogues, the situation is reversed and society itself becomes the victim of evil rather than its perpetrator. But in these works the moral issues are essentially the same as those on which the actual stories of Christian heroism center. In most of the period's fiction, Christian goodness, whether it is the direct focus of dramatic attention or not, is tested severely and then reaffirmed in a triumphant ending.

The role of Providence frequently is conspicuous in these narratives, a very great many of which purposefully counter the moral darkness revealed to empirical observation with a bright faith in providential interposition to secure the happiness of the good. The conventional happy ending works as expression of an implied higher reality which transcends the empirical reality of the beleaguered hero's experience. Usually such affirmation is achieved through the author's benevolent manipulation of the fictional world, and with considerable regularity this manipulation is explicitly characterized as divine intervention. Maneuverings of this kind may actually reflect the private beliefs of the authors, though as often as not they seem gratuitous, a matter of romantic convention. Occasionally, as in the works of Defoe, Fielding, Smollett, or even Charlotte McCarthy or Mary Collyer, benevolent manipulation by providential action becomes a crucial and quite integral part of the overall design of the narrative. Martin C. Battestin's controversial argument that some early eighteenth-century writers tried to form their own created worlds with the grand example of the divinely ordered "Book of Creation" in mind receives important support from the example of a great many popular storytellers.[23] Certainly, very few minor novelists took their works seriously enough to conceive of them as in any way analogous to some universal ordering principle. Nevertheless their repeated displays of the kind of deliberately providential plot design which rewards goodness and punishes wickedness provides at least indirect evidence of how really widespread was the contemporary understanding of the formally didactic function of art that Battestin has described.

Despite the intensity of the various problems of early eighteenth-century life that so deeply engaged the moral attention of its fiction writers, there were certainly many other and more positive features of the contemporary social scene. The doctrine of benevolence bequeathed by Shaftesbury and the seventeenth-century latitudinarian divines urged a kind of meliorism which resulted in such humane projects as the establishment of Captain Coram's Foundling Hospital for orphaned or abandoned children, General Oglethorpe's prison reforms, and the passage of Insolvency Acts designed to relieve the miseries of certain classes of debtors.[24] These and similar accomplishments represented real though modest improvements in the social welfare of the English people. The melioristic impulse which produced them seems to have derived from a distinctively (though not exclusively) middle-class interest in relieving suffering and removing temptations, especially those posed by poverty, so as to make it easier for people to be good. Fielding's friend Ralph Allen of Bath is only the most famous example of the self-made man turned benevolist, and his concern, like that of his fictional counterpart Squire Allworthy in *Tom Jones*, was that Christian virtue should be encouraged, and that the world should be made less hostile to it.[25]

At the risk of an annoying repetition, it must be emphasized that a substantial majority of the works of fiction published in the 1740s deal directly and even obsessively with the abiding question of how to be good in a world of real evils, or how to be a Christian hero. And in so doing they frequently reflect what was the central social conflict of the period: namely, the tension between a degenerate aristocracy, with its traditional license, and the middle classes themselves, with their new wealth, their social consciousness, and their sober Puritan morality.[26] This was an age whose didacticism was paradoxically countered by its promiscuity, and one in which a principle of social and economic aggression was in rather violent contention with a set of attitudes involving sentimental social benevolence and notions of sexual modesty and purity. These broad issues, as treated in the fiction of the 1740s, often reduce to a matter of rhetorical strategy: a spotless heroine is relentlessly pursued by a libertine male who is usually of a higher social rank, which frees him from conventional restrictions on social and sexual behavior.[27] The many variations upon this pattern only confirm its real importance. A fable of beleaguered virtue, it seems, even when rendered in terms of the simple moral imperatives typifying most of the decade's fiction, had a contemporary relevance that may escape us today. The author of *Leonora* certainly spoke directly to audience preoccupations when she wrote that her "chief Point in View" was to "regulate the Conduct of her own Sex, by guarding them against the treacherous ensnaring Arts of the other."

In the fiction of the 1740s the topics and strategies I have been discussing occur with insistent regularity in narratives of all kinds. Obviously, the storyteller's surest path to success lay in the exploration of the widest possible variety of contemporary interests. Among many writers and readers alike, the preoccupation with topical appeal seems to have diverted attention away from a concern with prose narrative as art, just as surely as did the prevailing attitude toward fiction as frivolous and "untrue." On the other hand, the responses by authors to the immediate interests of their audience inevitably brought fiction closer to the texture of real life than it had typically been in an earlier day. The various masks of truthfulness worn by so many storytellers over the years, although they constituted a literal denial of fiction as art, had enabled it to function in an atmosphere generally hostile to imaginative prose narrative. Prior to the great excitement generated by the publication of *Pamela* and *Joseph Andrews*, it was the exploration of fiction's various incognito forms as vehicles for the entertaining and instructive portrayal of familiar people and contemporary affairs that probably did most to gain it credibility and swell its audience. Meanwhile, the lawless conditions that prevailed in the marketplace unquestionably did their part to inhibit the production of native fiction of real distinction, as did the deplorable conditions under which most novelists had to work. In the long run, however, the lawlessness may have been beneficial. The situation was fluid, not frozen; experimentation was most certainly possible. The boundaries limiting the storyteller's energy and imagination really were determined only by what would succeed commercially. Within these boundaries a serious writer of great talent and a lively sense of the immediate scenes of life might work with considerable freedom and good fortune, as the simultaneous arrival of Richardson, Fielding, and Smollett in the 1740s proved conclusively.

These great novelists, different as they are, were surely enjoyed for many of the same reasons that their lesser contemporaries earned the favor of the public. Their works are in every important sense products of all the circumstances described in the preceding pages, circumstances which they reflect as clearly as any story by the most obscure hack, but with much greater originality. It is the imaginative intensity of their fresh approach to familiar materials that distinguishes Richardson, Fielding, and Smollett from the background against which they wrote and that justifies the attention they have received ever since their novels first began to appear. Their immense popularity in their day suggests that even less sophisticated readers appreciated their worth and seriousness. Meanwhile the fresh and venturesome adaptations of available narrative forms so visible in their stories, their convincing moral earnestness, their obvious craftsmanship and critical sensitivity—in Fielding's case the public proclamation of prose fiction as art—addressed cultivated tastes and certified that the novel was on the threshold of its future as a major new form of literature.

Without the benefit of historical perspective, few people of their own time could have fully realized the momentous importance of what Richardson, Fielding, and Smollett accomplished as innovators, though it is of no small interest that the clever novelist and critic Francis Coventry did not wait long to publish a pamphlet called *An Essay on the New Species of Writing Founded by Mr. Fielding* (1751). At the end of the decade of the 1740s most prose fiction was about as amorphous and commonplace in form and quality as it had been at the beginning, before the sudden appearance of Richardson's triumphant story of *Pamela*. This work, and the other great novels that followed it in such rapid succession, must have struck most people simply as amazing departures from what they had been accustomed to reading. But we are able to see now what those early readers could not have perceived: that during the critical ten years between 1740 and 1749 the course of the novel's development in England was irrevocably changed by three popular writers, whose half-dozen books showed in unprecedented ways what rich possibilities of expression lay open to gifted storytellers of fertile invention and genuine artistic integrity.

CHAPTER II

Romance and the "New" Novels of Richardson, Fielding, and Smollett

I N ENGLAND in the 1740s, most forms of prose romance enjoyed only a very dubious reputation. No one was any longer writing heroic romance of the kind popularized in the seventeenth century by La Calprenède, the Scudérys, and their numerous English imitators. Thomas Simon Gueulette's several vulgar imitations of the delightful oriental fantasies of Antoine Galland (*Arabian Nights*) and Pétis de la Croix (*Turkish Tales* and *Persian Tales*) were declining in public acceptance, although their fine originals were to remain extremely popular throughout the rest of the century. Fénelon's didactic romance of *Télémaque* (1699–1700) still had many readers, if the number of editions—five—in the decade is any indication, but native writers displayed little interest in developing this mode in new works of their own. The English reading public had not totally renounced romance, which was destined to enjoy an enthusiastic revival in some new forms during later decades. But for the moment, readers were more interested in works by Cervantes, LeSage, and Defoe, and they were greatly excited by the new novels of Richardson, Fielding, and Smollett. Interestingly enough, most of the avowed romances published in the 1740s were political fables and satires which actually reinforced fashionable hostilities toward romance. That is to say, despite their unbelievably valiant heroes, astonishing coincidences, and generally exotic dress these works seem to have concentrated less on the "marvellous" than on the topical. In some surprising ways, their claim on the public's attention coincided with and perhaps reinforced the claim laid by the works of the decade's major novelists, who were always topical and relevant but who certainly did not altogether exclude romance conventions from their fiction.

Heroic and Didactic Romance

Heroic romance, to be precise, may be described as dead in the decade inaugurated by *Pamela*, as far as new editions and translations are concerned. The 1730s had witnessed new folio editions of two seventeenth-century French originals in translation, La Calprenède's celebrated *Cléopâtre* and *Cassandre*, along with half a dozen or so French and English adaptations of more recent vintage.[1] None of the Gallic romances reappeared in the new decade, and of the eighteenth-century English adaptations only one was reprinted, an anonymous piece called *Celenia; or, The History of Hyempsal, King of Numidia* (1735–36).[2]

The early French examples of the type, and their many seventeenth-century English imitations, certainly offered little to attract an English audience in the 1740s. They were founded on the conventions of old chivalric romances like Don Quixote's favorite, *Amadis of Gaul*, and they had modified these conventions to place an emphasis not just on virtuous love and courageous conduct in battle, but on exalted aristocratic notions of morality and social behavior made fashionable in the salons of the *précieuses*. Basically discursive and structureless, they typically ran to many volumes. The usual skeletal story of suprahuman love and adventure was set in a remote, vaguely delineated classical (or sometimes oriental) locale, and punctuated with endless, pompous conversations and lengthy intercalated *histoires* exploring a variety of polite subjects from sentimental love to ethical philosophy, religion, history, and literature.

Adaptations like *Celenia* were much more in tune with contemporary needs. Like most recent romances of its kind, *Celenia* compresses its story within the space of two volumes instead of the three or eight or occasionally twelve required by the original models. Moreover, it translates the idealized salon morality of the French romances into contemporary terms. In his prefatory declaration that the work is fiction, the author cautiously justifies it on moral grounds, claiming that ten books like his own would be "more tolerable in a Christian Country, than one pretended true History, however solemnly introduced, whose Scope is, either by downright Forgeries, or misrepresented Facts, to poison the Principles, and misguide the Judgment of the Reader and to make Evil Good, and Good, Evil."

Doubtless *Celenia's* pointed moralism helped it to achieve a certain *réclame*, despite the fact that in almost every technical respect it is only the confused foreshortening of a typical seventeenth-century French romance. Furthermore, its strident Tory-Jacobite polemics against powerful ministers (meaning Sir Robert Walpole) and republican politicians (meaning the Whigs) gave it a topical immediacy; in revised and expanded form it reappeared twice (in 1740 and 1742) during the eve of Walpole's downfall.[3] The story of its various beleaguered heroic stereotypes seeks to demonstrate ideologically that the Tory-Jacobite cause must, by virtue of its own rightness and the Whigs' (and Walpole's) wrongness, win out in the end. Surely it is to the timeliness of this ideological appeal, and not to the book's generic affiliations or its interest as story (it has almost none), that we must attribute the considerable success *Celenia* enjoyed, though we have no perfect idea who its readers actually were.

In many respects the small heroic romance of *Celenia* closely resembles a related kind of early fiction, the didactic romance. Both of these types of avowedly invented narrative exploit unashamedly the chivalric conventions of noble action and inflated sentiments. The major difference between the two, and a primary reason why the didactic romance enjoyed an open respect often denied by large segments of the early eighteenth-century reading audience to other kinds of imaginative prose narrative, lies in the different degree to which they emphasize a moral function. The early heroic romances, at least, usually exalt the interest in the fable (and its discursive embellishments) over the claims of moral efficacy. Their didactic cousins, on the other hand, follow Boileau's famous pronouncements upon the moral function of epic, and seem to take quite literally Le Bossu's argument, in book one of his *Treatise of the Epick Poem* (1675), that the epic fable must be designed with a view to "the Instruction, and the point of Morality, which is to serve as its Foundation."[4] These didactic romances typically sacrifice narrative values to moral purpose. Specifically, they usually advance rationalist principles of ethics, theology, and politics as solutions to the problems encountered by a hero whose character is actually established as a suprahuman *beau ideal*. Apparently, their ideological appeal compensated adequately for the diminution of story interest. At any rate, didactic romances were in demand, though always in limited numbers, throughout the first four decades of the eighteenth century.

The most popular of all the didactic romances, and indeed the progenitor of the type, was Archbishop Fénelon's *Télémaque*, which enjoyed twenty or more English editions between 1700 and 1739. *Télémaque* set out to be a new kind of epic, as Fielding acknowledged in the preface to *Joseph Andrews*, offering in prose narrative a series of episodes allegedly omitted from Homer's *Odyssey*. Probably the most important reason for the work's continued popularity, besides its moralism, was the directness of its address to some of the pressing political and intellectual questions that occupied virtually all contemporary Englishmen.[5] The earliest readers were likely attracted by Fénelon's criticisms of the bellicosity and extravagance of Louis XIV's reign, criticisms which applied equally to the career of Louis XV. The archbishop's attacks on the French king, together with his quietist interpretation of Catholic theology and his implied assault on the Jesuits who dominated Versailles, held an inherent appeal for Englishmen who perpetually feared and mistrusted both France and the Roman Church. In a more positive vein, the humane and enlightened principles of government and individual conduct espoused by *Télémaque* conformed with much that was current in English philosophy and political thought. By means of the relatively simple device of tracing the virtuous Telemachus's difficult search for his father, Fénelon provided occasion for the display of some rather liberal-minded ideals characterized by a calm philosophic rationalism.

The extremely complicated plot of *Télémaque* does not require summary here. It is enough to point out that as Telemachus and his faithful tutor Mentor (an embodiment of the goddess Athena) pass through the many lands lying in their pathway—some of them, like the island of the lusty Calypso, as unreal or enchanted as any in Homer—the reader's attention is always focused on the lesson that the prince himself is learning. The lesson is that aggressive evil and carnal temptation wait around every corner; that in all of man's affairs prudence and reason must govern passion, and that man's public affairs are best conducted by kings whose control over their personal lives and over their foreign and domestic policies make them trustworthy servants not only of their own countries, but of all mankind. The central episodes concerning the newly founded city of Salente (books 8–17) are most crucial in this connection. While Telemachus is away on some heroic missions, Mentor instructs the city's ruler in a philosophy of government which virtually excludes the possibility of official corruption and unscrupulous ministers, and which thus protects the welfare and liberties of the citizenry. The story as a whole exalts the individual man as the author of his own rectitude and teaches the humane doctrines of benevolence and honesty, moderation and modesty in public and private conduct. Furthermore, the book boldly advocates policies of free enterprise and broad religious tolerance. These positions were anathema to the French regime the author once served, but they accorded with English moral philosophy and with the most popular policies of the Whigs. Fénelon's formal political views, as expressed in his romance, also paralleled jealously guarded postrevolutionary British ideals of a benevolent patriarchal government by consent. The government of the new city of Salente, as organized by Mentor, surely held attractions for all readers, of whatever class or political persuasion, who feared arbitrary power and disapproved of the methods of Sir Robert Walpole. Blessed with a wise and selfless monarch, unthreatened by ruthless ministers, and free from legislative factionism, Mentor's Salente is a utopian realization of the Lockean political ideals upon which the Whigs had supposedly founded their principles and policies of government. It was these ideals that, in the minds of many, Walpole (and George II) had overturned.

Despite an anachronistic indulgence in the *merveilleux* far exceeding even the improbabilities of the heroic romance, *Télémaque* (and similar didactic romances) had much to offer an English audience otherwise hostile to invented narrative and especially to frankly romantic fiction. Fénelon's popular work never generated many recognizable English imitations.[6] But over the years a number of Continental didactic romances, all of them close (and most of them avowed) imitations of Fénelon, did enjoy English versions. Some of these were moderately successful, and Andrew Ramsay's *Travels of Cyrus* (1727), a work which found its classical source in Xenophon's *Cyropaedia*, achieved a very considerable popularity. Ramsay was an expatriate Scot, the French-speaking tutor to the Stuart Pretender's children. His romance is much less gracefully done than *Télémaque*, but some seven English editions had appeared by 1745. Perhaps interest in the book was fanned by constant rumors portending a Jacobite uprising to be led probably by one of Ramsay's pupils, Prince Charles Edward Stuart.

Besides the works by Fénelon and Ramsay, the most popular didactic romance in the second quarter of the century was a translation of Bishop

Juan de Palafox y Mendoza's *El Pastor de noche buena* (1659). Long popular all over Europe, *El Pastor* was first translated from the Spanish into English in 1735 (with a subsequent Dublin edition in 1745, and many others thereafter), and given the title *The New Odyssey, by the Spanish Homer: Being the Travels of the Christian Hero, Ulysses Desiderius Pius, throughout the Universe*. Palafox's romance is a disjointed quietist fable. The central character, who is nameless in the narrative though not on the English title page, is a devout Christian to whose disembodied soul is exhibited a progression of instructive tableaux. In the preface to *Télémaque*, Fénelon had praised *The New Odyssey* highly, and had even identified it as one of his own models. The English translator, in an obvious ploy aimed at capitalizing on the popularity of *Télémaque* itself, did not fail to remind English readers of Fénelon's endorsement. *The New Odyssey*, says its title page, has been "vastly Recommended, as an inimitable Masterpiece of that fine Visionary and Allegorical Manner of Writing, by the late Archbishop of Cambray." But Palafox's narrative comes even closer to being Bunyanesque allegory, and it probably appealed directly to pious readers, whose education in devotion always included *Pilgrim's Progress*. *The New Odyssey* is pure spiritual fantasy. Its story is told by a worldly curate who, in an intense reverie one Christmas Eve, envisions himself set down before the infant Jesus and blinded by the radiant light from the manger. This affliction can be cured, so one of the attendant angels tells him, only by a spiritual pilgrimage to "those holy regions, where is to be seen the divine palace of that Princess, whom we intitle, The Science of Salvation, in which all the virtues reside." The Pastor is then led on a journey which is actually a course of study in the "Science of Salvation," and at its end he is no longer blinded by the Savior's radiance or the world's disguises.

Palafox's romance is charmingly couched in subdued tones, but it is in fact an aggressively polemical work conceived as a kind of *vade mecum* for novitiate Catholic priests and as an assault on the Jesuits, from whose hysterical antagonism the saintly bishop suffered throughout most of his career. The work's oblique attack on the most fanatical of Catholics may help to account for the reception it had in an England that was tense over the Roman murmurings of the most zealous and conservative Jacobites. *The New Odyssey*, of course, is also a story of personal salvation. Yet, despite the otherworldliness of its hero's visionary experience, its focus turns ultimately upon the way redemption may be put to use in this world.

Through the instruction offered to the Pastor, the narrative teaches how one may lead an exemplary life; how, by living the Christian virtues, the individual man may overcome the world's wickedness and preserve his moral integrity. In other words, Palafox's Pastor actually learns how to be a Christian hero. This, indeed, is what all of the heroes of early didactic romance become. The popularity of prose tales like those of Palafox and Fénelon surely helped to create and sustain a literary atmosphere receptive to other, less pretentious fictions of a Christian character. The shadow of *Télémaque* looms over pious narratives like the Rev. Philip Doddridge's *Some Remarkable Passages in the Life of the Honourable Col. James Gardiner* (1747). Moreover, because their works were avowed fictions, Palafox and Fénelon set an imposing precedent for writers like Penelope Aubin, the pious author of a number of early homiletic "novels" which set out to exemplify in tales of love and adventure the heroics of Christian virtue. It was not a very long step from the Christian heroines and heroes of Mrs. Aubin's fiction to those of Richardson, or even those of Fielding and Smollett.

⁂

Oriental Romance

Orientalism in European romance is at least as old as the Scudérys' *Le Grand Cyrus* (1649–53). In eighteenth-century England, however, a new and separate vogue for exotic tales of Eastern lands developed, principally under the impetus of Antoine Galland's *Arabian Nights* and Pétis de la Croix's *Turkish Tales* and *Persian Tales*.[7] These works were rendered into many European languages, and they generated a large number of imitations. Most of the imitations are inferior, but together with a numerous progeny of orientalized political fables and satires, they and their originals had many readers in England as well as France. This rather amorphous group of oriental tales and partisan allegories never moved into the mainstream of English fiction, but the significant numbers in which they appeared over the first half of the eighteenth century reflect a striking, if naive, contemporary fascination with Eastern history and customs, even when used as a thin cloak for discussions of contemporary issues.

The tales collected by Galland and Pétis de la Croix, are, of course, the purest fantasy. Directly adapted from genuine Middle Eastern popular literature and oral tradition, they are replete with authentic exotica, magic, metempsychosis, miraculous exploits, and the loves and intrigues of incredibly noble and evil characters. Nothing is based on real experience; even the frame tales are highly implausible. Each work employs a lone storyteller, like Galland's Scheherezade, who is required to spend countless hours, days, or nights beguiling a listener or listeners with a vast assortment of improvised narratives which, in fact, only the genius of a whole culture could produce. These fantasies, especially those of the *Arabian Nights*, are intensely imagined and unpretentiously narrated. Their richly human and yet lawless qualities as daydream help to explain their very warm reception among all kinds of English readers in an age of reason. Few of the tales are didactic, while many are mildly erotic. These qualities, it is true, may have given pause to pious readers, who would also be alienated by the Eastern doctrines of kismet and metempsychosis. However, the general tendency of these works is far from immoral or dissolute. Practically every story pits innocence against the villainies of consummately wicked viziers, lecherous sultans, scheming eunuchs, nomadic bandits, and so on. Many of the tales are love stories in which a luscious maiden becomes the symbol of goodness, threatened by masculine depravity or, sometimes, by an ambitious female who has renounced the "feminine" virtues and whose lust for power or sexual fulfillment makes her dangerous to everyone in her path. The tales of Galland and Pétis de la Croix, then, are even in eighteenth-century terms potentially moral fables. Addison saw them in this light, and further judged that a pleasing orientalism might be useful as the sugar coating on a moral or philosophic pill. He and his collaborators quickly put it to good use in some of the apologues and moral fables that appeared in the Spectatorial papers.[8] Meanwhile, the easy adaptability of oriental exoticism to purposes of moralized politics made it a popular feature of such partisan journals as the *Craftsman* (1726–47), to which Bolingbroke, Dr. Arbuthnot, Swift, and probably Pope frequently contributed.[9]

Most English fiction in the oriental mode is short. Neither the great popularity of Galland and Pétis de la Croix nor the sanctions of English periodical writers inspired more than a few full-length native works in the oriental vein during the first five decades of the eighteenth century.[10] And actually, after the *Arabian Nights* and the *Turkish Tales* and *Persian Tales*, most new collections of oriental fiction presented to English readers came from across the Channel, where the idea of the East was gradually extended to include Egypt, China, and distant exotic countries like Peru. In the 1730s and 1740s, the principal purveyor of oriental imitations was Thomas Simon Gueulette (1690–1766), a respected attorney and French political figure who also fancied himself an author. Gueulette's knowledge of the East was only tenuous, but he nevertheless turned out four popular collections of oriental tales between 1715 and 1733.[11] These efforts are all shamelessly derivative. They imitate the structure, the narrative conventions, and the oriental color and machinery of Galland and Pétis de la Croix, consciously departing from their models only in their more cautious eroticism and their unfounded prefatory claims of moral utility.

Gueulette was actually a clever vulgarizer of oriental romance, and in *The Oriental Tale in England in the Eighteenth Century* Martha Pike Conant accuses him of being everywhere extravagant in "the use of magic, fantastic in description and incident," and of "employing European legends freely and oriental colouring very slightly, sometimes moralizing, sometimes coarse, seldom satirical, imitating the faults rather than the excellences of genuine oriental translations" (p. 36). Given Conant's archetypal expectations of the oriental mode, this is all true, but apparently Gueulette's French and English readers entertained very different feelings. In the 1730s and 1740s Gueulette's works achieved a collective success exceeding that of any other variety of romance. In fact, the popularity of his oriental tales was almost unchallenged in England before 1745, the date of the last edition of any of his works for a number of years. About this time his vogue was decisively threatened by the Comte de Caylus. Interest in Gueulette would revive later; all of his stories would be included in Harrison's *Novelist's Magazine* (1780–89). But Caylus's clever *Oriental Tales*, as mocking parodies of Gueulette's romances, were somewhat more appealing to readers. They were not the first satires of their kind, but in succeeding years Caylus enjoyed a success approaching that of Gueulette himself.[12]

At least one extended native piece of new oriental fiction appeared during the 1740s, an anonymous narrative called *Memoirs of the Nutrebian Court* (1747). This long work departs from the example of Galland, Pétis de la Croix, and Gueulette by expanding the conventional frame-tale into a fully developed romantic story line, to which it gives its chief attention. It does interpolate a great number of brief stories, however, and otherwise demonstrates its derivative character by its pseudoexoticism and its fantastic flights into magic and mystery; one of its principal characters is a transmigrated butterfly named Papaglia, who appears as a sprite in miniature human shape. The *Memoirs'* apparent purpose is to provide a vehicle for its Tory author's glorification of the Jacobite cause, and for his simple-minded attacks on George II, the Whig oligarchy, and eighteenth-century English deists. It seems strange that in 1747, the year following the Stuart disaster at Culloden, any English fiction writer could have seriously engaged in an argument for so deflated a cause as Jacobitism.[13] An earlier and much more popular pro-Jacobite tale was Eliza Haywood's *The Unfortunate Princess; or, The Ambitious Statesman*. Originally published in 1736 as *The Adventures of Eovaai*, and reissued in 1741 under the altered title, this narrative is a full-fledged political romance. It is just as immoderate in its use of magic and mystery as the *Memoirs of the Nutrebian Court*, and even more relentless in its pursuit of a story line involving a kind of political allegory. But *Eovaai* aligns itself with the cause of the Patriot Opposition and takes direct aim at one man: Sir Robert Walpole, the infamous Ochihatou of the story. To exoticism Mrs. Haywood adds an eroticism designed to titillate susceptible readers and to defile her villain, who is cast as a hideous lecher assaulting the precious virtue of the maiden princess Eovaai, and hence the whole moral order.

In many respects *Eovaai* resembles the work of Claude-Prosper Jolyot de Crébillon, the most gifted and prolific, most elegantly venomous among a rather large number of orientalizing French romancers whose efforts had crossed the Channel in recent years. Mrs. Haywood may have consciously copied the manner of the Frenchman; in any case she followed a formula similar to his, adapting it to English politics and the moral preoccupations of English readers. Crébillon *fils's* orientalism, like Mrs. Haywood's, is always only tenuous, but it served his purpose of attacking the moral depravity of the courts of Louis XIV and Louis XV. In his exotic tales, which are also more than mildly erotic, the "prehistoric" kingdoms and Eastern personages, even the architecture of the palaces, all too closely resemble Versailles to pass for what they pretend to be. Crébillon obviously made no attempt to create a self-contained Eastern setting and fable that would possess the same intrinsic attractions as the authentic tales of Galland or Pétis de la Croix. On the contrary, he clearly employed oriental settings to afford greater freedom to his erotic fancy and to provide a certain distance from which to deal his blows of satire and personal vilification. One of his earliest and most popular works, a licentious piece called *Tanzai et Neaderné: Histoire japonaise* (1734), so slandered the French monarchy and the powerful Jesuits that the author was thrown into prison. In 1740 he published *Le Sopha*, an open, scurrilously brutal assault on the debased morality of the ruling echelons of French politics and society. This tale makes mere animal lust the symptom of a weak mind and a dull spirit, and nothing could be clearer than the political and personal implications of the empty-headed, lecherous behavior of the Sultan of the story, an indictment of Louis XV as a bored, debauched, inept monarch. *Tanzai et Neaderné* and *Le Sopha* both captured the attention of English readers in the 1740s, as did several other orientalized political fables by Crébillon *fils*. The topical value of these works surely provided one of their principal attractions for Englishmen alarmed over the spreading War of the Austrian Succession, in which the chief enemy was France. Joined with this appeal was the moral tendency of the stories, which righteously attack Louis and his court. Crébillon *fils*'s treatment of Louis could only have confirmed what Englishmen already believed, namely, that the French king was a base creature, who for the satisfaction of his own rapacious appetites preyed on innocent people and nations. Probably it was the overt moralizing and its political ramifications which made it possible for Crébillon's licentious tales to succeed with those many English readers who placed such a heavy emphasis on Puritan standards in sexual behavior. In these narratives the pornographic episodes, which must have appealed to the underside of Puritan morality, consistently work in support of a moral cause.

In his small book called *The Court Secret: A Melancholy Truth*, Fielding's friend George Lyttelton shrewdly adapted the methods of Crébillon *fils* and Mrs. Haywood as he launched an extremely vicious attack on Sir Robert Walpole. *The Court Secret* was printed in 1741, 1742, and 1743, and its popularity was well deserved, for it is one of the most skillful of the orientalized political fables. Lyttelton's work depicts Walpole as a self-seeking vizier named Behemoth who drives a gentle, virtuous man named Achmet to his grave. At the very outset, the narrative sets forth the beastly attributes of the despicable vizier: "—The Hog of *Noah* was not more sensual, *Eve's* Peacock more gaudy, or *Solomon's* Horse more proud; no Fox was more subtle, no Wolf more voracious, no Dog more fawning, no Hare more timorous, and no Cat more desperate." Driven (we are told) by inner fears of failure and loss, Behemoth has but one object: to perpetuate and increase his ill-gotten power by any means. Achmet challenges him on the grounds of political chicanery, fiscal corruption, and complicity with a hostile foreign nation; Behemoth destroys this good man in self-defense, tricking him into treason and finally suicide. *The Court Secret* perpetrates the most shameless kind of propagandistic satire: it capitalizes on all of Walpole's alleged failings, and viciously distorts recent events in order to support its slanderous thrusts. The historical record shows that the Earl of Scarborough, a onetime ally of Walpole who had begun to frequent Opposition assemblies, did take his own life in 1734, some years before the publication of Lyttelton's book. But there is no evidence that Walpole persecuted him, as Lyttelton charges, or that he tricked him into a treason that precipitated suicide. *The Court Secret*, then, is not a "melancholy truth," but an orientalized political myth about an obscure figure who is depicted as a paragon in the moral order that his persecutor schemes to destroy.

The Court Secret functions as romance in only a limited way. Like the other orientalized political fables, it lays claim to the notice of the public by addressing topical issues quite deliberately, thus directing attention to contemporary life and away from its own remote settings and fantastic occurrences. With the exception of Gueulette's exotic fantasies, the other kinds of romance I have described worked to similar effects. So far as this function is concerned, the appeal of such works coincided with the appeal of the "new species of writing" offered so successfully in the 1740s by Richardson, Fielding, and Smollett, whose own tendency in the direction of antiromance was surely encouraged by the general climate.

※≫≪※

Romance and the Major Novelists

All three of the major novelists of the 1740s characterized their works as antiromances of some sort, although in very different ways.[14] Richardson saw *Pamela* as the kind of new work that might neutralize the "pomp and parade of romance-writing."[15] He may have idealized his virtuous heroine, but he endowed her with a distinctive, sensitive personality that is finely delineated in the dramatic record of her experience. Later, in the preface to *Clarissa*, Richardson very carefully reminded his readers that in offering his heroine as "an exemplar to her sex," it was imperative she be "not in all respects a perfect character"; for it was "not only natural, but it was necessary, that she should have some faults. . . . To have been impeccable, must have . . . carried our idea of her from woman to angel" (1.14). Fielding, in his theoretical statements, stressed the comic qualities of his own works, and made Cervantes his acknowledged model. His mock-epic flourishes and his focus on ordinary people and contemporary affairs constituted a strong reaction to heroic romance.[16] He was emphatic on the desirability of mixed characters; the prefatory chapter to book ten of *Tom Jones* argues that in fiction nothing can be more convincing or "of more moral Use" than little "Imperfections" of character, since "such form a Kind of Surprize, more apt to affect and dwell upon our Minds . . . ; and when we find such Vices attended with their evil Consequence to our favourite Characters, we are not only taught to shun them for our own Sake, but to hate them for the Mischiefs they have already brought on those we love." Fielding is just as urgent on the question of believability in the fable as a whole. The introductory chapters to books seven, eight, nine, and seventeen of *Tom Jones* address this question directly. The introduction to book eight, for example, sneers at "that Species of Writing which is called the Marvellous," and then rules that every writer should keep "within the Bounds of Possibility." But Fielding's narrator goes on: "Nor is Possibility alone sufficient to justify us, we must keep likewise within the Rules of Probability."

Smollett made the most sustained attacks on romance of all three major novelists. The preface to *Roderick Random* indicts romance as the opiate of foolish minds. Its origins are identical with those of epic and tragedy, Smollett observes, but "when the minds of men were debauched by the imposition of priest-craft to the most absurd pitch of credulity; the authors of romance arose, and losing sight of probability, filled their performances with the most monstrous hyperboles." In the same preface, Smollett voices his admiration for Fielding's revered mock-romancer Cervantes, and announces that in his own novel he has followed a variation on Cervantean fiction as practiced by "other Spanish and French authors," and most particularly LeSage, whose *Gil Blas* had "described the knavery and foibles of life, with infinite humour and sagacity." Smollett's satiric portrayal of contemporary life is vivid, brusque, sometimes savage; nothing is idealized about the world through which his picaresque hero moves. Some of Roderick's adventures are quite extraordinary, but Roderick himself, as Smollett conceived him, is a young man of "modest merit struggling with every difficulty to which a friendless orphan is exposed, from his own want of experience, as well as from the selfishness, envy, malice, and base indifference of mankind."

Each of the major novelists of the 1740s tried in his own way to offer a convincing portrait of contemporary experience, dramatized in the lives of familiar characters. The familiarity of their characters was very likely as much a moral and epistemological as a literary matter. Different as the various heroes and heroines are, they are all struggling to preserve their moral identity against the threats of a hostile environment. Given the didactic emphasis in the major novels, the currency of works like *Télémaque* and Palafox's *New Odyssey* suddenly seems very relevant, although these romances unreservedly indulge in inflated characterizations and the *merveilleux*. The early latitudinarian argument for the "good man as hero" receives very emphatic, if varied, endorsement in the fiction of Richardson, Fielding, and Smollett, and that argument included a strong position on the moral efficacy of ordinary, believable exemplars as aids in the quest for Christian truth and the good life.

These three novelists generally dismissed the marvellous as unworthy and inappropriate, but they did not totally renounce romance. Their conversion to a mode of antiromance was only partial. Each of the major novelists made tacit concessions to a tradition that so recently enjoyed the favor of English readers, and that was to be renewed in the romances of the 1750s and after. Richardson, Fielding, and Smollett specifically rejected the extravagances of orientalized fiction, with its magic and improbable mystery—in *Tom Jones* (17:1), Fielding made plain his own objections to tales of "*Arabians* and *Persians*" with their "Genii and Fairies."[17] Romance conventions from other modes, however, recur in their works. In effect, the major novelists heightened and intensified the stories of their ordinary characters and familiar circumstances by appropriating some of the attitudes and strategies of romance.

Richardson's persistent treatment of the theme of sentimental love repeats a romance convention, which was also a convention of the contemporary theater and of the amatory novels of Eliza Haywood and her imitators.[18] Richardson's novels, however, focus narrowly on the moral dimensions of the theme and use it very precisely as a device for defining the moral worth of his characters. That is to say, in his stories requited love and happy marriage signify the rewards due to the virtuous at the end of a moral struggle, and marriage is seen as the earthly state nearest to heavenly bliss. The wedding of Sir Charles Grandison and Harriet Byron is a triumphant event. Mr. B. calls Pamela a "romantic girl," and the novel itself is a moralized retelling of the romantic Cinderella legend. Even Clarissa Harlowe's melancholy story concludes with a version of this same convention of a happy ending in matrimony, for the heroine goes as a "bride" to her "marriage" in heaven. In pursuit of his didactic purpose, Richardson tends to idealize his heroes and heroines so that they parallel those of romance in some important ways. But there are essential distinctions to be made between what the romances had done with character, and what Richardson was attempting to do in his "new species of writing." In *Rambler* No. 4 (March 31, 1750),[19] when speaking of the "works of fiction, with which the present generation seems more particularly delighted," Dr. Johnson carefully stated one overriding consideration distinguishing realistic narrative from romance. It is widely believed that Johnson was defending the author of *Pamela* and *Clarissa* in this essay. The "province" of this kind of writing, he observed, "is to bring about natural events by easy means, and to keep up curiosity without the help of wonder: it is therefore precluded from the machines and expedients of the heroic romance, and can neither employ giants to snatch away a lady from the nuptial rites, nor knights to bring her back from captivity; it can neither bewilder its personages in deserts, nor lodge them in imaginary castles." From this premise, Johnson argued that the "task of our present writers" properly demands, "together with that learning which is to be gained from books, that experience which can never be attained by solitary diligence, but must arise from general converse, and accurate observation of the living world." These writers are "engaged in portraits of which every one knows the original, and can detect any deviation from exactness of resemblance."

In other words, according to Johnson, the novelist's function is to hold the mirror up to life and human nature, and to reflect its general truths. But this is an ethical as well as an aesthetic problem. The authors of these works are "at liberty, tho' not to invent, yet to select objects, and to cull from the mass of mankind, those individuals upon which the attention ought most to be employ'd; as a diamond, though it cannot be made, may be polished by art, and placed in such a situation, as to display that lustre which before was buried among common stones." What Johnson's essay really discusses here is a variation upon the neoclassical ideal of *la belle nature*—the doctrine that the mirror of art should reveal an exemplary pattern, a generalized version of archetypal nature on which the eye might be fixed, and that this pattern must conform to the truth of empirical observation.[20] The extravagant characterizations of seventeenth-century French heroic romance, and those of didactic romance as well, were indebted to this ideal for their original sanction. The writers in these two modes, however, and especially the authors of heroic romances, distorted the ideal by imparting to their flat heroes and heroines suprahuman qualities which were not supported by the realities of life itself and which, with repetition, generated mere stereotypes having even less validity as representatives of general nature.

It is not clear just how aware of the ideal of *la belle nature* Richardson may have been. In his fiction he is not so close to it as Johnson implies in his comments; his allegiance to that ideal seems to have been partial and indirect. Richardson avoids the marvellous, and his technique is that of circumstantial fidelity to empirical reality. His heroes and heroines, as exemplars, or models, are very original portraits vividly drawn from ordinary life, and their particular heroism rests on a personalized, uplifting spiritual code of honor and on a conception of the unremitting pursuit of simple goodness as the highest courage. In these respects, they differ markedly from the personages of romance. But they are also extremely subjective creations, endowed with amazing and highly individualized beauty, endurance, and powers of mind. In addition, they tend to be relatively unflawed. In some striking ways Richardson's idealized characters resemble those found in *Celenia*, *Télémaque*, and *The Adventures of Eovaai*. Pamela Andrews, with all the wit, cunning, and energy that give life to her character, is nevertheless projected as an almost flawless creature, a heroine of romance recast as a serving maid. Some readers would have recognized that her name comes from Sidney's *Arcadia*. Clarissa Harlowe, although a more mature creation and a much more convincingly representative figure, is still very grandly romanticized as the ideal of female virtue. Even as he argues for his heroine's faults, Richardson declares that "as far as is consistent with human frailty, and as far as she could be perfect, considering the people she had to deal with and those with whom she was inseparably connected," Clarissa "is perfect" (1.14). Sir Charles Grandison strikes the reader as a most glaring monster of perfection, for he is almost without a blemish. *Grandison*, says Richardson in his preface, was written upon his friends' pleas that, having already provided the world with two matchless heroines, he should finally favor it with "the character and actions of a man of TRUE HONOUR."

In book three, chapter one of *Joseph Andrews*, Fielding declares "once for all": "I describe not Men, but Manners; not an Individual, but a Species." His endeavor, we are told, is to "hold the Glass to thousands in their Closets"—to depict general truths about human nature, so that his readers might confront the reality about themselves from within the world of his novel. In part, perhaps, Fielding was reacting to what he seems to have regarded as *Pamela's* undue glorification of an unrepresentative heroine. Richardson is assuredly one of those modern "novel" writers chastised earlier in this same chapter, writers who "without any Assistance from Nature or History, record Persons who never were, or will be, and Facts which never did nor possibly can happen." But this chapter of *Joseph Andrews* is interesting in the present connection chiefly because it suggests Fielding's own version of the neoclassical ideal of *la belle nature*, which he (as a comic writer) had extended to enable him to describe the "Actions and Characters" of all kinds and classes of men, from low life to high life. Fielding was steeped in neoclassical doctrines; his own idealized portraits may occasionally bear resemblances to those in recent romantic fiction, but (unlike Richardson's) they derive directly from the older tradition. Many are quite pictorial in their effects, and they attempt to render not only the particular aspects of visible human nature—what Erwin Panofsky calls common nature[21]—but also the general and the ideal.

The young titular hero of *Joseph Andrews*, a footman and paragon of male virtue, having been provided with a mock-epic lineage (1.2) is described (1.8) at the "one and twentieth Year of his Age" as a youth whose exact proportions and handsome mien, even to "those who have not seen many Noblemen, would give an Idea of Nobility." Joseph's beloved Fanny

Goodwill, a paragon of female virtue, is similarly described (2.12); of a perfect shape and plumpness, she is endowed by nature with a neck whose whiteness the "finest *Italian* Paint would be unable to reach," and blessed with a "natural Gentility, superior to the Acquisition of Art, and which surprized all who beheld her." Fielding is often very deliberate about mixing imperfections into his heroes, but the character of Parson Adams is an intensely visualized comic idealization of the "good-natur'd" man, a saintly creature whose naivete and little vanities over his excellences as preacher and schoolmaster in no way qualify his function as a "Character of perfect Simplicity." *Tom Jones* (4.2) introduces Sophia Western with a burlesque epic flourish ("Hushed be every ruder breath"), but calms to a modulated, deliberate description of the character, an exemplar of all natural beauties and virtues. Sophia was

> a middle-sized Woman; but rather inclining to tall. Her Shape was not only exact, but extremely delicate; and the nice Proportion of her Arms promised the truest Symmetry in her Limbs. . . . Her Neck was long and finely turned; and here, if I was not afraid of offending her Delicacy, I might justly say, the highest Beauties of the famous *Venus de Medicis* were outdone. . . . Such was the outside of *Sophia;* nor was this beautiful Frame disgraced by an Inhabitant unworthy of it.

Although Fielding's portraits are directly indebted to the traditional ideal of *la belle nature*, they are, like Richardson's, of familiar personages. Quite obviously part of the purpose of the idealized descriptions in the work of both novelists is to exalt familiar characters as moral exemplars. Furthermore, Fielding's pose as the author of "comic-prose-epics," while it suggests his rejection of heroic modes as inappropriate for contemporary writers, likewise serves to impart heroic status to figures drawn from ordinary life.[22] The pose has another aim, of course. Like Cervantes, Fielding is a comic romancer. As he implies in *Tom Jones* (8.1), when kept "within the Rules of Credibility" his mockery is a license to "deal as much in the Wonderful as he pleases," in order to "surprize the Reader," "engage his Attention," and "charm him."

Through his burlesque of romance and epic machinery Fielding actually imports elements of the marvellous into his own work. For one thing,

he endows Fortune with a very long arm. For another, moments like the
Upton Inn episodes of *Tom Jones*, while at least marginally plausible in the
events, stretch credibility by a mock-epic rendering that is itself a form of
the marvellous. But Fielding employs his epic machinery in the service of
his comic realism, as a device to heighten the significance of the real as he
presents it. Fielding also exploits the theme of sentimental love, although
he characteristically parallels it to his sweeping commentary on the contemporary world through which his characters journey. His repetition of
this romance convention, however, functions to virtually the same end as
it does in Richardson's novels. The rewards in love and marital bliss that
accrue to Joseph Andrews, Tom Jones, and Billy Booth serve as a measure
of their moral stature—for Jones and Booth they come after a long progress toward Christian heroism. The sudden reversals of fortune that
make the material happiness of these heroes possible also derive in part
from a tradition of romance plotting; all three heroes rise from a nadir
into wealth, while Joseph Andrews and Tom Jones learn their true identities and climb several notches in the social hierarchy, as well.[23]

Of the three major novelists of the 1740s, Smollett depends least upon
romance. The theme of sentimental love does enter *Roderick Random*,
though it is much subdued, as it is later in *Peregrine Pickle* (1751). Smollett
permits Roderick to idealize his beloved Narcissa, much in the manner of
a romancer: "So much sweetness appeared in the countenance and car-
riage of this amiable apparition, that my heart was captivated at first
sight" (chap. 39). The course of Roderick's mercurial career, like that of
Tom Jones, is abruptly brought to an end by a stroke of good fortune. He
discovers his long-lost father, now a wealthy resident of Brazil; his newly
won moral integrity is subsequently rewarded in happy marriage. To a
certain extent the novel romanticizes the picaresque hero himself as a
wayward but good-natured youth, driven by adversity into roguery, but
destined for moral nobility. These are all very rudimentary gestures in the
direction of romance. Smollett's first novel (and *Peregrine Pickle*, as well)
much more closely resembles the lively antiromance of *Gil Blas*. A modified picaresque fiction, it notices romance mainly by inverting it. Like
LeSage's work, *Roderick Random* focuses on an antihero, and seeks to expose through relentless satire the seamiest sides of contemporary life.

The concessions made by Richardson, Fielding, and Smollett to a romance tradition are important, and probably helped their "new species of

writing" to gain the notice of the public. Furthermore, as we have seen, the devices and strategies borrowed from the writers of romance and from related sources contributed to the enrichment of these stories of familiar life, and helped to heighten the significance of their characters' experience. But none of this really changes the major writers' stance in opposition to romance, which they tended to dismiss for what they regarded as its faulty and therefore dangerous vision of life. Any student of their remarkably fresh and original works recognizes the insistence of their topical relevance—Richardson's social myths, for example, or Fielding's anti-Jacobitism in *Tom Jones*, or Smollett's criticisms of the Navy adminstration in the Carthagena episodes of *Roderick Random*. The very topicality of these novels is a feature shared with romances like *Celenia*, *Télémaque*, and *The Court Secret*, which have already been described as antiromances, though in a very special sense, because of the kinds of interest generated by their frequent reference to topical issues. In the final analysis, of course, the novels of Richardson, Fielding, and Smollett differ fundamentally from these shamelessly exotic lesser works. For the major novels of the 1740s are essentially circumstantial records of man's broad social and moral experience, seriously conceived and carefully wrought as authoritative statements about observable life. As such, they achieved extraordinary success among their first readers. Our continued interest in them testifies to the clarity and permanence of their authors' vision.

CHAPTER III

Fiction as Contemporary History

T O A DEGREE unprecedented except in the important and influential work of Defoe, popular storytellers of the 1730s and 1740s focused their attention on what was observably true in contemporary life—on recognizable characters and distinctly English or European habits of daily living. As we have seen, even the avowed romances of the period leaned in this direction. Meanwhile a very numerous and conspicuous class of narratives, which actually includes the majority of all contemporary fictions, openly professed a historical or biographical function and claimed to deal with real places, actions, situations, and people. The obvious intention of the authors of these works was to authenticate what they had written, but most such masked fictions really did borrow their approaches to subject matter, their methods, their structure, and even their titles from genuine histories, memoirs, and court chronicles, all of which were respectable forms of prose narrative. The considerable popularity enjoyed by the many works of pseudohistory and pseudobiography provides dramatic testimony to the period's general preference for extended stories about familiar subjects.

The most important contribution of the remarkably varied works in this large class of narratives, from the point of view of the historian of the novel at any rate, is their elevation of private experience to the status of public history. This accomplishment reflects the age's new understanding of history as dynamic process set and kept in motion by the actions of individual people. But it also attests, and more precisely, to the importance of a closely related development, the new willingness—the eagerness—of readers actually to see the individual life, no matter how ordinary or extraordinary, as having some kind of real public value. With this

43

recognition arrived the idea of a moral law of consequences that figures so conspicuously in the novels of Defoe, Richardson, Fielding, and Smollett, who sent their familiar characters forth into their fictional worlds as agents of moral responsibility interacting with a tangible environment. An identical assumption about the moral impact of the individual life receives repeated affirmation in the works of later novelists, including Fanny Burney, Jane Austen, Charles Dickens, and George Eliot, and indeed it is one of those abiding concerns that have engaged serious fiction writers ever since the beginning of the eighteenth century.

Neither writers nor their readers in the early 1700s understood very clearly what we would now acknowledge as conventional distinctions between history and biography. The record of a battle, of a war, or of the reign of a monarch was obviously a work of history. But the story of a life, whether real or feigned, was considered an exercise in historical writing too, and many narratives of this kind were projected and even labeled as such. In many instances the label is at least marginally justified. Voyage narratives, for example, and memoirs of public careers, while they usually take a biographical or autobiographical form, clearly appealed to their audience in large measure because of the historical function they served, because of the information (oftentimes mostly invented) they professed to supply about exotic lands and peoples or about exciting political and military events. On the other hand, stories of private lives lived as exercises in pious devotion, or low-life tales of rogues and criminals in their impious personal wickedness, also made their appeal as history or pseudo-history, for they gave expression to important ideals or anxieties of the culture. Yet these narratives, in their approaches to character, are much more nearly biographical in the sense in which we usually mean the term, for the most sophisticated and interesting of them reveal a concern with day-to-day experiences and with the psychology of the individual as he or she relates to or resists (for the criminal character, we should say defies) the realities of the social and moral environment. Meanwhile, spy narratives and scandal chronicles boldly and with some justice proclaimed their value as history, though they deliberately sought to examine and usually to expose contemporary life as it was lived by individual people, many of them imaginary, whether at Court, in the important institutions of the day, or—in the case of spy stories especially—in a domestic setting.

The confusion of forms is real, but it interestingly reveals the degree to which the age itself was struggling toward important new assumptions about the relations between the individual and a changing world, relations that the novel would take as its great subject matter. It must be said that few of the fiction writers working in the modes of pseudohistory and pseudobiography had any real notion of the demands of formal realism. Some of them actually favored the devices of fantasy over the techniques of verisimilitude, and occasionally this preference was strategic, as in the case of exotic utopian voyage narratives or the more polemical scandal chronicles. Yet the most emphatically "factual" of these stories likewise fail, usually, to be convincing even as fictionalized history and biography. Apparently this deficiency did not trouble the eighteenth-century audience much, possibly because such narratives supplied a fantasy life that enabled their readers, as private men and women, to participate imaginatively in the great moral, social, and political concerns of the day.

Despite the bewilderment of contemporary writers concerning the boundaries separating the various branches of historical and biographical narrative in which they practiced, it is possible to sort out the many works themselves according to the emphases they develop, and to do so without seeming too arbitrary about it. It is a useful and instructive undertaking. As biographical histories of private characters whose moral experience elevates them to high public importance, the eclectic novels of Richardson, Fielding, and Smollett made their chief appeal to the contemporary audience on some of the same broad grounds as the many lesser historical and biographical fictions—they provide the same kind of fantasy life, though greatly enriched. *Joseph Andrews, Clarissa, Roderick Random*, and the other major novels of the 1740s earned recognition as triumphant products of the imagination, but in varying degrees their authors actually incorporated many of the conventions of the several kinds of pseudofactual narrative. The adaptations and transformations of such conventions achieved by Richardson, Fielding, and Smollett are often quite remarkable to observe, and are sometimes crucial to the purposes or design of their novels, as I shall try to show in the present chapter on fiction as imaginative history and in the next two chapters on fiction as feigned biography.

Spies and Scandalmongers

With the translation of Giovanni Paolo Marana's *L'Espion turc* (1684) in 1687–94, spy-letter fiction achieved an instantaneous vogue in England. Its popularity was later reinforced by numerous English editions of Montesquieu's *Lettres persanes* (1721), a brilliant adaptation of Marana's formula, and by the publication of a good many imitations of both Montesquieu and Marana. Spy fiction did not, in fact, enter fully into a popular decline until after it had reached its culmination in an English work which is perhaps the very best example of the type: Oliver Goldsmith's *Citizen of the World* (1762).[1] Public demand for this brand of pseudohistorical writing, which often took on an oriental coloring, initially anticipated and later paralleled that for oriental tales and romances. The collective success of the spy narratives never quite equaled that enjoyed by the efforts of Galland, Pétis de la Croix, and certain of their parasites and legatees. Yet in a very real sense the work of Marana and his early eighteenth-century imitators and adapters played a far more important role than did the oriental tales and romances in determining the direction that the best English fiction was to take beginning in 1740.

For the spy stories are not romances. On the contrary, they are essentially circumstantial, antiheroic satirical fictions that function most frequently as precise and detailed commentaries on the hard realities of contemporary life. The character of the spy himself is usually rather well defined. He is typically an urbane fellow of real wit and keen powers of observation, and he supplies the focal consciousness through which the substance of the narrative is filtered as he writes his epistles home. Sometimes the spy is merely a tourist, sometimes a diplomat or other foreign official, sometimes quite literally an espionage agent. Whatever his status, he is always an alien standing outside the pale of the host community's moral and social traditions. His situation thus automatically provides him with a perspective from which he can see clearly the virtues and, most importantly, the follies, vanities, and vices of the society under his scrutiny. Indeed, the function of the spy is to "see"—to experience, to interpret, define, and judge. In effect, he is a modern version of the persona of formal (and particularly Juvenalian) satire. Very often he is at once *vir bonus*, naïf, and hero.[2] The spy's letters characteristically deal with particular observations and thus rarely give any sense of a coherent narrative. Except for the many interpolated *histoires*, tales, and *nouvelles* (most often introduced as the illustration of some point of criticism or approbation), the usually thin thread of the central character's own career furnishes the only sustained story interest. But plot is decidedly secondary in importance, for the bent of this kind of fiction is satirical, and the quick, scrupulously circumstantial record of separate incidents is the most prominent feature of its narrative method.

Most of the spy fictions range over a whole social spectrum. They frequently give close attention to domestic scenery, but the typical spy takes as his special province the host society's politics and religion, its high life, its manners and morals as exemplified in its more important institutions and people. As exposés of fashionable life and as political satire, these works resemble the secret histories of Delarivière Manley and Eliza Haywood, but they rarely indulge in the vigorous personal slanders that enliven *Queen Zarah* or the *New Atalantis*. To a discerning reader, neither of these kinds of fiction could have been very convincing as history, although the narratives in each mode invariably claim to be fact faithfully recorded. At the same time, the best works in both types share in a real seriousness of purpose by establishing a fictionalized perspective from which they can take direct aim at specific aspects of contemporary life. That their historical function provided certain satisfactions is attested by their steady popularity among all kinds and classes of readers in the early years of the eighteenth century. Spy narratives in particular enjoyed considerable prestige. Only the well-to-do could even have afforded the eight volumes (in four) of *The Turkish Spy*, which, despite the astronomical price of one pound, reached its twelfth edition in 1748. The very high quality and wide popularity of Montesquieu's *Lettres persanes* lent a real respectability to this mode of writing, and probably helped to attract to its practice the likes of Marlborough's biographer, Thomas Lediard (*The German Spy*, 1738), and such established figures as George Lyttelton (*Letters from a Persian in England*, 1735) and Oliver Goldsmith.

Marana's *Turkish Spy* was the most popular of all spy fictions in England. It was also the source book for most later tales of its kind. Marana's work begins with some elaborate editorial claims regarding the authenticity of the Arabic manuscript from which the narrative was allegedly translated.

47

The spy is one Mahmut, a Turk sent by the sultan of the Ottoman Empire to report on European courts. Disguised as a Moldavian priest throughout nearly half a century ("from the Year 1637, to the Year 1682") as an espionage agent, he spends most of his time in France, spying on the courts of Louis XIII and Louis XIV. Mahmut proves himself an astute political observer, but he is likewise an extremely sensitive, reflective man whose intense curiosity brings him to report also on the strangeness, the decadence, and often the absurdity of local manners. An admirer of Descartes, he is a skeptic who punctuates many of his dry official communiqués with penetrating comments on the tensions rending French Catholics, on Gallic social hypocrisy, and on the amorous intrigues among the upper crust. Mahmut particularly enjoys (while condemning) the pomp and vanity of a social elite whose false splendor contrasts vividly with the ugliness and squalor of so much of the rest of French national life. He records these musings usually by rather faithful reproduction of the scenes which sparked them, and he sometimes reflects comparatively—and not always favorably—on the customs and institutions of his own country. Mahmut becomes so preoccupied with the inconsistencies in what he sees that he is moved to write numerous descriptive, critical letters to a variety of friends and relations. These sometimes intensely personal epistles balance the typically matter-of-fact official ones, and they reveal the human personality behind the journalistic, detached sensibility of the spy. Mahmut's private correspondence grows in frequency and volume, and this aids significantly in the definition of his own rather complicated character. In the latter sections of the work, which may not have been written by Marana, satisfaction of friendly inquiries from acquaintances at home sends the spy off in all directions.[3] He goes to remote corners of Switzerland, Spain, Germany, and Albania, where he researches a diverse array of historical, social, and religious curiosities which come to occupy a considerable portion of his time and energies. The narrative is at length brought back into very sharp focus near its end, when Mahmut manifests an increasing preoccupation with himself, with his personal life and his growing fears of assassination at the hands of a hostile Turkish faction. The work thus ends as it began, with a concentration on Mahmut's personality and observations as a spy.

The Turkish Spy enjoyed a steady following in England throughout most of the eighteenth century. Its long-lived vogue is quite remarkable in view of its exceptional length and high price. Doubtless much of its appeal for English readers of the period consisted in its distinctive formula, which offers close observation of French high life and public figures, as well as a great variety of narrative episodes, some sensational and amorous, some domestic and sentimental, some dealing explicitly in political intrigue and social exposé. In addition, the characterization of the spy himself strikes an interesting contrast to the blustering heroes of the romances popular at the time of his arrival upon the scene. Mahmut is a humane man of quick intelligence, but he is quiet and contemplative. Moreover, though he hails from an exotic land, he is quite ordinary in many ways, including his appearance. In the very first letter he describes himself as a person of "low Stature, of an ill-favour'd Countenance, ill-shap'd, and by Nature not given to Talkativeness." Such a character must have seemed quite an original creation to English readers in the late seventeenth century; by the 1740s the unpretentious, "ordinary" Mahmut was very much in the mainstream that was to be navigated also by the creators of characters like Clarissa Harlowe, Roderick Random, and Billy Booth.

The Turkish Spy generated many imitations, including two by a French aristocrat named Jean Baptiste de Boyer, Marquis d'Argens. D'Argens's *Lettres juives* (1736–38) and *Lettres chinoises* (1739–40) both adhere faithfully to Marana's formula. Translated as *The Jewish Spy* (1739–40) and *Chinese Letters* (1741) respectively, they enjoyed numerous English editions over the next several years. Both works are stale copies of Marana, but d'Argens was a skillful literary mimic and his narratives achieve a certain slickness of finish. Apparently, English readers did not worry much about fine discriminations between Marana's original and d'Argens's competent but uninspired imitations. Along with these narratives by d'Argens, however, Englishmen particularly admired two sophisticated adaptations of Marana, Montesquieu's *Lettres persanes* and George Lyttelton's anti-Walpole fiction called *Letters from a Persian in England to his Friend at Ispahan* (1735), which is an imitation of Montesquieu. Oddly enough, neither book seems to have been reprinted in the 1740s, although Lyttelton's had gone through four editions within a year of its initial publication, and Montesquieu's was a perennial favorite of eighteenth-century English readers. Nevertheless these two works continued to be admired in the decade, and together they contributed much to the contemporary status of fiction.[4]

Montesquieu and Lyttelton depended fundamentally upon Marana's topical formula, but the *Lettres persanes* (or *Persian Letters* as it was called in John Ozell's English translation) in particular is distinguished for its tighter narrative framework, its yet closer delineation of character, and for the gentle irony with which it views the foibles of its central personages. In its treatment of the spy Usbek especially, the *Lettres persanes* presents a figure even more introspective than Mahmut, and one whose own failings of pride and ambition (he so neglects his domestic life that it collapses disastrously, to his great sorrow) receive such emphasis as to make him an extremely interesting figure in his own right. In fact, the book centers almost as much upon Usbek as on the objects of his satire. Lyttelton attempts the same kind of effect with his character Selim, a friend of Usbek who practices his espionage in London and writes his topical epistles home to an associate named Mirza. The book is clearly derivative, and its author manages to do little that his model had not done before him in the way of satirical commentary. Political, legal, and ecclesiastical institutions all come under direct attack, as well as certain stereotyped figures: the cunning lawyer, the venal merchant, the cuckold, and especially the corrupt clergyman and the debased, striving politician. Walpole, perceived as the principal enemy of English liberty and the sacred Constitution, is a special target. As commentator Selim is thoughtful, judicious, and urbane, although he lacks the wit and fire of Usbek. Frequently his letters become just a forum for the Patriot sentiments of the author, and in fact the overbearing emphasis on the polemical function of Selim's character serves rather to suppress than to reveal and underscore his human qualities. Yet it was probably the extreme topicality of Lyttelton's book that did most to occasion its broad initial popularity.

The most impressive new piece of spy-letter fiction to appear in the 1740s was *Letters Written by a Peruvian Princess* (1748), the work of a French gentlewoman named Françoise d'Issembourg d'Happancourt de Graffigny. Translated from *Lettres d'une Péruvienne* (1747), this work was enormously popular in its native country, and it gained a considerable following among English readers as well. The heroine (and letter-writer) is Zilia, a young Peruvian princess and "Virgin of the Sun" brought to France by a rescuer after the Spaniards had conquered Peru and inflicted their barbarities upon that country's people, customs, and treasures. Like Montesquieu's Usbek, Zilia is permitted to view French customs with the innocent detachment of one wholly unacquainted with them. A feminist at heart, and endowed with a ready sensibility, she attacks the restrictive social sanctions governing French women, but is even harsher on the women themselves, who seem to her hard, insensitive, fatuous, and devious. "In the different countries that I have passed thro'," she says of the French, "I have not seen any savages so haughtily familiar as these. The women, in particular seem to have a kind of disdainful civility that disgusts human nature, and would perhaps inspire me with as much contempt for them, as they shew for others, if I knew them better" (Letter 14). Zilia's judgments arise from close observation of people and events, and her capacity to portray domestic scenery is particularly noteworthy. She writes to the moment, and her letters therefore have the added interest of her immediate involvement in what they record. But Zilia's strictures on French manners and morals are woven by Mme de Graffigny into a fully developed love story which actually forms the dramatic center of the narrative. Zilia may be a *femme philosophe* and a judicious social critic, but she is also an extremely sensitive young girl, desperately (and, as it turns out, hopelessly) in love. Throughout, she is enchained by her passion for a noble young Peruvian named Aza, a captive of the Spanish and the addressee of most of the letters. Her fidelity to Aza will not permit Zilia to yield to the honorable proposals of the worthy Chevalier Déterville, her savior and protector. Torn between despair over Aza's silence on the one hand and gratitude to the virtuous young chevalier on the other, her life turns into a round of loneliness. Partly for solace and diversion, Zilia occupies herself with observation of the scenes about her. Late in the story she learns to her dismay that Aza has betrayed her love; he has taken up Catholicism, renounced her, and betrothed himself to a Spanish woman of fortune. At first overcome with grief, the heroine summons her strength and resigns herself to her fate. The thirty-eighth letter recalls the despairing, departed Déterville (he had joined the celibate order of Malta) to live near her in simple friendship. She can never give herself to him in marriage, but together they can renounce passion and retreat into the joys of reason and philosophy, of science and the arts.

The Peruvian Princess is a sentimental tale of almost unrelieved melancholy. It pits the virtuous heroine and the faithful Déterville against a variety of adverse forces—their own passions, the Spanish atrocities, the grim follies of French society, the sinister Catholicism that steals Aza's soul and mind, leaving Zilia wretched. Though tortured by these forces, the heroine and her generous benefactor rise above them in the end; their victory is moral and thus consonant with the current notion of Christian heroism, which held that one could control his own fate in a grotesquely wicked world by exerting a kind of moral self-control and simply having the courage to be good and true. It is easy for such a paragon as Zilia to say of the hypocrites of France: "I suspect this nation not to be what it appears; for affectation seems to be its ruling character" (Letter 16). But no one could make such a statement about Zilia herself, or about the faithful Déterville.

The success earned by *The Peruvian Princess* in England, it is likely, may be to some extent explained by its moral ideology, and also by the explicit topicality of its feminism, its assaults on French society, and its implied attacks on the Roman Church.[5] But the work has considerable merits, too, and these should not be left out of account. Mme de Graffigny exploits not only the formulas established by Montesquieu and Marana, but also the attitudes popularized by two more recent French fiction writers, Marivaux and Prévost. *The Peruvian Princess* is indebted at least partly to the influence of Marivaux for the prominence given to sentiment in Zilia's interpretation of every event of her life, to Prévost for the role that an enslaving passion plays in determining those events. The success with which she weaves these effects together proves Mme de Graffigny to be a skillful and serious writer. In some respects she resembles Richardson, a much finer artist, whose *Clarissa* began to appear in the same year that *The Peruvian Princess* was published in Paris. As a rule the character of Zilia is consistently controlled and, despite her failure to be convincingly Peruvian, she is vividly portrayed and quite human. The hysteria of the letters written during the Spanish invasion is genuine and moving; Zilia is no less credible when the hysteria subsides, yielding successively to the bafflement, the clear vision, the quiet despair, and the calm philosophy of the later epistles. The conclusion of the story may seem somewhat improbable out of context, but it comes as no surprise to the reader of Zilia's letters. The resolution is in every way consistent with the character of the heroine, and in fact is made to seem inevitable. In *The Peruvian Princess*, spy fiction reaches a kind of culmination, surpassed only by Goldsmith's *Citizen of the World*. But Goldsmith's work mines almost exclusively the vein of Marana, Montesquieu, and Lyttelton, whereas Mme de Graffigny pursues an eclectic method that radically expands the boundaries of spy fiction. *The Peruvian Princess* is a transitional work, showing the passage of this kind of fiction from satirical observation of public actions and people to a central concern with private and personal experience.

As feigned records of scandal and foolishness in places high and low, the spy fictions of Marana, Montesquieu, Lyttelton, and Mme de Graffigny all belong to the same family of pseudohistories, which also includes a prominent cousin, the secret history, or *chronique scandaleuse*. Secret histories by writers like Delarivière Manley and Eliza Haywood were more controversial than the circumspect spy fictions, although the two kinds of feigned history closely resemble one another. The chief difference between the two is that the secret history usually treats a much more limited range of familiar issues and public characters, for more specialized purposes. Following the example of original French models like Mme d'Aulnoy's *Mémoires de la cour d'Angleterre* (1695), the typical *chronique scandaleuse* is an episodic work purporting to tell the "real truth" about certain thinly disguised figures in contemporary politics, Court, and fashionable life.[6] Narrower in scope than the more urbane spy story, this type of work trades in personal scandal and political invective. That is, if the work of Marana and Montesquieu functions as a modern adaptation of the Juvenalian attitude, the secret history perverts that attitude. Furthermore, its writers reject conventional standards of taste. Whether motivated by genuine partisan interests or mere lust for success in the marketplace, they deal more in character assassination than in real political or moral discourse, more in licentious gossip than in fruitful satire of the actual manners and machinations of the real people they "expose."

Most secret histories published in the early eighteenth century superimpose upon their real, contemporary subjects the filmy pretext of an ancient or remote civilization. Such a pretext allows them to criticize and scandalize with complete abandon. In this respect they parallel the licentious orientalized political satires of Crébillon *fils*. Some secret histories pretend to deny their contemporary relevance by having the "editor" question the authenticity of the "manuscript," and insist on its antiquity. The preface to part two of Mrs. Manley's *Secret History of Queen Zarah* (1705), one of the earliest, most influential, and most durable English works in this vein (it was revived in editions of 1743, 1745, and 1749), ironically protests against the widely held view that the previously pub-

53

lished part one had launched an attack on Sarah Churchill, Duchess of Marlborough. The "whole *Story*," the "editor" suspects, "is a *Fiction*." There is "no such Country" as the Albigion depicted in the tale, "nor any such Person now Living, or ever was, as Zarah, or the other Names Characteriz'd, either in This or the First Part." The "manuscript," therefore, written before there were civilizations or governments, can only be a prophecy of "something yet to come." For it is impossible, the "editor" concludes, that "any Nation under the Moon ever cou'd produce a Creature of so little Use to the rest of the Creation besides herself, as this Wonder of her Sex, Queen *Zarah* is feign'd to be. That alone is sufficient to persuade me this Story is all a Romantick Tale of a Tub."

Although less famous than the same author's much longer *New Atalantis* (1709), *Queen Zarah* provided a kind of immediate native model to which future secret histories were to pay the homage of at least partial emulation.[7] The preface to part one makes a clear distinction between such "little Pieces" as *Queen Zarah* and the extravagant, ill-contrived heroic romances so justly "cry'd down" at present by all "Persons of good Sense." A work like the present one, by contrast to such romances, observes the "Probability of Truth, which consists in saying nothing but what may Morally be believed." In *Queen Zarah*, we are told, nice delineations of character are preserved; and when the characters speak, they do so in the "easie and free Manner" of everyday discourse and not in the rhetoric of romance. Yet despite Mrs. Manley's ostensible commitment to moral and mimetic ideals, her work is hardly a sober return to real life. On the contrary, it is a scurrilous Tory indictment of the Duchess of Marlborough and the Whig politicians of Queen Anne's reign. Despite the author's insistent claims of moral utility, the logic of the work is that vice is best censured by titillating exposure. The method of *Queen Zarah* is to exhibit very transparent, stereotyped personages—prowling *grandes dames*, lecherous statesmen, wicked libertines preying on imperiled virgins, and so on, all of them copied from a Theophrastian sketchbook—wallowing in scandalous love affairs and indulging in boudoir politics. These characters are the vehicles of partisan invective. Given their polemical function, it is not surprising that except for their ironic treatment, their visible eccentricities, familiar mannerisms, and open eroticism, they are hardly distinguishable from the inflated characters of romance attacked in the preface to the work.

Queen Zarah moves episodically, interrupted by little novellalike tales that pause over the dissolute escapades of readily recognizable figures such as the Earl of Godolphin and the Duke of Marlborough. Many later secret histories, while remaining essentially faithful to the example of *Queen Zarah* and the *New Atalantis*, compressed their bulk into slim volumes or pamphlets. But for Mrs. Manley, the more and juicier the episodes, the better the partisan purpose was served. In such works as hers, as every contemporary reader would have intuitively understood, the only ordering principle lies outside the world of the narrative, in the society that is being reflected in this special manner. The works themselves are only loosely held together by the presence of a presiding narrator. In *Queen Zarah* and the *New Atalantis*, and in their numerous close imitations, a ubiquitous persona moves in and out of salon and court, closet and bedroom, functioning as a kind of invisible spy who details the intrigue, the amorous machinations, the erotic confrontations in which the characters involve themselves. To this end, the separate scene frequently assumes greater importance than the story of which it is a part; this is especially true with Mrs. Manley and later Mrs. Haywood, both of whom were playwrights as well as novelists. The descriptive, judgmental, editorial voice of the narrator, however, always directs the reader's responses. Mrs. Manley's Intelligence, with the help of her mother Virtue and most especially of Astrea, speaks as the final authority on all of the amorous behavior observed at the Court of Atalantis.[8] The first-person narrators of *Joseph Andrews* and *Tom Jones* derive ultimately from a different narrative tradition, but the familiarity of some readers with the methods of Mrs. Manley and others like her would help to prepare them for Fielding's mannerisms.

Mrs. Manley's formula was simple, but very successful. *Queen Zarah* and the four volumes of the *New Atalantis* enjoyed a vogue that lasted for several decades. Apparently they were also politically effective, earning their author the gratitude of her fellow Tories.[9] The popularity of Mrs. Manley's secret histories generated a number of derivative works, the most successful of which were John Oldmixon's *Court of Atalantis* (1714), a Whiggish reply to Mrs. Manley, and Eliza Haywood's many *chroniques scandaleuses* of the 1720s. By the 1730s, however, the demand for such works had declined, and the new decade could count only seven or eight pieces that can technically be called secret histories. Except for the *New*

Atalantis itself ("seventh edition," 1736) and the fourth edition of Old-mixon's work, booksellers reprinted none of the once popular titles, either English or French. Instead, the 1730s offered mostly original native works, all of them undistinguished.

Much the same situation obtained in the 1740s. A slightly greater number of secret histories appeared, perhaps a dozen. Among these were the reprints of *Queen Zarah*, but the rest were inferior efforts, all but a very few of them new works by English writers. At least some of the decade's new native secret histories, while they are of little intrinsic interest, yield readily to the investigator who would discover their allusions. One work, which describes itself as an "Atalantis Reviv'd," is not really a secret history at all, for it is completely devoid of contemporary relevance. *The Young Ladies and Gentlemens Amorous Amusement. Being Memoirs of Several Illustrious Persons of Distinguish'd Quality of Both Sexes; or, The Atalantis Reviv'd* (1745–48) is actually a collection of novellas framed in a set of imaginary memoirs of such historical personages as Margaret of Parma, Charles Beaudon (Henry VIII's Duke of Suffolk), and the Duchess of Mazarine (niece of a French cardinal and mistress to the exiled Charles II of England). By 1745, the *New Atalantis* was something of a classic within whose shadow R. Thompson, the supposed author of the *Amorous Amusement*, was quite content to appear. It may be that Mrs. Manley's continuing reputation resulted from the sustained antagonisms between Tories and Whigs; or perhaps, judged by later performances, her works were felt to possess some literary merit.

The two major political figures of the 1740s, Sir Robert Walpole and Prince Charles Edward Stuart, both occasioned secret histories. Walpole, in fact, was the subject of at least four, two of them little scurrilous slanders that take direct aim at the prime minister. One of these two is entitled *A True and Impartial History of the Life and Adventures of Some-Body*. Published in May of 1740, *Some-Body* was followed exactly a year later by *A Court Intrigue; or, The Statesman Detected. A Genuine Story, Delivered by the Oraculous Ship. Address'd to His Honour and the Countess of Y——R——H.* *Some-Body* is a crude and obscene character assassination, in the expected manner of such works. *A Court Intrigue* is only slightly less malicious, though it does focus on political rather than personal slander. It poses as an ancient Greek tale and employs the background metaphor of the "ship of state." The alleged narrator is an inanimate object, the "Oraculous Ship," which traces its "life" back to Jason's voyage for the Golden Fleece.

Captained by one Hiram (George II), it is treacherously piloted by the wicked but trusted Gomorrah (Walpole). The story echoes the usual charges made against the prime minister, charges of political extortion, graft, violations of treaties, and so on. But the attack centers on Walpole's attempt to use George II's favorite mistress, the German Countess of Yarmouth (Lady Medea in the narrative), to persuade the king that the nation's progress toward the War of Jenkins' Ear should be reversed. The outcome of the scheme, as related in the story, is altogether predictable. At first so obliging, Lady Medea develops a conscience and exposes the wicked Gomorrah; in the end, all good "sailors" and "passengers" share the moral triumph of seeing him "hung up at the Yard-Arm," swinging (as Fielding's Jonathan Wild was later to do) "amidst the Acclamations of a shouting Throng." The degree of fantasy in this secret history is indicated by the role of the countess, who in real life completely avoided political involvement.

Probably the most pretentious of the decade's secret histories is a rambling two-volume narrative called *Memoirs of the Nobility, Gentry, & c. of Thule; or, The Island of Love. Being a Secret History of Their Amours, Artifices, and Intrigues.* This work takes on not only "His Honour" and the Georgian court, but also Carteret (Walpole's immediate successor), the principals in the religious establishment, and indeed the entire elite of England. Surely its wide-ranging topical references helped toward its success; the work was issued at least twice in the 1740s, once in 1742 and again in 1744. In this narrative, Thule, of course, is England, which is equated with the ancient island first described by the Greek navigator Pytheas in the fourth century B.C. In his elaborate prefatory discussion, the "editor" vouches for the truth of the tale, but dedicates his work to "Lady Fancy," whom he ironically denominates the mother of Chaos and Old Night and thus the ancestress of Dulness. The *Memoirs* is obviously modeled upon the *New Atalantis.* Unfortunately, however, its author possessed neither the wit nor the fancy of Mrs. Manley.

The one remaining secret history requiring attention is a curious piece entitled *The Amours of Don Carlos. A True History. Translated from a Manuscript Privately Handed About at the French Court* (1749). Despite the typical pretense of foreign authorship, intended, no doubt, to lend spice to the story, this anonymous work is very likely by some pro-Jacobite English hack. The "Don Carlos" of the narrative is a thinly veiled picture of Prince Charles Edward Stuart, a figure whose presence was as much felt in the latter half of the 1740s as was Walpole's a few years earlier. *The Amours of Don Carlos* is the decade's only secret history to deal with a person whose character and exploits, one would think, might have prompted a number of such works. And even this story is a conventional scandal chronicle only in its early pages, where the author "exposes" (but not harshly) some minor love affairs of the hero. The remainder of the book may best be described as a sentimental love story which concludes with the virtuous prince's reward in happy retreat, after his defeat, into the arms of his beloved.

The truth is, by the 1740s the secret history was near the end of its days as a successful literary commodity. From the beginning, this form of pseudohistory had been limited in its possibilities of development and growth. It had now been mined of all it could yield in the way of freshness and originality. The form was by no means abandoned for dead in this decade. Later writers would return to it, but rarely and with small enthusiasm, and their works would only echo Mrs. Manley. We may assume that the secret history had helped to familiarize the reading audience with the interests of a narrative literature drawn from the sources of contemporary life, and by its appeal as sensational exposé had encouraged a taste for the same. But it was eclipsed in popularity by the more flexible mode of spy fiction, and even more spectacularly by pseudohistorical voyages and adventure narratives, which appeared in increasing numbers as the second quarter of the eighteenth century progressed. These stories, insistently reflecting the expansiveness as well as the felt turbulence of English national life at the time, encouraged readers to extend their own "historical" curiosity far beyond the doings at Court and in Parliament to encompass the high seas, new and strange lands, the battlefields and harbors of English military exploits, and most importantly, the public experience of private travelers, soldiers, and exciting contemporary folk of all kinds.

Voyagers and Other Adventurers

In the first half of the eighteenth century in England, works by actual adventurers and voyagers recounting real (though often exaggerated) ex-

periences and discoveries appeared in great numbers. Many were translations, but the vogue for travel literature was fostered by a growing English spirit of commercial and colonial imperialism.[10] Most such narratives
offered, in the manner of the memoirist, the matter-of-fact observations
of a brave and resourceful but otherwise quite ordinary sailor, trader, or
explorer as he detailed the dangers he had survived, or described the lands
he had seen and the unfamiliar people, customs, and institutions he had
encountered. Relatively little was known at the time of nations and
peoples beyond Europe. Some writers deliberately capitalized upon the
susceptibilities of naive readers, and stretched the basic truth of their narratives with inventions that brought them to the borderline of fiction.
This practice was already widespread in the earliest years of the century.
In the *Characteristics* (1711; 1713) Shaftesbury taxed "this race of Authors"
with the inability either to lie or to tell truth consistently, and with the
objectionable habit of creating things both unnatural and monstrous. In
the following decade Swift published *Gulliver's Travels* (1726), which functioned in part as a devastating restatement of the same objections.

With the tempting example of the popular authentic works before
them, it is not surprising that fiction writers should have produced large
quantities of imaginary voyages.[11] By its very nature, with all its possibilities of invention without detection, the voyage narrative must have
seemed a ready vehicle for the author and bookseller sensitive to current
prejudices against fiction. The imaginary voyages, like their authentic
models, typically present a central character who returns from his travels
to tell (or write) of what he has seen. The narrator-hero, or memoirist, is
most often a pleasant personage of middling cultural or intellectual attain-
ments, articulate and endowed with a pragmatist's curiosity, practical ingenuity, and a large capacity for endurance. Some of these unpretentious,
ordinary voyagers become the satiric tools of their creators—Swift's Le-
muel Gulliver is the most notable example. A few, gifted with genuinely
reflective minds, descend directly from Sir Thomas More's Raphael
Hythloday. Most fictitious voyages in the eighteenth century are documentary in character; that is to say, they combine startling adventures and
real information, drawn from experience or from books of travel. But the
fecund tradition of voyage literature also spawned a substantial number
of satirical utopias which functioned as commentaries on English or European society, politics, and intellectual or religious life.

All of these works, both documentary and utopian, incorporate elements of the surprising or the bizarre, and of adventure into the unknown. The voyage often becomes in effect a metaphor for life itself, without ever losing touch with some aspect of familiar experience. The various trials and dangers represent moral crises pitting good against evil in a contest from which the hero, who almost always is emphatically a good man (or Christian hero), usually emerges triumphant. The characteristic moral ideology of these narratives is identical with that of most other popular fiction published in the period. Strange as some of them are, the imaginary voyages are not romances, though they frequently indulge in the *merveilleux*. In fact, they are at once biographical stories of ordinary men and historical narratives that develop an insistent pattern of allusions to contemporary political, social, and religious issues. At the same time, their preoccupation with the remote and (often) the improbable also exploits a taste for fantasy. In an important sense, the imaginary voyages are romance made "real."

The most popular among the several documentary voyages published in the 1740s were reprints of Defoe's early successes. *Robinson Crusoe* (1719), in combination with the *Farther Adventures* (1719), enjoyed at least two editions (1740 and 1747); *Madagascar; or, Robert Drury's Journal* (1729) reappeared in 1743, and perhaps again in 1747; and *Colonel Jacque* (1722) was reissued in 1741 and 1743. *Captain Singleton* (1720) and the *New Voyage round the World* (1724) had both been reprinted in 1737. It would be hard to overestimate the influence of Defoe on this kind of minor fiction in the 1740s. The persuasive force of his example seems to have dominated voyage literature for many years after his death in 1731. Moreover, his work was likewise popular on the other side of the Channel. Even the single French work in this mode to appear in English translation during the 1740s, LeSage's *Adventures of Robert Chevalier, Call'd de Beauchine* (1745),[12] is a potpourri of devices, characters, and episodes obviously copied from *Crusoe* and *Madagascar*, larded with some of the quasi-picaresque piratical elements of *Singleton* and *Colonel Jacque*.

A number of early native imitations of Defoe ranged close behind his works in collective popularity among readers in the 1740s. Peter Longueville's *The Hermit; or, The Unparalled Sufferings and Surprising Adventures of Mr. Philip Quarll, an Englishman* (1727) was reprinted in 1746 and 1748, and Longueville's book ran through at least fourteen more English editions during the latter half of the century.[13] *The English Hermit*, as the work is called in its running title, builds rather exactly and unimaginatively upon the successful Crusoesque formula of the desert island adventure narrative combined with elements from Puritan spiritual autobiography. To this formula it adds a slight variant upon the utopian features of Swift's *Gulliver*. Longueville, in the guise of "editor," negatively acknowledges his models in a preface that takes aim at their "untruthfulness" and obviously means to defend the "factuality" (and hence the moral utility) of his own production. "*Truth* and *Fiction*," Longueville remarks, have lately been too "promiscuously blended together" in works like *Crusoe* and *Gulliver's Travels*. By contrast, he is ready to affirm of his own "*surprising Narrative*" that though it "be not so replete with *vulgar Stories* as the former, or so interspersed with a *Satirical* Vein, as the last of the above-mentioned Treatises; yet it is certainly of more Use to the publick, than either of them, because every Incident, herein related, is real Matter of Fact." These remarks are a subterfuge. The success of Longueville's book doubtless resulted from its author's skill as an imitator. That is, the work clearly copies Defoe in its exploitation of the popular desire for knowledge of remote parts (in this case, the Caribbean), and it delineates an ordinary man who, like Crusoe, against all odds triumphs over adverse forces and creates a personal utopia. Its very moral ideology is Crusoesque. The "autobiography" was written, says Quarll, not to "exalt my Parts, but to keep me in mind of the many Mercies I have receiv'd from Heaven ever since my Youth, and to record the wonderful Effects of Providence."

Of the many narratives in the life-and-adventures school of Defoe to appear in the 1730s and 1740s, the most interesting is William Chetwood's *Voyages, Travels, and Adventures of William Owen Gwin Vaughan, Esq.* (1736).[14] *Singleton* is clearly Chetwood's model, yet *Vaughan* strikes out in some new directions of its own. Like *Singleton*, it begins with an account of the hero's early life, but extends this stage of his career to occupy virtually a third of the whole story. The voice throughout is that of a mature, reflective Vaughan, who manages to invest his autobiographical narrative with a mixture of melancholy, bemused irony, and a certain rudimentary psychological penetration. In the early pages we learn of a distressed childhood that begins inauspiciously with the death of the hero's mother as she gives him life, and then lingers over the tortures inflicted upon him by a hostile family dominated by a rapacious stepmother and her aggressive son Jack. A number of these domestic scenes are rendered with considerable dramatic immediacy. The young Vaughan suffers the agonies of neglect and abuse, but as his older self clearly recognizes, his own record is not spotless. As a perpetually angry and brutal youth, he commits numerous acts of violent aggression against his stepbrother and rival, Jack, and even gives a vicious beating to a local schoolmaster who had already been a frequent victim of his cruel pranks. At length rescued by a kindhearted maternal uncle who had perceived both his misery and his superior intellectual gifts, Vaughan receives a genteel education and an introduction into polite society. He soon develops into an adult rogue of sorts, and his uncle, in a misguided effort to subdue and civilize him, sends him off on a Grand Tour that takes him not only across Europe but to many remote parts of the globe.

The Tour and the conventional voyage adventures, which are quasi-picaresque in character, comprise the third stage of Vaughan's life and occupy almost half of the narrative. They constitute the work's primary appeal, which is that of *Crusoe* and *Madagascar*, and thus amply justify placing Chetwood's story among other voyage fictions, though it prominently features some of the devices of the picaresque tale and the domestic novel. *Vaughan* was not the first work to import these alien narrative conventions into an otherwise uncluttered pseudohistorical account of adventurous travels. It fails to bring all the hybrid elements into a coherent thematic or structural pattern (the three discrete stages of the hero's career exist almost independently), but makes an unusually ambitious attempt to treat adequately a complex domestic situation. In this respect, it looks forward to a much finer work, Smollett's story of Roderick Random, whose domestic plight parallels Vaughan's. Each hero is a Scot, each is motherless, each plagued by a usurping rival named Jack and tormented by a schoolmaster whom he finally thrashes. Furthermore, the hero of each work is rescued by a benevolent uncle who packs him off on extensive travels leading to mercurial picaresque adventures, rapid changes in fortune, and final happiness in love and affluence. Both Chetwood and Smollett depict the progress of a somewhat culpable hero past obstacles and pitfalls towards a moral equilibrium. LeSage's *Gil Blas* probably had the stronger influence on Smollett, but the similarities between *Vaughan* and *Roderick Random* should not be lightly dismissed, especially since Chetwood's work was current when Smollett came down from Scotland in 1739. Gaylord R. Haas suspects that Smollett may even have borrowed from Chetwood. But the real significance of the discoverable parallels between the two stories is, as Haas rightly suggests, that *Vaughan* is a "transitional work, standing . . . between the novels of Defoe and one manifestation of the new fiction of the 1740s in which there is a much greater interest in states of mind and complex behavior."[15]

Chetwood's *Vaughan* is very different from the utopian voyages that appeared in the 1740s. Variously modeled on older works like Lucian's *Veracious History*, More's *Utopia*, Bacon's *New Atlantis*, James Harrington's *Commonwealth of Oceana*, and (most immediately and importantly) Swift's *Gulliver's Travels*, these narratives give an unqualified emphasis to the fantastic as opposed to the more nearly mimetic. There are many variations, but a typical procedure in works of this kind is to leave a conventional adventurer-hero stranded in some isolated culture, whose characteristics then function as vehicles of satire or argumentation. Usually, the descriptions of these remarkable societies are very detailed. Their locations, however, range from the just barely imaginable to the wholly impossible: the heart of the African desert, the moon, and the center of the earth are among the settings chosen. Only the very susceptible could have been tricked into belief by the almost mocking protestations of authenticity characterizing the utopian voyages. Such readers would have little concerned authors whose primary purpose was not to entertain, but to argue and instruct. These writers conceived of their narratives as historical in a very special sense, and they addressed their claims of truth to sophisticated readers who could perceive the intellectual and moral realities in which they dealt.

The utopian voyages of the 1740s include a curious piece by John Kirkby (Gibbon's tutor) called *The Capacity and Extent of the Human Understanding: Exemplified in the Extraordinary Case of Automathes* (editions in 1745, 1746, and 1747), which is actually a hybrid incorporating elements of both desert-island and utopian fiction; and a translation of Baron Ludwig Holberg's *A Journey to the World Under-Ground* (1742), a most ingenious imitation of *Gulliver's Travels*. Both of these works promote doctrines of philosophical and theological rationalism. Automathes, stranded on a remote island as a child, uses his powers of reason to deduce the existence of a Prime Mover or First Cause, the Artist of the universe. By the time he is rescued, he has turned into an intelligent, knowledgeable, pious young Anglican gentleman. Holberg, whose imagination was much more fertile than Kirkby's, projects a subterranean world organized into nations inhabited by such Swiftean grotesques as rational tigers, monkeys, ice-blocks, musical instruments, and mouthless human figures who communicate by passing gas in rhythmical patterns. The land of Potua is particularly interesting, for it exhibits a race of trees who, despite their lack of ritual and a scripture, have discovered God and His truths and have become pious, humble worshippers. Unlike the implied deism of *Automathes*, the Potuan faith parallels the arguments of liberal orthodox apologists like George Berkeley and Joseph Butler. The formal theology of the Potuans is in fact, whether Holberg intended it or not, quite a Berkeleyan interpretation of the function of reason as the means by which, in response to the material world, the human mind formulates ideas of God. In this respect, Holberg's *Journey* closely resembles another important utopian voyage, the *Memoirs of Sig^r. Gaudentio di Lucca* (1737; reprinted in 1748 and many times after), a piece that for almost fifty years was regarded as the work of Bishop Berkeley, but is actually by an obscure writer named Simon Berington.[16]

Berington's narrative, like Holberg's, founds its arguments upon the principles of right reason and natural law. It depicts its own utopia, located deep into the African desert, in which sanction is given only to those customs and habits that may be justified on liberal rationalist grounds. This land, a virtual paradise called Mezzorania, is the home of a Semitic race of believers in a universal spatial and moral order of which the sun is both the physical and symbolic center. The Mezzoranians have organized their populated areas according to the universal pattern of concentric spheres, while their political and family structure is modeled after the patriarchal order of the universe, of which El (God) is the head. The role of Pophar in the state parallels that of El in the universe, and the father of a family functions as the patriarch of his own little empire. All authority is absolute, yet the society is free at all levels from injustice and inequality, tyranny and brutality. Berington's continued insistence upon the ideal quality of moral and political life in Mezzorania constitutes an extended and severe attack upon conditions in England. No reasonably alert reader could have missed the implications of this utopian vision, which emphatically defines the value of the work as an example of historical narrative. From natural phenomena, the gentle and good Mezzoranians have deduced the existence of El, the Supreme Being to whom they faithfully refer all moral and ethical questions. Gaudentio finds the theological rationalism of these people profoundly attractive, but inadequate to answer man's spiritual needs. Over the years, he converts many Mezzoranians to Catholicism (that is, Anglicanism) and thus, in the manner of More's Raphael Hythloday, brings a final spiritual perfection to this already faultless society.

Gaudentio's chief attractions as utopian fiction reside in its concreteness of representation, in the shrewdness of its insistent political criticism, and in the generous, benevolent spirit that pervades it. The hero is a competent and engaging memoirist; his descriptions are exact, his satire and moral judgments quite pointed, and his own character rather fully delineated. Furthermore, the numerous trials and dangerous adventures to which he is subjected, and from which he emerges triumphant as a Christian hero, make him the familiar ideological agent of conventional morality. Berington's narrative as a whole is unoriginal, its format taken from earlier utopias such as those of More and Harrington. But when accepted on its own terms as fantasy, *Gaudentio* may be understood as a meaningful work of fictionalized contemporary history. The world Berington creates (like the world of *Gulliver's Travels*) defines a convincing intellectual and moral reality. It is a reality given life even more by the energy and eloquence of the author's ideas than by his intensely imagined people and places. And as a fictional construct it is made relevant to eighteenth-century readers by its more than oblique commentary upon what they could not have failed to know about the less than utopian qualities of their own land, with its squalor and poverty and decadence, its class tensions, its debased and corrupt politicians, and (as many believed) its spiritually impoverished Church.

Voyagers like Gaudentio di Lucca were not the only adventurers whose stories captivated English readers in the 1740s. Another species of pseudohistory dealing with the exploits of public figures in politics, the military, and society enjoyed equal popularity. Tales of this kind are usually grounded in fact, but they are at least marginal works of the imagination, for their authors do not seem to have felt very strictly bound to actuality. These narratives typically adopt a loosely biographical mode, but they all disregard the interior life and the particulars of daily existence in favor of a strategy which allows their authors to use the dramatic external facts of personal experience to illuminate, or comment upon, important contemporary events and controversies. For want of a more precise term we may call such works, whether genuine or feigned, by the name of historical biographies. Their ancestors are to be found among the examples of a species of popular military and political narrative that flourished in the late seventeenth and early eighteenth centuries. None of the distinguished originals reappeared in the 1740s—neither Phillipe de Commines's *Mémoires*, nor Bishop Burnet's *Life and Death of the Right Honourable John Earl of Rochester* (1680), nor the soldier Edmund Ludlow's three volumes of quasi-fictional *Memoirs* (1698–99), nor other seventeenth-century narratives of this kind, formerly very popular. Indeed, since about 1720 a majority of such works published in England were new native pieces like Defoe's *Memoirs of a Cavalier* (1720), *The Military Memoirs of Captain George Carleton* (1728; usually attributed to Defoe), and the anonymous *Memoirs of Capt. John Creichton* (1731). In this kind of writing novelty seems to have been a requirement. Except for a few translations from undistinguished foreign pieces, the many narratives in this vein published during the 1740s were all new English productions. Most of these prove to be copies from earlier models, but they are manifestly inferior, and their quality signals a marked decline from the performance of Defoe and his best imitators.

Among the new English originals the great subject was the Jacobite Rebellion of 1745–46. Curiously, neither the period's parliamentary maneuvers nor the long War of the Austrian Succession generated much in the way of fictionalized political or military historical biography, unless we count the secret historicans' slurs on Walpole. The cataclysmic events of the 'Forty-Five, however, riveted the attention of the English people, and with only a very few notable exceptions the chroniclers of the adventures of contemporary public figures fixed their own eyes on Prince Charles Edward Stuart and others who played some part in events connected with the Rebellion.

One of the remarkable exceptions is a celebrated work which details the private experiences of an alleged aristocrat: James Annesley's *Memoirs of an Unfortunate Young Nobleman* (1743–47). Annesley claimed to be a disinherited nobleman, son of the Irish Lord Altham, suffering deprivation and degradation at the hands of his usurping uncle Richard—who, according to young James, had betrayed him, sold him into American slavery as a child, and stolen his rightful title. There was in 1743, and still is, much doubt about the truth of Annesley's claim; he may have been, as his uncle said he was, his father's bastard.[17] The narrative, however, indicates that the subject himself suffered no doubts about his legitimacy. Annesley's story, the title of which sounds like a novel, is an interminable affair (it was published in three substantial parts) written from the third-person point of view, but with very little detachment. The book serves partly as a public indictment of Annesley's uncle Richard and the system which supported his perfidy, partly as a self-aggrandizing portrait of the young hero, or the "Chevalier James," as he is called throughout. All those who support Richard's case appear as consummate blackguards, while the wretched uncle himself possesses "all the Vices center'd in his Composition: he was proud and mean at the same Time—vain-glorious yet avaritious—ungrateful for good Offices—revengeful for even imagin'd Injuries—treacherous when trusted—mischievously inquisitive when not so—without the least spark of Honour, Pity, or even common Humanity—incapable by Nature of doing *any Good*, and qualified by an extreme *Subtility* for *all kinds of Evil*." The Chevalier James, on the other hand, emerges as a character complete in his perfection—handsome, loving, compassionate, noble, courageous, strong in his pursuit of the right. All those who second him simply sparkle as lesser stars in the celestial sphere he inhabits. In pursuit of its polemical purpose, the work incorporates a wealth of circumstantial evidence, but little of it is imaginatively employed. Potentially interesting as the account of the hero's deprived childhood is, it reads as though it were part of a legal brief. The thirteen years of Annesley's slavery receive lengthy treatment, yet except for the narrator's intermittent diatribes against cruel masters we get little sense of what it was like to be a slave in the Delaware River Valley. Annesley spends the mature years of his life gathering evidence for his cause, and this period is lovingly (and tediously) detailed. An army of worthy souls, some of them former allies of Richard, join the hero, and their aim is to help him gain justice and to protect him against the uncle's murderous attempts on his life and character. Several lengthy courtroom scenes punctuate the remainder of the narrative.

So clumsy a work as the Annesley *Memoirs* seems hardly worth the attention it received from contemporary readers. But the Annesley case was famous. Especially for middle-class readers increasingly conscious of class privileges and discrimination, it must have held an inherent interest. The work itself underscores the social drama of the actual case by a moral ideology pitting the unblemished common man against the dangerous wiles of a thoroughly villainous, conniving aristocrat. Interest in the Annesley affair even justified a vulgar plagiarism from parts one and two of the *Memoirs*, a piece called *Fortune's Favourite: Containing, Memoirs of . . . Jacobo Anglicano, a Young Nobleman* (1744). Readers could also buy an account of *The Tryal of James Annesley and Joseph Reading for Murder* (1742), and a popular pamphlet entitled *The Case of the Hon. James Annesley, Esq.* (1744).[18] Not all of Annesley's admirers were vulgar scandalmongers, however. Tobias Smollett saw Annesley's work as an important commentary on the times, and in chapter 106 of *Peregrine Pickle* (1751) he gave it sympathetic attention. *Roderick Random* itself is the story of a dispossessed heir, though the hero's rank is much lower than Annesley's, and though in the end he finds his lost father and is restored to fortune.

In its special concern with the conflict between the private individual and an arbitrary social establishment, the *Memoirs of an Unfortunate Young Nobleman* emphasizes what I have already suggested was a main preoccupation of contemporary fiction—the elevation of the private person to public stature. The functions of biographical and historical writing merge completely in a narrative like this one. A better work than Annesley's, and one which views the private character in a similar light, is *The Life and Adventures of Mrs. Christian Davies, the British Amazon, Commonly Called Mother Ross* (1739–40). The story of Mrs. Davies, which enjoyed a second edition in 1741, certainly stands out as the most sophisticated of all the decade's original works in this mode. It is clearly an imitation of Defoe. In its competent use of the autobiographical form, in its piling up of circumstantial detail, its portrait of a vital, energetic character, and its vigorous plain-style, the work closely resembles the *Memoirs of a Cavalier*. Like Defoe, also, the anonymous author borrowed facts, rearranged and embellished them, imaginatively blending truth and fiction in a first-person narrative. There really was a Mother Ross, and she had a real career as foot-soldier and dragoon first under William III and later under Marlborough.

The Mother Ross of this work, as a representative of the lower classes, possesses the appeal of the familiar or ordinary character who endures the trials and enjoys the pleasures of extraordinary experience. As a deflowered maiden, she marries young, and when her husband is pressed into military service under the Duke of Marlborough, she dons man's garb and sets out to find him. She is a convincing female picaro in disguise, and after numerous adventures along the road she joins the army and shortly distinguishes herself for valor on the battlefield and in the boudoir (she is astonishingly thought to have sired a bastard). Marlborough even makes her his favorite. At length she finds her husband in the arms of a whore, whose nose she cuts off in anger, and having dispatched him as well, she returns to battle, whereupon she is wounded and her sex revealed. She remains in service, now as a cook and campfollower who lives chiefly on plunder and booty. Twice widowed, she retires to private life as proprietress of a public house and marries one Mr. Davies, keeping him and her customers in check by occasional display of her former warrior ways. In her declining years, she enjoys a pensioner's residence at Chelsea College together with a sergeant's rank in His Majesty's Army and the attention and benefactions of distinguished company.

The first-person method of *Mrs. Davies* is consistent with the work's claim that the story is taken from the heroine's "own Mouth," although it is most likely by an anonymous hack. Surely this record of remarkable adventures takes considerable liberties with the facts of the real Mrs. Davies's career.[19] The work's topical immediacy (England was just going to war in 1739–40) and its extravagant adventures, straightforwardly rendered, doubtless recommended it to readers, as did some of its particular merits as pure story. Furthermore, many of the numerous military characters are treated with Theophrastian zest and succinctness, and some of the important adventures have the vividness of lively recollection. The numerous battle actions in particular are closely and graphically detailed, although the author cannot equal Defoe's success with this kind of description in *Memoirs of a Cavalier*. But *Mrs. Davies* possesses no moral dimension whatever. The work's ethical shallowness results largely from the character of the heroine, who is throughout most of her story a woman of action, not reflection. Her experience does not teach her, and she does not grow; her claim on the attention of readers resides chiefly in her resilience, her zest for highjinks, her capacity to endure as a resourceful woman in a man's world. Only when her story is nearly over, as she grows old and infirm, does Mother Ross develop the kind of depth which can command human sympathy. The "Expense of Coach Hire," she laments very near the end, "as both my Lameness and Age increase, for I cannot walk ten Yards without Help, is a terrible Tax upon their [her benefactors'] Charity"; my "former Substance is greatly diminshed from what it was." The last pages of this marginal novel show us something of a reflective heroine, conscious of the sad irony of her present invalid, dependent state and her past life of energetic action, independence, and glory—a glory for which she is still celebrated, but which she can recover now only through memory. There is a poignancy in this that vaguely adumbrates the kind of richness English novelists were soon to learn how to exploit.

Except for Annesley's *Memoirs* and the story of *Mrs. Davies*, the most interesting of the new fictionalized biographies of public figures appeared in the wake of the 'Forty-Five, which they took as their subject. A few of these works bear some relevance to the major fiction of the decade, although none is up to the mark of quality established earlier by *Mrs. Davies*. A majority of the dozen or so stories in this group feature various Scottish lairds and ladies who gave aid and comfort to the Young Pretender, or the Young Chevalier, as Prince Charles Edward Stuart was often called. English readers apparently found the Chevalier's Scottish supporters peculiarly interesting because of the mystery surrounding the Highland gentry and nobility, who were popularly regarded as romantic barbarians. Following the decisive battle of Culloden, many of these apparent eccentrics were brought to trial in London, and received considerable attention from the English press. A small handful of the fictionalized biographies treating the Jacobite uprising are six-penny pamphlets that deal with bona fide heroes from the middling class of people. One of these, John Drummond's *The Affecting Case, and Dying Words of Mr. Arch[ibald]. Oswald, an Ensign in the Young Pretender's Service* (1745), briefly recounts the heroism of a youthful Scottish soldier who died of three musket shots at the Battle of Preston-Pans. Another outlines the career of an ordinary young Englishman named Charles Radcliffe, who, before he was slain in battle, rose briefly to become secretary to Charles Edward.[20] Although the number of works dealing with the Rebellion is relatively small, narratives detailing the careers of ordinary soldiers actually outnumber those occupied with the gallant and occasionally spectacular prince himself. The life and adventures of the Young Pretender received major treatment in newspapers and popular ballads, but apparently, when the contemporary reader turned to historical biography, he preferred something closer to his own experience.

The two historical biographies taking Prince Charles Edward for their subject are both lengthy and ambitious productions, but surprisingly pedestrian and slipshod in the performance. One of these, a hastily written work of almost 300 pages called *Ascanius; or, The Young Adventurer. A True History* (1746), is possibly by Dr. John Burton, whom Sterne unfairly portrayed as the ridiculous Dr. Slop in *Tristram Shandy*. *Ascanius* is actually a kind of miscellany which begins by presenting a brief historical account of the Rebellion, then devotes most of its many pages to the extended story of the "Young Adventurer" himself before concluding with summary sketches of a few of the prince's more notorious supporters. By slyly offering his book as a translation from a manuscript "privately handed about at the court of Versailles," the author hints at its authenticity as an account written by some insider possessing special knowledge. There can be no doubt that this conventional pose of the surreptitious fiction writer is adopted so as to provoke interest in the centerpiece of the book, the sensational chronicle of the prince's hair-raising exploits and narrow escape from capture and certain execution. The portrait of Charles Edward himself is clumsily drawn and most unsympathetic, and the narrative as a whole is fiercely but crudely polemical, even moralistic, in its attacks upon the Jacobites. But *Ascanius* is, at least, varied as well as purposeful. While protesting that he writes history and not fiction, the author actually looses his imagination upon his subject, repeating battle plans, letters, confidential conversations, and private reflections that are obviously the products of invention. Throughout, the effect is always to distort the truth about the prince and his Scottish and French allies, who are wrought into monsters of evil by the cheapest devices of exaggerated characterization. Mercifully, there are a few lively scenes that succeed in displaying the Chevalier's instinctive military cunning and the intense loyalty he inspired among his fanatical followers.

The intended appeal of *Ascanius* is transparent: the work invites its readers to exercise their deeply felt hostilities against the whole Jacobite enterprise, with its long history of threats against the Constitution, the established Hanoverian succession, and the public welfare. It projects Charles Edward as an archetypal villain of almost mythical proportions, as a fig-

71

ure whose presence endangered moral order itself. Yet the work actually reflects the abiding fascination felt by so many English citizens as a response to the gallantry of the young prince. In his attempt to vilify the Pretender as a wicked, ambitious adventurer, the author only makes him a glamorous, royal rogue—a kind of highborn Mackheath of political criminality. Surely this accounts for the fact that *Ascanius* was by far the most popular of all the many narratives inspired by the 'Forty-Five.[21] Like Fielding's portrait of Jonathan Wild, also, the version of the Chevalier presented in *Ascanius* is appealing partly because of the sheer bustle of his activity, the imaginative energy he brings to his schemes against conventionally accepted ideas of the political good. This author was not alone in the unacknowledged sentimentality of his reaction to Charles Edward; it was common enough in popular ballads and prints issued on both sides of the Jacobite controversy.[22] The prince was all the more dangerous for his very real attractions, as the Fielding of the *True Patriot* and the *Jacobite's Journal* was well aware. But *Ascanius* gives no overt sign that it was designed to assault the evils of Jacobitism by exposing the appealing attributes of its leader as fraudulent, or that any other kind of subtle strategy was intended. The only controlling vision in the work is a simply polemical one. The complications introduced—tentatively, it must be said—into the characterization are all inadvertencies; or if they are not, they are clever swindles designed to beguile members of a susceptible, agitated audience into reading and then encouraging others to read a timely book about a celebrated public figure toward whom many people felt a mixture of admiration and detestation.

Some of the several narratives dealing with Charles Edward's Scottish allies are equally interesting (if no more skillful) contrivances. A small book called *Memoirs of the Lives and Families of the Lords Kilmarnock, Cromarty, and Balmorins* (1746) offered sensational sketches of three of the most famous Highlanders who had lent their support to the prince and been hanged for it. They were barbarians all as presented by the author or authors of these accounts, but a measure of the public fascination with such characters may be taken by noting the publication in 1747 of a most curious pamphlet whose title will reveal the actual nature of its appeal: *An Account of the Apparition of the Late Lord Kilmarnock to the Rev*[d] *Mr. Foster. . . . To Which Is Added, The Second Appearing of the Late Lord Kilmarnock, to a Clergyman of the Church of England.* Apparently, at least some readers were ready to believe the romantic Highlanders capable of most amazing feats of endurance. In the same year another book, much more ambitious, offered 368 octavo pages of fictionalized memoirs treating *The Female Rebels: Being Some Remarkable Incidents of the Lives, Characters, and Families of the Titular Duke and Dutchess of Perth, the Lord and Lady Ogilvie, and of Miss Florence M'Donald.* These ladies and their families were close to the Young Pretender, and this association is the source of their interest.

The Reverend Archibald Arbuthnot was the author of two substantial historical biographies of celebrated figures from the 'Forty-Five. His *Memoirs of the Remarkable Life and Surprizing Adventures of Miss Jenny Cameron* (1746) gives us the fictionalized life story of a roguish vixen, a lively Scottish girl who, in her mid-forties, became mistress to Prince Charles Edward and followed him through the whole course of the Rebellion. In his anti-Jacobite's zeal to expose Jenny Cameron as a woman of no moral or political principles, Arbuthnot accidentally imparts to her fictionalized counterpart some of the attractions of a female picaro. Indeed, even though sketchily drawn, the Jenny Cameron of this book emerges as a mixed character whose hoydenish qualities are offset by her strength of mind, her wit, and her animal vitality. She clearly possesses some of Mrs. Davies's most engaging charms. The last forty pages of the book deal explicitly with the liaison between Jenny Cameron and the prince. Here Arbuthnot uses his trumped-up heroine to express simple moral indignation, with the aim of discrediting the Young Pretender's principles, character, and cause.

Jenny Cameron appeared almost simultaneously with another narrative by the same author entitled *The Life, Adventures, and Many Great Vicissitudes of Fortune of Simon, Lord Lovat* (1746).[23] Arbuthnot's partisan account of this famous Scottish Jacobite is fairly faithful to the basic facts of its subject's life, but it outrageously heightens and ridicules his eccentricites. The author especially makes comic capital of Lovat's notorious cowardice, which stirred huge sneering crowds at the time of his trial and imprisonment in the Tower and, later, at his execution. This book does the same kind of thing as *Jenny Cameron*. For almost 300 pages it develops the details of a distorted portrait of a well-known Jacobite figure in an attempt to cast serious aspersion on the Jacobite cause itself. Neither of Arbuthnot's two books has any real literary merit. Like all of the contemporary historical biographies of this kind, they aim only to satisfy a popular taste for tales of the more spectacular Scottish rebels, and to stimulate the growing hatred and fear of them—in effect, to help bring about what later happened, the disarming of the Highlanders, the depreciation of their culture, and the reduction of the powerful feudal chiefs to figureheads. A main reason for restoring such works to view is to demonstrate in yet another way that readers in the mid-century period were accustomed to fiction in the guise of history that took a partisan view of recent events and issues, and gave a sense of participation in the same.

Richardson, Fielding, and Smollett:
Private Experience as Public History

The broad relevance of the various kinds of pseudohistory and historical biography should be obvious to anyone familiar with the works of Richardson, Fielding, and Smollett. Each of these writers styled himself a historian in a fictional mode, and it is easy enough to see that the popularity of their novels coincided with and perhaps was even reinforced by the currency of spy fictions, secret histories, and feigned memoirs and lives of private people whose experience had imparted to them some kind of real public importance. Such works, we will remember, professed to renounce the extravagances of romance, and they contributed importantly to the climate of interest in narrative accounts of familiar life and contemporary affairs, while they almost invariably proclaimed a moral commitment to the ideals of Christian virtue. Throughout their own novels, Richardson, Fielding, and Smollett exhibit their very serious interest in the historical functions of prose fiction. Our labors, said Fielding of his story of *Tom Jones* (in 9.1)—and his words apply equally well to the two other major novelists of the 1740s—"have sufficient Title to the Name of History," for they draw upon the vast materials furnished to the observant eye by life itself, which is interpreted in these fictions by a transforming moral imagination. The exactness with which the authors of *Pamela*, *Joseph Andrews*, and *Roderick Random* reflect the texture of life in their period, the social and moral tensions and the actual feel of day-to-day living, suggests the degree to which they shared some of the impulses of the lesser writers

74

whose works are discussed in earlier pages of this chapter. Their superior gifts and vision enabled them to avoid the limitations of mere topicality and voguishness, but Richardson, Fielding, and Smollett were simply the most able and important among a larger community of writers of prose narrative whose varied approaches to the business of representing the realities of public and private life were mutually reinforcing.

The term *history*, as used in the title of *Tom Jones* or *The History of Clarissa Harlowe*, actually suggested a biographical as well as historical method to readers of the day, and the novels of Fielding, and of Richardson and Smollett as well, possess considerable interest as fictionalized history in both important contemporary senses of the term. Like the popular spy fictions and secret histories, they not only register significant truths about familiar life, but sometimes deliberately enter areas of experience hidden from ordinary view. Fielding and Smollett in particular are satiric writers who aim to expose certain ludicrous or odious people and institutions to their readers' scrutiny and derision.

The heroes and heroines of the major novels are all somehow strangers, at least in a moral sense, to the scenes of wickedness and corruption they encounter. Their resemblance to the moralizing spies of Marana and Montesquieu may well have seemed more than just casual to the first readers of their stories. Always innocent in some degree, characters like Pamela Andrews, Abraham Adams, and Roderick Random are outsiders in the real world, where they are confronted by hypocrisy, venality, and cruelty. The role of Richardson's Pamela, as letter-writer and moral agent, is in part that of an observer, a shrewd, articulate, unspoiled country girl whose virtue makes her a kind of alien in genteel society. Her futile efforts to enlist the aid of her captor's neighbors in Lincolnshire reveal the moral shallowness of the country gentry and their upper-class indifference to the rakish carryings-on in their own neighborhoods and their own social circle. In *Clarissa* the picture of life in country houses is narrower than in *Pamela*, but presented in greater depth, and when the novel shifts its scene to London, Richardson bares the inner workings of a circle of libertines and whores as they victimize his beleaguered heroine. The tone of Clarissa's own letters does not differ significantly from that of the epistles written by Mme de Graffigny's Peruvian princess, although they are composed with even greater intensity of personal feeling.

In Fielding's comic "histories" of *Joseph Andrews*, *Tom Jones*, and *Amelia*, it is the narrator who leads the reader behind the façades of contemporary life, but the effect often approximates that of the spy fictions. In the early scenes of *Joseph Andrews*, for example, the author dramatizes the experience of the innocent and therefore alien hero as a means of exposing the vagaries of Lady Booby and her fashionable household. In the same novel he employs Parson Adams as a device for stripping away the mask of an inept, debased clergyman like the swinish Parson Trulliber (2.13), and later draws a vivid picture (in 4.5) of the kind of stupidly depraved country justice with whom Fielding the lawyer was well acquainted and who could, if bribed, "commit two Persons to *Bridewell* for a Twig." Trading justices, in fact, as well as other commonly corrupt public servants (lawyers, physicians, prison bailiffs, clergymen), are from this time abundantly examined in Fielding's fiction.

Smollett's "friendless orphan" Roderick Random, as a young Scotsman, is most definitely an outsider in the scenes that come under his view. Smollett's novel generally follows rather closely the model of LeSage's picaresque romance of *Gil Blas*, but it bears the same relationship to spy fiction as *Gil Blas* does to the same French author's *Le Diable boiteux*, a fantastic adaptation of Montesquieu which Smollett translated in 1750.[24] Roderick lacks the detachment of the typical spy, and his own knavery qualifies his reliability as a witness, but his narrative abounds with graphic accounts of country families in strife, of the follies and vices of provincial pharmacists and innkeepers, the twistings of government bureaucracy, the dishonesty of aristocratic ministers, the machinations of gamblers and fortune-hunters. The extended autobiographical episodes describing the ill-fated expedition to Carthagena in 1741 (chaps. 24–37) supply what is probably the most detailed and damning account ever written of the realities of eighteenth-century Navy life. Smollett's journalistic instincts were strong, and his novel reports with great intensity upon the cruelties of the press-gang, the brutishness of common sailors, the sickening food and the filth of shipboard life, and the incompetence of officers like the *Thunder*'s Captain Oakum and surgeon Mackshane.

The savagely satiric treatment of Captain Oakum, moreover, is a stroke much in the manner of a secret historian as well, for it surely reflects upon some ship's captain, now impossible to identify with any certainty, of the fleet in which Smollett served aboard the *Chichester* during the Carthagena disaster. A number of real people regarded themselves as wounded by the portraits drawn in these episodes, where the author fictionalizes real events for at least the partial purpose of ridiculing public figures.[25] Smollett undertook similar treatment of real-life characters in the long prison chapters of his novel (61–64) where he avenged himself on Lord Chesterfield, who had once denied him patronage, and on Quin, Garrick, Lacy, and Rich, the actors and theatrical managers who had refused to produce his unactable tragedy *The Regicide*. He boldly drew their caricatures in the silly figures named Earl Sheerwit, Bellower, Marmozet, Brayer, and Vandal. It was this "set of scoundrels" who had driven the deserving poet Melopoyn to poverty, despair, and jail.

Like Smollett, Fielding more than just occasionally engaged in a gesture recalling the methods of the secret historian. The Beau Didapper of *Joseph Andrews*, to name but one important example, is clearly John, Lord Hervey, Baron Ickworth, the effeminate, diseased, painted courtier whom Fielding loathed for his loyalty to Walpole, and who was known to his enemies by Pope's contemptuous epithet "Lord Fanny." (Fielding, of course, ironically dedicated *Shamela* to Hervey in the person of "Miss Fanny.") Beau Didapper is that "little Person or rather Thing" who, though immensely rich, chose for the "dirty Consideration of a Place of little consequence" to submit his "Conscience," "Honour," and "Country" to the capricious will of a "Great Man" (4.9).[26] In this instance, Fielding's intention is identical with that of Mrs. Manley in *Queen Zarah* or the *New Atalantis;* he aims to embarrass a public person and expose him to ridicule, all for partisan purposes.

Fielding probably read the "*Atalantis* Writers" he sneered at in *Joseph Andrews* (3.1). He certainly despised them, and he would have had no need to turn to them for instruction in the creation of a character like Beau Didapper, or Peter Pounce, or the many other comic figures he drew from real life into the worlds of his fictions for the purpose of ridiculing them. Dryden, Swift, and Pope had all used similar tactics in modes of writing that would have been more likely sources for his inspiration. The point is that the satiric strategies of the secret history were still current in popular fiction, as were the conventions of spy narrative. Richardson, Fielding, and Smollett, as alert members of the reading public, could hardly have been ignorant of these two voguish modes of pseudohistorical writing, or (for that matter) of the degree to which the occasional attractions of their own novels as exposés overlap with the appeal of works like

The Turkish Spy and *Queen Zarah*. There is no clear evidence to suggest that they borrowed directly from specific conventions of the spy narrative or the *chronique scandaleuse*, but then neither did they, in composing their own works, entirely renounce all association with important attractions of these kinds of popular fiction.

The various forms of historical biography—the lives of all kinds of public figures and of adventurers at sea or on the battlefield—are much more relevant to the novels of Richardson, Fielding, and Smollett than are the spy fictions and secret histories. All three major writers made deliberate attempts to tell stories celebrating the importance of individual men and women, showing how any person, however humble of origin, might rise to a kind of conspicuous moral eminence. Joseph Andrews and Abraham Adams have their counterparts in the Bible, a simple but ingenious allusiveness by which Fielding certifies at once the timeliness and the universal value of their comic experience. The names Tom Jones and Roderick Random in different ways suggest the broad application of the particularized characters they identify and describe—Tom Jones by its very commonness; Roderick Random by its combination of a Christian name drawn from romance and thus hinting at the native nobility of Smollett's hero, with a surname pointing to the dangers of the potentially erratic quality of individual moral life in a vexing, chaotic world. Roderick, like Tom, is projected as a kind of everyman. The epistolary story of Clarissa Harlowe is an intensely autobiographical fiction, and so of course is the first-person tale told by Roderick Random. Yet, as we know from Richardson's emphatic authorial comments, Clarissa herself was conceived as a representative figure whose exemplary function as Christian heroine, in the author's mind, gives her imagined life high public importance. In the novels of all three major writers, whatever their other attributes or uses of popular narrative conventions, private experience as it touches upon the felt reality of familiar life is deliberately rendered as a special kind of contemporary history—moral history, we may call it, or (in the case of Fielding and Smollett) comic history.

None of this is really news. Every modern reader of *Joseph Andrews*, *Clarissa*, *Roderick Random*, and the other major novels of the 1740s has acknowledged at least the general appropriateness of their claims to a historical function. Their very first readers were surely just as sensitive to the justice of these claims. But the members of the eighteenth-century audience would have read the novels in a context of popular historical biographies, to which they relate in some very interesting ways, and some of these readers—the more sophisticated ones, anyhow—would therefore have enjoyed an enhanced appreciation of their methods and of their authors' performance as contemporary historians in a fictional mode.

There can be no question but that Richardson, Fielding, and Smollett exploited some of the conventions of historical biography, though of course their own complex purposes as artists and as moralists never coincide perfectly with the more limited aims of Simon Berington, or James Annesley, or the author of *Mrs. Christian Davies*, or the other writers of similar narratives. This point may be easily illustrated. The novels of Richardson, Fielding, and Smollett, in pursuit of their didactic purposes, all deliberately employ the motif of the journey, either literal or spiritual, as an extended metaphor for life's entanglements. Furthermore, one might argue that each of the major novels subscribes to an idealism that works itself out in the protagonist's moral progress toward a final reward, usually represented by the happiness to be found in a rural utopia. Clarissa Harlowe's reward comes in heaven, of course, but the principle is the same: like Pamela and the heroes of *Tom Jones*, *Joseph Andrews*, and *Roderick Random*, she ends her journey in a place which, by its very perfections, implies strong criticism of the vexing world through which she has moved. The appeal of this manner of resolution overlaps with the general utopian attractions of a work like Simon Berington's account of the travels of Gaudentio di Lucca, although the kind of ending we find in *Clarissa* had its ultimate origins in pastoral traditions and Christian homiletics, not in utopian voyages, which use a different strategy involving a journey from the real world to a utopia and back again. Clarissa's passage through life to heaven is much more closely related to Christian's journey in *Pilgrim's Progress* than to contemporary travel narratives.

The specifically utopian qualities of the major novels are important, however, and must not be discounted or diminished. Richardson, Fielding, and Smollett were all Christian idealists, though in varying degrees, and surely they were all three aware of the long tradition and continued currency of utopian travel literature, which may have at least indirectly influenced their vision of the meaning of their characters' experience. A more cautious comment, perhaps, is that their Christian understanding of moral life coincided with the idealism expressed in utopian narrative, and that this very real parallel may have been to some degree deliberately emphasized in their novels as an ingredient of their formula for popular success. We may only speculate whether this is so, but the very obviousness of the parallel must have helped to fire the enthusiasm of contemporary readers long since accustomed to the pleasures of utopian tales and to other kinds of stories—the pious novels of Penelope Aubin, for example—that resolved the crises of their beleaguered heroes and heroines' progress toward fulfillment by imposing a Christian utopian vision upon the hard empirical realities of their fictional worlds.

Other kinds of adventure narratives bear much more directly on the practice of the major novelists. In *Jonathan Wild*, Mrs. Heartfree's long story (4. 7–9, 11) of her scarifying experiences with her abductor Wild, of her escape and subsequent adventures on high seas and foreign shores, is Fielding's tongue-in-cheek version of a conventional imaginary voyage. Wild's own adventures after Mrs. Heartfree's departure burlesque the same mode (2.10–13). Earlier in the book Fielding parodies the Grand Tour (and its literature) by devoting to his "hero's" travels the less than two pages of a "very short chapter" containing "not one adventure worthy the reader's notice" (1.7). In his *Journal of a Voyage to Lisbon* (1755), Fielding would offer a voyage narrative worthy of admiration, as he declared in the preface, because not disfigured either by the introduction of monsters and improbable adventures in unimaginable places, or by the dilation of trivial experience into many dull pages. The voyage narrative, Fielding explained, as a species of historical writing, ought to tell the truth, it ought to be artfully done, and it ought to instruct as well as delight. In *Jonathan Wild* he sought, as did Swift in *Gulliver's Travels*, to expose some of the absurdities of familiar voyage and travel literature. And yet Fielding's purpose, like Swift's, was more complex. By the extravagance and vanities of Mrs. Heartfree's tale, he obviously meant to mix in some foibles that would qualify her otherwise unblemished character, thus bringing it closer to his own theories of characterization. At the same time, he was perfectly serious at another level. Mrs. Heartfree's tale of her trials—of abduction, slavery, leering advances, attempted rape, and so on—illustrates her moral strength and functions as a parable of persecuted virtue triumphant.

Fielding's two great novels of the 1740s, the histories of Joseph Andrews and Tom Jones, present stories of energetic adventurers possessing great personal resilience and powerful moral and emotional interest as ordinary people struggling through life's entanglements. Because the aims of these two works are so very complex, they far surpass anything achieved by the author of the historical biography of Mother Ross or by James Annesley in his autobiographical *Memoirs of an Unfortunate Young Nobleman*. But *Joseph Andrews* and *Tom Jones* do deliberately incorporate some of the same interests as these lesser works. *Tom Jones* does so most conspicuously. The novel is sprinkled with allusions to the Jacobites, and Tom's escapades on the road to London are actually thrown into relief against the turbulent background of the 'Forty-Five. Fielding's lively youth even joins the Hanoverian cause as a soldier ready to die in order to protect the kingdom from the Jacobite invaders. This is all obvious. But the important thing is that for a time at least, the very identity of Tom as familiar hero is partly defined by his direct connection with a great public controversy.

In his last novel, *Amelia*, Fielding exploits still more conspicuously the appeal of the popular historical biographies of military characters in treating the experience of his wayward soldier Billy Booth. Booth is the central figure in a considerable cast of military characters. Though weak and vacillating in his domestic relations, he is a responsible officer who fights valiantly and is wounded at Gibraltar. We see only slightly more of Booth's actual soldiering than we do of Tom Jones's experiences as a military man, but we are led to believe that he was courageous. It is of course impossible to know the degree to which Fielding may have intentionally tried to call to mind the many fashionable tales of soldiering adventurers, but to any reasonably alert reader *Amelia* must have seemed more than just remotely related to works like *Mrs. Davies* and Defoe's *Memoirs of a Cavalier*. Fielding's novel effectually turns the formula of the military memoir inside out. The hero's adventures occur mainly in Admiralty offices and the prisons and coffee houses of London, and his enemies are mostly domestic. But the specific effect of the novel's treatment of this gallant soldier is toward defining a higher kind of heroism. Booth, an ordinary man who has benefited from hard experience and finally from the wisdom of Isaac Barrow's sermons, achieves in the teeming world of London what he could not attain in the isolated, remote world of the battlefield, where the dangers were only physical: the status of a Christian hero. In fact, Fielding seems to say in *Amelia* that the real battles, the important moral struggles, are fought in the everyday world, and it is there that they must be won. The circumstances of Booth's seemingly hopeless poverty and his terrible frustrations in trying to get a promotion expose the abuses of privilege in the prevailing military system, and therefore function in the fabric of the novel's social criticism. They link the world of the battlefield with that of daily affairs, which is the novel's main arena, and thus join with Fielding's exposure of a large variety of other social ills—corrupt justices, prison abuses, official favoritism, inadequacies and cruel inequities in the treatment of debtors, the irresponsibilities of an indifferent aristocracy, and so on—in defining the world's resistance to goodness and charity. By surviving his adventures, Booth actually becomes not a warrior hero but, in a very rich sense indeed, a Christian soldier and thus a triumphant figure important to our understanding of Fielding's conception of the deepest meaning of heroism and of his own role as moral historian in a vein of comic fiction.

In *Roderick Random* and *Peregrine Pickle*, with their large casts of fighting sailors, Smollett approaches more nearly than Fielding ever does the actual formula of popular military memoirs. Smollett is a kind of panoramist, and his sailors are less subtly drawn than the soldiers in *Amelia*. Not one of them possesses the depth of Billy Booth, although Peregrine Pickle's benefactor Commodore Hawser Trunnion, in all his delightfully grotesque eccentricities, belongs among the most memorable military characters in eighteenth-century fiction. But Smollett's sailors were drawn from firsthand observation, and what they lack in subtlety is made up for by the accuracy and vividness of the portraits. The shipboard scenes of *Roderick Random*, the battle descriptions, and the accounts of military strategy have the convincing ring of authenticity, and link the Carthagena episodes of the novel very closely to the memoirs of public careers. In fact, throughout these pages Smollett almost duplicates the formula of Defoe, allowing for changes in literary fashion. Roderick himself, by his direct association with such great events and by virtue of his privileged role as their chronicler, inevitably proclaims the public importance of his own life. In a quite spectacular way, his performance in giving his account of the Carthagena affair merges the functions of biographer and historian. Smollett's hero thus demonstrates dramatically how nearly inseparable the two functions could sometimes be in this period. In an extremely explicit manner that neither Richardson nor Fielding ever quite attempted, Roderick's story also reveals how very intimately the two dimensions of private and public life were thought to touch upon one another. Viewed in this light, the Carthegena chapters of *Roderick Random* appear to be a deliberate as well as complete paradigm of the most crucial interests cultivated by all the contemporary kinds of pseudobiographical and pseudohistorical stories. To say the least, Smollett made capital use of what he knew about these minor but important works of narrative literature as he readied his own first novel for the press.

The numerous and varied works of pseudohistory and feigned historical biography were, as I have already suggested, deliberate responses to public tastes. In a kind of circular process familiar enough to anyone who has studied literary history at all, by catering to those tastes with such energy and enthusiasm writers inevitably helped to reinforce them, actually deepening the yearnings of their audience for more of the same. Apparently, contemporary readers could never get enough of stories offering a fantasy life which exalted private experience, gave it public visibility, and emphatically affirmed its importance. Certainly that is the lesson of the popularity earned by the kinds of narrative studied in this chapter, and the same general appeal, though in different manifestations, characterizes the more strictly biographical accounts of social outcasts and pious heroes and heroines to be discussed in the next two chapters. It also, of course, was the chief appeal of the new form of the novel as it emerged in the 1740s. If authors had not tried to satisfy popular tastes—an almost unimaginable possibility given the general opportunism of the writing and publishing businesses in the period—then presumably the novel as we know it would have had to await a later birth. Popular stories in historical and biographical modes were rarely the acknowledged products of the imagination, but by sheer repetition they familiarized their readers with important conventions and a kind of subject matter to which novelists like Richardson, Fielding, and Smollett found it easy to turn when composing their own more able and ambitious works.

It is not necessary to argue the degree to which these three major novelists may have copied this or that convention from this or that type of popular history or biography. What they do borrow they adapt or transform, usually quite radically, making it their own. Sometimes their borrowing is very direct, most often it is not so direct, and occasionally (as in the case of the naval chapters of *Roderick Random*) one of their works will combine the attractions of several kinds of narrative in a single episode, a concentrated series of related scenes, and so forth. Nor would it be useful to debate the broader question of whether the ingenious eclecticism of the major novelists was in every instance of its complexity a calculated response to, or borrowing from, some mode of pseudobiography, or pseudohistory, or (for that matter) romance or novelistic narrative. In the present connection at least, it is much more meaningful simply to observe that the biographical histories of Richardson, Fielding, and Smollett were written in a context which included many other lesser works that made something like the same general appeal even while disguising themselves (however transparently) as true stories of real people. The currency of these forgotten tales, we may say, despite their inferior literary quality, very likely helped encourage the chroniclers of the lives and times of Pamela Andrews, Tom Jones, and Roderick Random to write in the manner they all three adopted.

CHAPTER IV

Fiction as Contemporary Biography: Tales of Low Life

I N THE CURIOUS taxonomy of narrative types available during the early years of the eighteenth century, secret histories, spy stories, and the various kinds of historical biography took the regions of high life, controversial public events, and worldwide adventures as their subjects of concern. As a result, such works show little interest in the psychology of the characters they present, or in the mundane particulars of daily existence. Meanwhile, those life writers who approached most nearly to our modern understanding of the function of biography tended to focus on characters and circumstances closer to the actual experience of their readers. Apparently, these writers judged it easier for people to be interested in the interior life and routine habits of a familiar criminal, or a convert to the Wesleyan religious persuasion, than in any similar human particulars of an energetic adventurer like Mrs. Christian Davies. Defoe, of course, especially in *Robinson Crusoe* but to some extent in the *Memoirs of a Cavalier* as well, managed to join the attractions of historical adventure with those of a subtle and penetrating portrayal of human character, at the same time successfully passing off his stories as true. This is a tribute to his talent, and to the ingenuity of his use of the devices of verisimilitude. Few other authors in the modes of pseudohistory and pseudobiography possessed his skills, or his boldness.

Novelistic writers, including Eliza Haywood, Mary Davys, Jane Barker, and Penelope Aubin, generally restricted themselves to domestic conflict in stories of amorous adventure, often larded with at least superficial representations of the inner torments suffered by their impassioned characters. But in effusively sentimental tales like *Love in Excess* (1719) and *The Life of Madam de Beaumont* (1721) Mrs. Haywood and Mrs. Aubin made extravagant use of the license given by their avowal of their works as products of the imagination to expand the usual geography of novels so as to test the virtue of their persecuted heroes and heroines in all manner of strange and exciting places—dark caves in Wales, the Barbary Coast, Continental dens of iniquity, and so forth. Novels in general, it seems—that is, to define the term broadly, works about familiar domestic characters, acknowledged as fictions—were less strictly bound to any particular conventions of circumstantial realism (most of them very flimsy anyway) than the kinds of pseudohistories and pseudobiographies seem to have been. Surely this explains in part their greater range of interest in the varied dimensions of human experience. Novels were repeatedly condemned as untrue and therefore dangerous, but the different expectations with which readers approached them as works of the imagination enabled a writer like Henry Fielding to style himself as comic historian of the world in general while also posing seriously as a biographer of a poor footman, a lowly foundling, an impoverished soldier and his wife.

The true-to-life accounts of impious criminals and rogues, and of pious heroes and heroines, reflect popular interest in private experience as it gained public value by simply measuring important preoccupations of contemporary culture. The works in the second of these classes of pseudobiography must await a later chapter for discussion in depth, but it will be useful here to mention them in an introductory way, alongside their apparent opposites. As I have already suggested, the appeal of both of these types of life writing was in an important sense as much historical as biographical. Thieves, swindlers, murderers, whores, rapists, conniving rogues, indeed all kinds of deliberate offenders against law and moral order were everywhere to be seen in the cities and on the highways of early eighteenth-century England, and they were feared and despised as public menaces. Yet, the popular attitude toward such aberrant characters was deeply ambivalent, if we may take as evidence the fiction written about them—and we may add here a reference to the ballads and prints inspired by the most notorious of them. They commanded extraordinary interest as people. No doubt this was partly because they were often spectacularly deviant, partly because they answered a normal desire for vicarious experience of the forbidden accompanied by a deep public curiosity about the criminal mind. This curiosity is seldom satisfied in any meaningful way by popular fiction, but all except the most rudimentary chapbook sketches acknowledge it by providing at least some superficial insights into the motivations and feelings of those whose life stories they relate.

The popularity of criminal biography actually coincided with the great celebrity enjoyed by Continental picaresque fictions such as LeSage's *Gil Blas*. The picaresque bears much in common with the stories of criminals, but it is of course a species of satirical rogue narrative deriving from a different tradition. In works like *Gil Blas* and the prototypical Spanish tale of *Lazarillo de Tormes*, the rogue is an outcast, buffeted about by a hostile environment, making his way by the use of his wits in a villainous world whose corrupted and decayed institutions are treated very cynically as the targets of usually severe satire. Like the criminal, the picaro typically exults in his roguery, although he is basically a decent fellow, not willfully deviant. As a character, the picaro possesses little interest—that is, he is not engaged in any kind of moral progress; he does not grow. He is merely surviving, and his resourcefulness in the enterprise excites the admiration of readers as they observe his movement through an episodic succession of difficult experiences. Criminal lives, on the other hand, are a native species which originated in the coney-catching pamphlets of the Elizabethan period. They sometimes project their characters as the victims of circumstance, but they almost always condemn deviant behavior precisely because it directly violates accepted standards of conduct, even threatens the stability of those standards. The criminal may be a product of social corruption and inept institutions, but the fundamental validity of conventional values and established order is not questioned. The criminal narratives, we may say, unlike the picaresque tales, assume the permanence of traditional ideals of society and morality, and are actually a literature of affirmation—the criminal is invariably undone in the end, or else transformed and united with his surroundings.

Probably few readers in the early eighteenth century cared very much about fine distinctions between the picaresque as an established literary form and the popular criminal stories as a species of sensational rogue biography. From their perspective, we may assume, it appeared that booksellers offered for sale a great and interesting variety of rogue narratives, some telling stories of spectacularly wicked robbers and murderers who break the law but always get their comeuppance, some reciting the lively adventures of attractive rogues who may flout conventional morality or even the law itself, but who emerge triumphant over the visible corruptions of the world. The author of *Roderick Random* took the famous *Gil Blas* as his model, thus lending his first novel a certain respectability as an acknowledged work of fiction, but it is doubtful whether this meant very much to anybody except the more sophisticated readers who could appreciate the literary implications of Smollett's avowed discipleship and the interesting complexities of his adaptations. *Roderick Random* is not the tale of a thoroughgoing criminal; this much is obvious to any reader, although Smollett's young Scottish hero does frequently break the law, he is sometimes criminally violent about it, and he is eventually punished sharply for his transgressions. But in 1748 the story was very likely read by most people as yet another tale of energetic roguery—livelier than most, to be sure, richer and more interesting because of its hero's scourging of the society which makes him miserable, and embellished by the introduction of a sentimental love story with a happy ending; but still the story of an adventurer who does the forbidden and, for a time at least, gets away with it.

The conspicuous presence of a literature of rogues and criminals tells us something important about the period, or at least about certain vital preoccupations of the popular audience that read such works. Meanwhile the social decadence, the political corruption, and the general wickedness decried in so many sermons and periodical essays made those deeply pious men and women who struggled successfully to maintain their integrity against all the world's hostilities look heroic indeed. The inner conflict of their progress toward faith and Christian resolution—or in some cases the trauma of their attempts to sustain faith and resolution—provided a kind of emotional excitement not usually available in tales of soldiers and traveling adventurers. In the hands of at least some of the fictionalizing biographers of such pious folk, the record of spiritual experience was transmitted in such a way as to raise the subjects to great eminence as private people deserving to be recognized for the public value of what they had achieved.

The works of criminal biography and the stories of spiritual life are, when seen from one point of view at least, moral histories, though one kind retails the adventures of the impious and the other celebrates the pious. The characters of these works are projected as real people, and indeed some of them are real; but their authors reveal the workings of the imagination by frequently endowing them with the proportions of almost allegorical figures. They are the broad representations of perfect depravity, or corrupted decency, or complete goodness, or suffering virtue. Most of the stories themselves very probably were received as true, but this is only because writers and readers alike were confused over the demarcations dividing the factual life from the fictionalized one. Donald A. Stauffer has remarked upon the many "strange hybrids" published in the period, which suggest to him that at this time "neither biography nor the novel had attained artistic certainty."[1] Such uncertainty is, of course, a major reason why a writer like Defoe could assume the role of biographer or memoirist so credibly and with such tremendous popular success. But Defoe, when pressed to defend *Robinson Crusoe* as fiction, did so in terms of its function as moral history. His words apply equally well to the pious lives popular in his day and after, and in a special sense to at least the most sympathetic biographies of rogues (including his own *Moll Flanders*) as well. The story of *Robinson Crusoe*, he argued in the preface to the *Serious Reflections*, "though allegorical, is also historical; and . . . it is the beautiful representation of a life of unexampled misfortunes, and of a variety not to be met with in the world, sincerely adapted to and intended for the common good of mankind, and designed at first, as it is now farther applied, to the most serious uses possible."[2]

Defoe's statement is a most important early sign of what was to happen in the 1740s when Richardson, Fielding, and Smollett came to demonstrate in their various ways that allegorical history might be true; that a fictional life might, without concealing or denying the function of the imagination, justify itself as a true account of the general experience of mankind rendered in particular terms.[3] It is precisely this justification upon which Fielding rests his own lives of Joseph Andrews and Tom Jones. "To invent good Stories," Fielding remarks,

> and to tell them well, are possibly very rare Talents, and yet
> I have observed few Persons who have scrupled to aim at
> both. . . . Hence we are to derive that universal Contempt,
> which the World, who always denominate the Whole from the
> Majority, have cast on all historical Writers, who do not draw
> their Materials from Records. . . . Though as we have good
> Authority for all our Characters, no less indeed than the vast
> authentic Doomsday-Book of Nature, as is elsewhere hinted,

our Labours have sufficient Title to the Name of History. (*Tom Jones*, 9.1)

As general types of moral history, the many popular rogue biographies and records of spiritual life are extremely relevant to the novels of Richardson, Fielding, and Smollett, even though a good many of them are only marginal fictions. The remarks from Defoe and Fielding suggest one reason why we may say this is so. There are other reasons. The most interesting of these minor works, because they often turn their attention to the inner lives of their characters—that is, to regions accessible only through the vigorous uses of the imagination—develop something like the emotional or moral intensity that characterizes *Clarissa*, *Roderick Random*, and *Jonathan Wild*. In turn these major novels, different as they are, actually repeat many of the conventions of popular biography, and they do so in some very particular and interesting ways. *Roderick Random* and *Jonathan Wild*, obviously, offer themselves as rogue narratives, and though these two works represent markedly different manifestations of the form, they might never have been written at all without the example of the similar stories which appear so conspicuously in their background. *Clarissa*, like *Pamela* before it, may be understood as the record of a heroine whose experience provides for Richardson's readers an intensive exercise in devotion—which is precisely what the pious lives of saintly men and women were intended to do. Such connections as these could hardly be altogether accidental. They are real, they are important, and they are worthy of exploration in depth.

A "Secret Satisfaction": The Lives of Criminals and Other Rogues

In the 1740s the pseudobiographies dealing explicitly with the exploits of robbers, swindlers, rapists, murderers, whores, and other rogues totaled nearly three dozen, or better than one-tenth of all the fiction published in the decade. This body of work assumes a certain importance by its very size. The narratives themselves range from the simplest, most skeletal

summary life to the full-fledged biography that displays an interest not
just in its subject's crimes or rogueries, but in his feelings and motivations.
Practically every one of these stories is told by a detached, impersonal
narrator whose most conspicuous function is to urge the moral dimension
of the conflict between the criminal and the society whose values he
threatens. Typically, the characters themselves are generalized figures
bearing quite ordinary names—Robert Ramsey, Gilbert Langley, Paul
Wells, and so on. Their familiar habits and usually local spheres of activity authenticate their experience and give them real immediacy, though
the stories about them are often the purest fantasy. The detailed repetition
of the sensational exploits of the various rogues constitutes the most basic
appeal of such works, along with their moral pretensions. The moralizing
is a matter of convention, but it sometimes goes beyond mere platitudes
and outraged diatribes against lawbreakers and other wicked types. In a
few of the more ambitious narratives, the subject is projected almost sym-
pathetically as the product of a deterministic environment, and the tale
actually develops as a study in how a decent fellow, his good nature overwhelmed by hard circumstances, can fall into the trap of evil and suffer
the miseries of really deep personal misfortune. Such a work is, most
conspicuously, a moral history. But very few of the stories taking this
interesting approach achieve much in the way of subtlety; they are more
sentimental than astute in their portrayal of character. And they lead invariably toward the same almost obligatory conclusion as the rest of the
narratives in this numerous and varied class of pseudobiography. The
criminal is a force for disorder in a world deeply concerned about the
need for order and stability. He is the agent of chaos, and he must always
pay for his weakness or his wickedness, either through suffering—leading
finally to repentance and reform—or, in the case of the more hardened
criminal type, through apprehension, trial, conviction, and execution.

The anonymous author of *A Full and Particular Account of the Life and
Notorious Transactions of Roger Johnson* (1740) perhaps best explains the attractions works like his own held for their readers. "Natural Curiosity,"
he writes,

> incited in us a Desire of enquiring into the Lives and Actions
> of those who have, in any Shape, render'd themselves famous
> or infamous in the World: when a Jonathan Wild, or a Macray,

meet the just Reward of their Villanies, tho' we approve their Punishment, and abhor their crimes yet, at the same Time, *it is a secret Satisfaction to hear an Account, how such Men have perpetrated those Villanies*, and gull'd the Unwary, as it may, in some Measure, enable us to be upon our Guard, if any such Attempt should be made upon us. (p. 3)

Narratives like this one arose originally from what John J. Richetti has called a "native journalistic instinct for the notorious and the sensational," and they appealed to "a burgeoning market for reading matter that is bluntly free of any evasions or euphemisms."[4] The beginnings of rogue narrative in sensational journalism of the Renaissance and seventeenth century coincide with the earliest stages in the development of modern realism, which eventually gave birth to the novel as we know it. But, as Richetti has reminded us, works like *Roger Johnson* and its precursors were not sent into the world "merely to prepare the way for the novel proper" (p. 23). I have earlier observed that the importance of such stories has just as much to do with their extreme emphasis on conventional morality. Authors seem to have been no less ambivalent in their attitudes toward their subjects than the public itself. As fantasy, the criminal narratives often glamorize their rogues and whores, and they as often impart to them almost mythic status as hero-villains, fearsome enemies to received values whose exploits provide for vicarious experience of the forbidden and therefore fascinating, and whose capture and execution or reform at once justify and purge the fascination. Goodness, in this case society itself, always triumphs in the moral histories of defeated criminals. In their moral ideology at least, and in their preoccupation with familiar subjects, such works parallel and reinforce the interests revealed in the novels of important writers as different as Penelope Aubin, Samuel Richardson, Henry Fielding, and Eliza Haywood.

From the late sixteenth century to the heyday of Defoe a majority of criminal narratives, whether genuine or feigned (initially, most were probably genuine), were two-penny pamphlets printed on cheap paper, adorned with much-used woodcuts, and aimed primarily at an audience of the barely literate. After the Restoration, the audience for criminal narrative began to swell.[5] In the eighteenth century many rogue biographies—*Moll Flanders* and *Roxana*, for example, and numerous lesser pieces—were longer and more complex than anything earlier periods had seen in this vein. Obviously they were addressed to more sophisticated readers than the pamphlet or summary lives.[6] The latter, in fact, were now relegated mainly to papers like Applebee's *Original Weekly Journal*, of which Defoe himself was editor from 1720–26, and to collections like *The Lives of the Most Remarkable Criminals* and Captain Alexander Smith's *History of the Lives and Robberies of the Most Noted Highway-Men, Foot-Pads, House-Breakers, Shop-Lifts, and Cheats of Both Sexes in and about London and Westminster*.[7]

Aside from the journalistic summary lives, the most rudimentary examples among the separately issued criminal narratives of the 1730s and 1740s are really little more than bare sketches variously augmented by elaborate prefaces, by documents and testaments relating to the subject's offenses and victims, by moralizing disquisitions on his particular crimes and the threats they pose to society, or by any combination of such paraphernalia.[8] Frequently the extraneous matter occupies more space in the given narrative (usually of thirty, forty, or sometimes fifty pages) than does the life itself. Fielding's *The Female Husband; or, The Surprizing History of Mrs. Mary, Alias Mr. George Hamilton* (1746) is one such augmented sketch. This piece of journalistic hack-work, written from a desperate need for money, is patched together—as Sheridan Baker learned during his successful endeavor to establish Fielding's authorship—from court records, newspaper accounts, and hearsay, all of which are duly recorded in the course of a dull, flatly circumstantial, moralistic narrative.[9] Given its author's skill, *The Female Husband* is more rewarding to the reader than most works of its type, but it shares with them a method that resembles Edmund Curll's characteristic way of quickly and efficiently putting together a book on some controversial subject or contemporary character.[10] In 1741 Curll himself brought that method to the treatment of a criminal subject in *The Confederacy; or, Boarding School Rapes*, a 2s.6d. volume dealing with the lives, conspiracy, and trial of a group of reprobates charged with seducing one Mary King.[11]

Crude works like *The Confederacy*, and even Fielding's *Female Husband*, deserve little attention. More interesting is the larger group of narratives that may be called full-fledged fictional studies in rogue biography. These, in their concern with deviant psychology, give more comprehensive treatment to their subjects, and sometimes they come very close to presenting the given criminal or rogue as an attractive adventurer. A few of them are little more than summary lives that have been padded with conventional picaresque adventures and the crudest sort of psychological analysis. *An Account of the Life, Adventures and Transactions of Robert Ramsey, Alias Sir Robert Gray* (1742) is a case in point. The "unhappy Subject" of this pamphlet was a notorious real-life forger and robber. The author obviously intended to portray him as a perfect monster of wickedness, but instead made of him a rather engaging fellow by focusing upon his exuberance and his amazing cleverness. Ramsey was an extremely resourceful crook, adept in many fields of crime. According to the story, which is allegedly taken from an account supplied by his brother John, he was sometimes an alchemist, or a false, jewel-thieving bedside physician, or a pretended nobleman defrauding a fawning innkeeper. Like Fielding's Blifil, he even allowed himself to be converted by the Methodists, in this case so that he might reap the benefits of their alms and enjoy their women. There is some penetration into the recesses of Ramsey's mind as the author tentatively explores his motivations and reveals the makings of his ingenious schemes. Ramsey remains throughout a stereotype of the arch-criminal, but the reader actually approaches fairly close to him as a gifted and complex human character. The conclusion of this work gains some strength from this strategy, for it urges everyone to deplore the terrible misapplication of Ramsey's considerable talents, and meanwhile to enjoy a sense of release as his real threats to society and moral order are ended with his decline and execution.

Works like *Robert Ramsey* move haltingly in the direction of redeeming their subjects as human beings, but really succeed only in romanticizing the unbalanced criminal mentality. A work called *An Authentick Account of the Life of Paul Wells, Gent.* (1749), though brief, is a much more sympathetic, detailed, and analytical treatment of a real criminal's career. Wells was a wayward but frail young man, and the crime for which he was executed amounted to no more than changing a number *2* to a *3* on an old receipt. He was thus not a very romantic figure, and in fact the biography—"written by a Gentleman of Corpus Christi College, Oxford"—kindly treats him as a terrified youth quaking in fear before an awesome fate. Indeed, this work deglamorizes the criminal and manages also to be a rather close study of personality. Some of the scenes in the short narrative are rendered with genuine compassion and considerable dramatic intensity. We see the young Wells as he faints upon receiving his sentence, hear his laments as he languishes in prison awaiting the results of his plea for a pardon, and watch as he collapses at the very moment he is to mount the scaffold. As a criminal biography *The Life of Paul Wells* is overbalanced by its extreme pathos, which obviously registers the influence of Richardson's currently popular *Clarissa*. But the work nevertheless marks the more expansive dimensions of the new criminal biography, while it also signals the contemporary audience's growing sympathy for social deviates.

If *Paul Wells* is extremely sentimental, *The Secret History of Betty Ireland* (1741) and *The Fortunate Transport; or, The Secret History of the Life and Adventures of the Celebrated Polly Haycock, the Lady of the Gold Watch* (1748) are outrageously sensational. Each of these stories charts the episodic progress of an unregenerate female whose life begins with a luckless childhood and proceeds to an adult career of riotous whoredom, thievery, and general wickedness, finally culminating in a remorseless old age. We are told of Polly Haycock that she was "begot by Chance, came into the World with Life in spight of her Mother, nursed by Charity, brought up among Pickpockets, transported for Felony, and in spite of all that, now rolls in Ease, Splendor, and Luxury; and laughs at dull Moralists, who would persuade Mankind that the Way to be happy is to be good; and the Way to be great, to be wise and prudent." These two whore biographies represent attempts to emulate the achievement of *Moll Flanders* and *Roxana*. *Betty Ireland*, in fact, prefixes a crude little verse whose first line makes Defoe's influence perfectly clear:

> Read Flanders Moll, the German Princess scan,
> Then match our Irish Betty if you can;
> In Wit and Vice she did 'em both excel,
> And may be justly call'd a NONPAREIL.

But neither *Betty Ireland* nor *The Fortunate Transport* approaches the quality of Defoe's similar narratives; that is, they could hardly have appealed by their merits.[12] Such pleasures as they offered must be attributed to their specious combination of criminal biography with licentiousness and sensationalism.

The Fortunate Transport may have possessed yet another kind of appeal, for it develops an interesting variation upon the typical pattern of criminal biography. The story of this female rogue is explicitly designed to flout conventional moral values while appearing to uphold them. Polly Haycock herself is unmitigatedly wicked, in a superficial way almost a grand and perfect villainess, and she is duly punished for her crimes. But the punishment neither defeats nor changes her. She remains to the end a perverse character whose continued resistance to the supposedly wholesome influence of the society she had offended (but which helped to make her what she became) gives her an interesting and unusual vitality. It also suggests her author's particular and quite unambivalent notion of the hardened criminal character as incapable of sudden transformation. Polly simply thumbs her nose at the self-righteous posturing of those who banish her. The ironic touches hinted at in the passage I have quoted remind one of Fielding, if only vaguely. In fact, the character of Polly Haycock emerges as a kind of Jonathan Wild in petticoats, although her author's social and moral vision is much darker than Fielding's, for in the end the world gains no meaningful relief from the threat of what she represents.

Without overrefining this rather crude tale of *The Fortunate Transport*, we may say that it brings into fairly sharp focus what must have been an unacknowledged attraction of all the works of its type. As society's own creation, Polly Haycock exposes to view the depraved, dark, undisciplined side of man's moral nature. But the author, whether intentionally or not, complicates this picture by showing that such real and permanent attributes as are embodied in his Polly cannot easily be restrained by the law or diminished in their power to influence human behavior by the mere repetition of moral platitudes. At a more obvious and elemental level, this lively whore's derisive laughter "at dull Moralists" makes her all the more reprehensible, but it is a kind of triumphant laughter too. It mocks orthodoxy, including the orthodoxies of criminal biography. In a world dominated by evil, Polly's story seems to say, the wicked have a much better chance at "Ease, Splendor, and Luxury" than do the good, the wise, and the prudent.

Interesting as it is, *The Fortunate Transport* remains a clumsy story which probably deserves less attention than I have given it. Yet its qualities as a maverick within its type do help to illuminate other biographical tales of criminals and rogues. The work's unconventional approach to the criminal mentality, and to the meaning of the criminal as a social and moral fact, imparts a special importance to the private character as it functions within a public arena. Very likely this was all quite accidental on the part of the author, who gives no conspicuous signs that he consciously intended anything other than a lively, sensational book that would sell many copies. He appears to have miscalculated, by the way, for there is no known second edition of the story of Polly Haycock.

The author of *A Full and Particular Account of the Life and Notorious Transactions of Roger Johnson* approaches the criminal in a much more deliberate but also more orthodox way. This work transforms a notorious figure from real life into an engaging fictional character whose roguery is seen not just as a manifestation of inherent evil nature, but as a product of adverse circumstances and an adventurous spirit. Though relatively brief, the account of Roger Johnson enters with some vigor into the experience of its subject, and along the way provides some quite spirited narrative passages and some occasionally shrewd analyses of motive and behavior. Johnson learns in his childhood how to cheat and con, and as an adolescent he begins in earnest a career which carries him through a varied course of roguish activity: he becomes a swindler, a pickpocket, a smuggler and a highwayman before he graduates to the more sophisticated role of a confidence man exploiting rich women (who find him enchanting) through his disguise as a clergyman. Eventually he is caught and committed to Newgate, and at first undertakes to swindle as many of the prisoners as he can. Readers of Fielding will recognize the Roger Johnson of *Jonathan Wild* (4.3), and in fact this story was published in the fall of 1740, while Fielding may have been at work on a draft of his own ironic effort in the mode of criminal biography. At last, a more reflective Johnson grows soberly aware of the past misuse of his talents, whereupon he offers his services as legal counsellor to his fellow prison inmates and as trustworthy agent of the prison keepers. When finally he is pardoned, this reformed crook sets up as a hardworking, honest pawnbroker, and lives out his life in respectability.

The resolution of the moral history of Roger Johnson is wholly affirmative: an imprudent man, chastened by hard experience, comes to accept conventional standards of social and moral behavior. Through its conventional plotting, this story—like many others of its type—reflects the criminal biographer's typical complacency about the realities of radically deviant behavior as it touches upon society at large. It is just this compla-

97

cency, born probably of unexamined ambivalence, that the unorthodox author of *The Fortunate Transport* challenges. In works such as *Roger Johnson*, the kind of fantasy experience provided is restrained by a strong didactic impulse. The seriously deviant character attracts attention precisely because his very activity affirms—often violently—his individuality, but such radical affirmation cannot be tolerated. If he is to survive the consequences of his own actions, the criminal must prove himself susceptible to the gentling influences of civilized values; the only alternative is banishment or execution.

A surprisingly large number of criminal biographies, most of them probably altogether imaginary, choose the devices of assimilation as a means of resolving the conflict between the thief or swindler or rapist and a threatened society. This is despite the truly extraordinary number of public executions that really did occur throughout this early period. One would expect the writers of popular narrative to reflect the widespread fascination with these scenes of horror and to bring all tales of crooks and murderers to a conclusion at Tyburn. But that is not what happens at all. Hangings may have been great events in those days, attended by huge throngs of people gathered to celebrate their collective triumph over some wicked desperado.[13] But in the imaginary literature of roguery at least, the power of society to command submission, usually in the form of religious conversion and repentance, appears to have been thought a greater power than that expressed by the carrying out of an execution. In many stories of criminals there emerges a discernible narrative pattern of personal defiance followed by defeat and surrender, or complete transformation of the deviant character. This pattern plays out a kind of wish-fulfillment, and since it always concludes with a gesture of assimilation it can safely permit the treatment of the criminal as an energetic adventurer, deeply wicked and dangerously anarchic perhaps, but capable of reformation. In an extreme manifestation of the pattern, a very curious story called *News from the Dead; or, A Faithful and Genuine Narrative of an Extraordinary Combat between Life and Death, Exemplified in the Case of William Duell* (1740) tells of an imaginary rapist hanged for his crime at Tyburn but later revived so that he might repent and be redeemed.

A fundamental difference between the accounts of William Duell and Roger Johnson and, say, the stories of Fielding's Tom Jones and Smollett's still more roguish Roderick Random lies in the greater complexity of these major authors' intentions. Neither Tom nor Roderick is truly a depraved criminal, of course, but both commit extremely reprehensible acts, and both must adapt to accepted standards of social and moral behavior. Fielding repeatedly emphasizes how nearly his hero approaches to these standards from the very beginning of his life, how his basic decency and inherent good nature actually define and affirm them always, even though appearances may suggest otherwise. As a comic writer of moral history, Fielding traces out an integrative process. He propels Tom into motion and makes him discover his true moral identity by striving toward its mirror reflection in the person of Sophia Western. Smollett, though in very different textures and tones, develops a similar pattern throughout his story of *Roderick Random*, whose hero erratically quests after the ideal distantly represented in the figure of the heroine Narcissa until finally he is united with it.

The more ambitious writers of criminal biography, like the author of *Roger Johnson*, are certainly no less didactic than Fielding or Smollett, and they do relate at least remotely similar moral histories of rogues transformed. But the transformation of the criminal, the acceptance of assimilation, is always something imposed entirely from without by a moment of crisis—conviction, imprisonment, execution itself in the case of the remarkable William Duell. While engaged in their careers of crime, the protagonists in these tales define themselves radically as individuals, but only by their actions, or occasionally by their motivations and their attitudes toward their actions. This is as true of the most attractive rogue as of the most hardened murderer. Typically, such characters sprout feeling hearts and a moral sense—the rudiments of a real inner life—only in the end, when extinction or exile threatens. The wrenching of things that occurs at the conclusion of so many criminal narratives signifies the clumsiness of the authors, perhaps, and their limited understanding of how to portray the complications of human character. But writers really needed no such understanding so long as they could perform the necessary rhetorical tricks. A story of a crook or rogue must be exciting, it must be packed with scarifying action, and it must threaten the world with disorder and with domination by the dark and often violent forces of evil; but at last the criminal must be destroyed or displaced, or must become reflective and penitent, so that society might be seen exercising its power to redeem the world and, in many cases, the criminal as well.

The high-spirited, imaginary *Life and Adventures of Gilbert Langley* (1740) may be mentioned as a final illustration of the observations I have been developing over the last several pages. This is a skillful work, and a fairly substantial one—it is almost a hundred pages long. Langley, a convicted highwayman, narrates the history of his own life while in Maidstone Gaol under sentence of transportation (he had been scheduled for execution, but the sentence was rescinded). Throughout, his story is lively, interesting, and dramatic; the accounts of some of his escapades are given in lavish detail, and are both readable and convincing. But for most of the book Langley reveals little about his character except that he has always been energetic and ingenious in pursuit of a life of crime. In the very last paragraphs, however, he turns contemplative in the obligatory way, managing also to interject a note of real poignancy. The many climaxes of his eventful life have passed, and there is nothing left now but remorse over his past folly, his moral stupidity. The society whose values he had mocked by his very existence has trapped him, and has now won him over. His final words are an admonition to others: "May all young Men read [these pages] with a proper Disposition to avoid by my Example, the miserable State I have brought myself to. A State too frightful to describe, and the very Thoughts of which stops the Pen. Yet a State to which Numbers are running, as full of Mirth and mad Joy, as if their Fools Paradise was a real One. The Royal Mercy hath saved me from an ignominious Death, and I humbly trust in GOD, that he will give me his Grace to amend my Conduct, and by a thorough and sincere Repentance save me from Death everlasting."

When read in the context of the work as a whole, the conclusion to *Gilbert Langley* seems terribly contrived, but it is nonetheless moving. And it suggests that the attitude which produced and gave popular support to stories of its kind was to some degree religious; the connection between certain criminal biographies and contemporary spiritual autobiography is an important one, as G. A. Starr has shown.[14] Life in prison is represented, sometimes only very tentatively, as a hellish condition of physical and spiritual anguish, and sincere repentance and conversion can bring both tangible and intangible rewards to the most guilty of sinners; it is through Providence that Gilbert Langley, like Moll Flanders before him, is reprieved from the death sentence. It is largely because of such maneuvers that we are justified in calling the stories of these usually impious characters moral histories. Furthermore, if the self-righteous conclusions to most criminal biographies may be taken as evidence, it appears that the very business of capturing criminals and bringing them to justice reflects the interventions of Providence working through the arm of society's legal institutions. The conventional admonition "to avoid," as Gilbert Langley puts it, "by my Example, the miserable State I have brought myself to" suggests an inexorable law of retribution ordained to reward goodness but punish wickedness. A character like Roger Johnson or Gilbert Langley, or for that matter Moll Flanders, thus functions as a negative exemplar who, because lowered at last to a wretched condition of defeat, doubly reflects and enforces the age's interest in the ideals of Christian heroism and the happy exaltation to which it can lead.

Jonathan Wild, *Roderick Random*, and the Uses of Roguery

The novels of Samuel Richardson, Henry Fielding, and Tobias Smollett are all moral histories of quite ordinary personages from their birth, through struggle with a hostile world, to happy resolution in ease and tranquility. In *Pamela*, and also in *Clarissa*, which ends with its heroine's triumphant ascension to the perfect regions of heaven, Richardson most emphatically develops this pattern. He limits his focus to extremely concentrated periods in his heroines' lives, but still aims to study—and in great emotional and psychological depth—the tensions that occur when the individual will is asserted against a mystifying and sometimes almost overpowering world. Richardson, of course, affirms the biographical function of his novels to a degree beyond what Fielding and Smollett chose to do, posing as editor of collections of letters. But all three novelists urged the value of their works as historical accounts of familiar, private people importantly engaged in moral interaction with the world at large as it looked in their own time. No doubt they selected a biographical mode in part because it was already popular in several manifestations when they sat down to write. But as serious artists whose stories of Christian heroes and heroines were thoughtfully intended to edify as well as amuse their readers, they approached the matter of life writing with an earnestness of literary as well as moral purpose foreign to other writers in the same mode. A genuine and powerful didactic impulse, in other words, surely had as much to do with the biographical form of their novels as their awareness of the various popular species of pseudobiography.

Fielding and Smollett appear to have been particularly responsive to the interests revealed in the many biographical accounts of criminals and rogues. *Jonathan Wild* and *Roderick Random* are both triumphant expressions of their authors' sensitivity to the issues raised in these works, and to the conventions of the tales themselves. Following the publication of *Roderick Random*, Smollett pursued his concern with the aberrant character in *Peregrine Pickle* (1751) and *The Adventures of Ferdinand Count Fathom* (1753). Fielding remained deeply fascinated by the criminal throughout his life, at least in part because of his work as lawyer and magistrate. The prison scenes of *Amelia* attest to this abiding preoccupation, and *Tom Jones* actually reflects elaborately and playfully upon the whole idea of the criminal character. Tom, we are told, after having begun life by "robbing an Orchard, . . . stealing a Duck out of a Farmer's Yard, and . . . picking Master *Blifil*'s Pocket of a Ball," was cursed by the "universal Opinion of all Mr. *Allworthy*'s Family, that he was certainly born to be hanged" (3.2). Fielding's novel thus starts out to be an ironic life of a "criminal" hero, and it parallels the formula of criminal biography to the end, when Tom, who is indeed about to be hanged, is reprieved—and in this comic novel's scheme of things, it is clear, the reprieve comes partly because the hero has repented of his past and redeemed his life. The comic reversal, for which we are prepared over some hundreds of pages, is the exposure of Master Blifil, who comes to a bad end at the moment when his rival and intended victim is exonerated.

Even Richardson reveals a deep interest in the impious criminal villain. In his dazzlingly wicked Lovelace he presents a character whose moral crimes so darken Clarissa's world that she can no longer live in it. In the manner of a criminal biographer, Richardson reduces Lovelace to ignominy and sentences him to death for his numerous disguises, seductions, kidnappings, and other violations of the law and received morality—most of all, of course, for his rape of the angelic heroine. Lovelace's crimes are actually punishable in the courts, though he is never put on trial. Clarissa is several times bidden to prosecute her tormentor, and although assured of almost certain success, she refuses because she knows that a higher kind of retribution is reserved for him through the workings of Providence. By deliberately incorporating the decidedly familiar narrative pattern of energetic criminal activity followed by inevitable punishment, Richardson greatly furthered his didactic purposes. The moral history of Clarissa Harlowe is also the instructive moral history of the vile libertine who persecutes her and wrecks her life. Lovelace is of course an aristocrat, elegant and refined, and so he is not at all a conventional criminal hero-villain drawn from low life. Obviously, part of the moral and social purpose of the story is to show that the sphere of criminal activity in the contemporary world is not bounded by the back alleys and dark streets of London, though Lovelace has his connections in those regions, and his accomplice, Mrs. Sinclair, could easily be the subject of a whore biography. Yet Richardson's deeply sinister and amazingly resourceful villain actually represents the most artful, complete, and astute portrayal of the criminal mind to be found anywhere in the fiction of the period. It is impossible for us to tell just how much the author of *Clarissa* may have known about the many tales of thieves and rapists that so captivated early eighteenth-century readers, but his success as an innovator exploiting the interests they develop is undeniable. And it is worth observing that, besides *Clarissa*, only *Jonathan Wild* and *Roderick Random* among the major novels of the mid-century years reveal closer ties with this popular kind of biographical narrative.

In *The Life of Mr. Jonathan Wild the Great* Fielding turned his attention directly to the popular biographies of criminals. His book is the only really fresh and original new work specifically in this mode to appear in the 1740s, and of course it is an ironic adaptation in the form of a severe parody. It is also political criticism directed at the "Great Man," Sir Robert Walpole, and, in book four, at his successor in the prime ministry; and it is social criticism too. In this remarkable product of his wit and wisdom, Fielding ingeniously multiplies and transforms the aims of the usual criminal biographer, and along the way develops an elaborate and utterly serious theory of life writing. Even more conspicuously than his other novels, *Jonathan Wild* reveals how deeply and with what intensity of moral and aesthetic concern Fielding always reacted to the world around him, and how adept he was at using the materials of popular fiction in fashioning his own artful compositions.

Aurélien Digeon is correct when he says that it was "a part of the tradition" of criminal biography that "tales of thieves should be told with a smile."[15] It is certainly true, as both Digeon and William R. Irwin have shown, that many of the popular accounts of the real Jonathan Wild were written with tongue in cheek, as Fielding's was.[16] The effect of this mannerism was to mock the criminal, thus reducing him to a less threatening figure than he might otherwise have been. But as we have seen, a great many criminal biographies were written without the benefit of any such strategy, as apparently sober, moralized tales in which the criminal career is often made an adventurous affair, full of the thrills of danger and complete with abundant opportunities to exercise ingenuity at the expense of fools, the whole brought to an abrupt and morally satisfying conclusion. *Jonathan Wild* deliberately repeats the major conventions of popular criminal biography: the obligatory account of the villainous hero's lineage and the almost deterministic story of the circumstances which made him a criminal, the detailed record of crimes committed and victims undone, the pictures of gang life and of the horrors of capture and imprisonment, the visits of the Newgate ordinary, the final disposition of the criminal in an appropriate end. But of course Fielding hilariously inverts all of these conventions in what is surely one of the most brilliantly sustained pieces of ironic writing we possess. As parody, *Jonathan Wild* expresses its author's thoroughgoing disapproval of the mode of criminal biography.[17] It is at least as skillful an exercise in literary mockery as *Shamela*, and much more ambitious. Presented as an ostensible panegyric upon a complete reprobate, the narrative cleverly distorts the usual practice by which the personal experience of criminals was given high public visibility in stories about them, and by strategically mismatching style and subject it very closely approaches the burlesque.[18] The most obvious aim of this ironic moral history of a very "great" man is to explode the "heroic" criminal figure, to reduce him by ludicrously exalting him, thus making it impossible for any reader sensitive to the method ever again to see him in a glamorous light.

Part of Fielding's purpose, it is clear, is to convict the criminal biographers themselves of moral shallowness and to shame them for their cynical exploitation of the public's almost morbid fascination with the lowest of low life. In *Jonathan Wild*, the criminal becomes the true exemplar of "greatness," which, as Fielding's narrator says, "consists in bringing all manner of mischief on mankind" (1.1)[19] Wild is actually a representation of the Christian hero completely inverted; he is deliberately made out to be an energetic, attractive figure whose scheming ambition falls "little short of diabolism itself" (2.2): "I had rather stand on the summit of a dunghill," he tells Count la Ruse, "than at the bottom of a hill in Paradise" (1.5). Like Milton's Satan, Fielding's work deliberately suggests, the criminal as a figure of evil is fascinating precisely because of his vitality and boldness in the enterprise of challenging moral law, and because he expresses a side of human nature which decency and morality teach mankind to suppress in the interest of preserving communal life. Possibly because he was able to acknowledge some ambivalent attitudes of his own, Fielding held that it is the allurements of evil that make it so insidious and pernicious. *Jonathan Wild* unmistakably declares that the attractions of the popular criminal biographies, for all the sobriety of their punishment or reformation of the characters whose exploits they record, are likewise a threat to a gullible public.

If in *Joseph Andrews* Fielding would "hold the Glass to thousands in their Closets" and laugh them out of their deformity (3.1), then in *Jonathan Wild* he would, by the high-spirited, farcical exposure of the most ludicrous conventions of the criminal biography, laugh readers out of their foolish addiction to that kind of writing. This is serious business, for the hardened criminal is no amiable rogue like Gil Blas. As Fielding represents him in the character of Wild, he is a consummate blackguard, almost perfectly consistent in his dark villainy—though, as Fielding's narrator slyly says, the "sharp eyes of censure" might indeed be able to "spy out some little blemishes lurking amongst his many great perfections" (1.1). Incapable of remorse, Wild is also unable to be touched by the divine promise of rewards or punishments in the hereafter, as we learn during the episode (2.11) following the French captain's decision to cast him into the sea. "If there should be another world it will go hard with me, that is certain," Fielding's criminal tells himself; "I shall never escape for what I have done to Heartfree." And then: "If there be no other world, why I shall be in no worse condition than a block or a stone; but if there should— d——n me I will think no more about it" (2.11).

For all his humanity, and for all his devoted interest in the reform of institutions so that they might make it easier for men and women to be good in this world, Fielding toyed with the possibility that while some people were innately good-natured, others were innately depraved, and that it might even be impossible to educate the depravity out of the latter.[20] He repeatedly expressed his commitment to a doctrine of mixed characters, but the point of *Jonathan Wild* is that a confirmed criminal, whether depraved by nature or by circumstances, is not a likely candidate for conversion to a redeeming faith; the proof of faith and good nature is in good deeds, and the criminal's life is one long succession of wicked deeds. The sudden conversion so typical as the conclusion to criminal biographies reminded Fielding of the antinomian doctrine of salvation by profession of faith alone, and it must have corresponded to what he liked contemptuously to call "good humour," the hypocritical art of putting on at will the false face of good nature. Wild himself is not converted. "If I should believe all you say," he tells the prison ordinary who comes to counsel him regarding divine rewards and retributions, "I am sure I should die in inexpressible horror." But the ordinary, who is nearly Wild's equal in hypocrisy, promises him mercy anyway in thanks for a compliment paid to his "vast learning and abilities." "It is true you are a sinner," he replies to Wild, "but your crimes are not of the blackest dye: you are no murderer, nor guilty of sacrilege. . . . Happy is it indeed for those few who are detected in their sins, and brought to exemplary punishment for them in this world. So far, therefore, from repining at your fate when you come to the tree, you should exult and rejoice in it" (4.13). The entire episode, with its hilarious exposure of blatant hypocrisies given in the absurdly fragmented form of a blotted record of the conversation between prisoner and chaplain, expresses Fielding's scorn for this particularly insidious convention of criminal biography.

The conclusion of the moral history of Jonathan Wild brings the hero to a glorious end justified by his many and unalloyed perfections. Upon "the day of execution," or "apotheosis (for it is called by different names)," Wild reaches, without remorse, the "highest consummation of human GREATNESS" (4.14). Just in case any reader may have missed this point, Fielding reemphasizes it in the concluding chapter on "the character of our hero." We must not omit, says the narrator, "what indeed ought to be remembered on his tomb or his statue, the conformity above mentioned of his death to his life; and that Jonathan Wild the Great, after all his mighty exploits, was, what so few GREAT men can accomplish—hanged by the neck till he was dead" (4.15). The ironic consistency of the plotting and action of the book serves Fielding in his role as political satirist and as commentator on crime as social problem, but it also functions importantly as part of the parodic strategy. As a species of life writing, criminal biography is in *Jonathan Wild* made the object of some of the very same kinds of criticisms of biographical writing in general raised in *Shamela*. Life writing, says Fielding in the first paragraph of *Jonathan Wild*, "may be justly and properly styled the quintessence of history." Especially in the lives of great men,

> when delivered to us by sensible writers, we are not only most agreeably entertained, but most usefully instructed; for, besides the attaining hence a consummate knowledge of human nature in general; of its secret springs, various windings, and perplexed mazes; we have here before our eyes lively examples of whatever is amiable or detestable, worthy of admiration or abhorrence, and are consequently taught, in a manner infinitely more effectual than by precept, what we are eagerly to imitate or carefully to avoid. (1.1)

This double-edged statement expresses Fielding's notion of the high purposes of life writing, whether in fiction or in genuine biography. But of course when taken in the context of the narrative of *Jonathan Wild* itself, the statement is richly ironic. It is qualified in the first chapter of the book by Fielding's sneers at the biographers of the mighty heroes Alexander and Caesar, biographers who had mitigated the perfect villainy of their subjects by foolishly "and indeed impertinently" introducing little hints of "their benevolence and generosity, of their clemency and kindness" (1.1). The author of *The Life of Mr. Jonathan Wild the Great* will be guilty of no such foolishness or impertinence. Biographical writing, for Fielding, is clearly a matter of telling the literal truth about human beings, but it is also a matter of exercising judgment in the interest of arriving at the moral truth about the subject's life, whether real or imaginary. Fielding commits himself to this ideal in *Jonathan Wild*, and he sustains the same commitment in *Shamela*, *Joseph Andrews*, *Tom Jones*, and *Amelia*.

The role of the imagination in *Jonathan Wild* is revealed by the presence of the ironic narrator, and Fielding's unembarrassed acknowledgment that his work is a fiction—though based on a notorious figure from real life—represents one of his most significant departures from the practice of other criminal biographers. Fielding actually re-creates the conventions of criminal narrative in fashioning a comic fiction. *Jonathan Wild* has often been described as a formal satire, an angry Juvenalian attack on the corrupt people and institutions of Fielding's time. The book is satirical, it is angry, but the distancing effects wrought by a liberating wit and irony relieve the anger and soften the impact of the moral hideousness that dominates the fictional world over which Wild presides for so many pages. The role assigned to Providence—or Fortune, or Nature, as this force is variously called—signifies that the work is a comedy. The comedy is dark, and in fact it is very close to what we nowadays call black comedy, the mode which wrenches us incongruously into searching and unsettling laughter at the bizarre, the hideous, the grotesquely wicked and threatening in life. Wild himself is a moral anarchist who does not prevail in the end; it may take providential intervention to get him his comeuppance and redeem the world from him, but the manipulations of Fortune dramatically suggest Fielding's confidence in the permanence of those values—chiefly honesty, Christian love, and benevolence—by which human society coheres and will survive in a moral universe.[21] As Mrs. Heartfree says in concluding the account of her hair-raising adventures after Wild had abducted her, "PROVIDENCE WILL SOONER OR LATER PROCURE THE FELICITY OF THE VIRTUOUS AND INNOCENT" (4.11).

In the criminal biography of Jonathan Wild, wickedness itself defines the ordering principle which governs the characters' experience. This repetition of a convention of the mode Fielding mocks is only partially ironic. The apparent order of the fictional world is an order of disorder which initially makes goodness appear an aberration even more weak and ineffectual against the center of things than the aberrant Trullibers, Didappers, and Blifils of Fielding's other novels, where the values are not inverted. The Heartfrees, we are told in grimly playful words, belong to that pitiful class of creatures "who are in contempt called good-natured; being indeed sent into the world by nature with the same design with which men put little fish into a pike-pond in order to be devoured by that voracious water-hero" (2.1). They are very limp and passive figures—flat characters, or pasteboard abstractions, as so many of Fielding's readers have observed. It seems to me wrong, however, to assume that Heartfree is nothing more than a frail negative exemplar of positive human values, or an artistic failure, as some critics have suggested.[22] It ought to be noticed that this virtuous fellow of a merchant, powerless though he truly is, possesses the sturdy resolution of a Christian hero. When Wild gets him thrown into the Fleet and then tries to entrap him further by proposing robbery and perhaps even murder as a means of escape, Heartfree responds vigorously, stating his own unalterable rule of conduct, which consists "OF DOING NO OTHER PERSON AN INJURY FROM ANY MOTIVE OR ON ANY CONSIDERATION WHATEVER." And, speaking of the "one permanent and complete" reward for such honorable conduct, he even abuses Wild: "Dost thou think then, thou little, paltry, mean animal (with such language did he treat our truly great man), that I will forego such comfortable expectations for any pitiful reward which thou canst suggest or promise to me?" (3.10).

Heartfree and his family may be seen most accurately as dramatically appropriate, effective creations, allegorical figures really, set down in the midst of an environment that is almost perfect in its hostility to what they represent. In such a world, powered and given definition by evil itself, goodness can only seem a theoretical abstraction. The conspicious role given to the Heartfrees signals another of Fielding's important departures from the practice of more conventional criminal biographers, who usually focus almost exclusively on the exploits of the criminal himself. The author of *Jonathan Wild* obviously knew that villainy takes on its truest colors when seen in light of the real consequences to its victims. His story gives meaningful representation to those victims, whom it also celebrates as the actual embodiment of a set of moral values antithetical to the grotesque amorality of the criminal. From the beginning of book two forward, the author's interest centers increasingly on the relationships between the arch-criminal and his helpless but resolute victims. Ultimately, in moral terms at least, these quite ordinary people are raised to an eminence even greater than that occupied by Wild himself.

The figure of Jonathan Wild stands at the center of a complete, comprehensive order of vile deceit and hypocrisy which includes the idle, frivolous "aristocrat" Count la Ruse as well as low, base creatures like Bagshot and Fireblood. In his function as political satirist, Fielding extends the boundaries of criminal wickedness to include rampaging conquerors and corrupt prime ministers. "In civil life," Wild tells the count, "doubtless, the same genius, the same endowments, have often composed the statesman and the prig. . . . The same parts, the same actions, often

109

promote men to the head of superior societies, which raise them to the head of lower; and where is the essential difference if the one ends on Tower-hill and the other at Tyburn?" (1.5). The source of the prig's (or the statesman's) deceit and hypocrisy is ambition, and the result of his machinations is power, power over a gang, a political party, or a whole society. The wickedness of the great thus consists of their abuses of power, which is as often ill-gotten as it is inhumanely wielded. Fielding, as George Sherburn has demonstrated, thought of society as an organic whole, its organization stratified by classes but dependent for its survival upon the positive contributions of all its members:[23] those who are rich and those who are poor, those who "use their own hands" at work, to borrow Jonathan Wild's own categories, and those who "employ the hands of others." In *Jonathan Wild*, and again in his *Proposal for Making an Effectual Provision for the Poor* (1753), Fielding makes it plain that social responsibility is for him an ethical issue of paramount importance, and the greatest sin of "great men"—conquerors, absolute princes, statesmen, and prigs alike—is that they "employ hands merely for their own use, without any regard to the benefit of society" (1.14). They are thus deadly parasites upon the social organism, deadly in the sense that their actions disrupt social and moral order and violently threaten goodness, as *Jonathan Wild* so graphically shows.

This corruption—it is even profanation—pervades the world of *Jonathan Wild*. It is no wonder that, given this perspective, innocence seems powerless to assert itself and gain dominance. The voyage adventures of Mrs. Heartfree, while they effectively mock a type of popular travel narrative, serve also to extend the picture of wicked deceit and corruption beyond the confines of London. The actual topos of *Jonathan Wild*, however, and the center of its universe, is Newgate Prison. "The truth is," Fielding says in the advertisement to the second edition of the work (1754), "as a very corrupt state of morals is here represented, the scene seems very properly to have been laid in Newgate." The prison itself remains throughout little more than an abstraction, the "castle" of the heroes who prowl and plunder in the streets outside its walls. But it is the place where, as Fielding tells us in the final chapter of book three, "most of the great men of this history are hastening as fast as possible," some of them stopping along the way at Mr. Snap's house, which is a Newgate in miniature.

Though not at all visually represented in the novel, Newgate teems with a multitude of villains, chief among them Roger Johnson and Wild himself, vying for the powerful position of preserver of the "liberties" of the place—*liberties* being a euphemism for privilege and the right to plunder. The political criticism of the prison episodes of book four is blunt and devastating, though not unrelievedly cynical. In the preface to the *Miscellanies*, possibly with these episodes in mind, Fielding remarked that "without considering *Newgate* as no other than Human Nature with its Mask off, . . . a Thought which no Price should purchase me to entertain, I think we may be excused for suspecting, that the splendid Palaces of the Great are often no other than *Newgate* with the Mask on."[24] As has been widely noticed, the prison scenes convey Fielding's new conviction (first expressed in his poem *The Opposition: A Vision*, 1741) that the system of government spawned by Walpole, who is represented in these episodes by Johnson, will not be much improved upon by his successor Carteret, a one-time member of the Opposition Fielding had supported in his political journalism, but here (it seems) represented by Wild. Newgate thus serves Fielding as a device for concentrating, in microcosmic form, his expansive definition of the evils rampant in the world at large, a world dominated by prigs who are statesmen, or statesmen who are prigs—the terms are interchangeable. But Newgate also serves the narrative as the alien place, the nightmarish "castle," where the arch-hero of villainy literally imprisons goodness in the person of Heartfree. The faint but distinctive echo of a romance convention cleverly suggests the helplessness of the victim in the dungeon, and also indirectly justifies the seemingly miraculous release that comes at the end, not by supernatural means of course, as in a romance, but nevertheless providentially, through the benevolent actions of an honest magistrate.

Fielding carries his irony straight through to the end of the hero's career, whereupon Wild empties the attending parson's pocket of a bottlescrew just before swinging out of this world. However, he also subtly but unmistakably shifts the focus, especially during the progress of book four, so that the reader's eyes are fixed on the Heartfrees, who after all were not destroyed by Wild. As the pitiful and contemptible exemplars of good nature, they of course do not deserve to be hanged; that exaltation is denied them, and in this the narrative is perfectly consistent with the ironic terms of the scheme of rewards and punishment pursued throughout. But

Fielding reserves for them another kind of exaltation. He virtually aban-
dons his irony in the last pages of the concluding chapter, becomes a
straightforward moralist, and presents an image of the Heartfrees which
everyone is sure to remember after the book has been read. Heartfree, we
are told, together with "his wife, his two daughters, his son-in-law, and
his grandchildren, of which he hath several, [now] live all together in one
house; and that, with such amity and affection towards each other, that
they are in the neighborhood called the family of love" (4.15).

The idea of a "family of love" is at the end a powerful one in *Jonathan
Wild*. It is profoundly important, too, for it provides a counterbalance to
the cynicism, the lovelessness, self-seeking ambition, and hypocrisy characterizing the "families" of thieves—the Snaps, Wild and Laetitia, the
gangs themselves, all of them represented as the instruments of social and
moral disorder. Indeed, the "family of love" brings together the values of
benevolence, honesty, and loyalty on which so much of the meaning of
the book comes to rest. These values are made to reside in ordinary
people, an honest merchant and his wife who possess a natural nobility in
virtue. Fielding's providential manipulations in the last pages of *Jonathan
Wild*, as he brings the hero to his highest glory upon the hanging tree,
actually represent the completion of his transformations upon the conventions of criminal biography. In his story the criminal is not redeemed, but
rather the victims of his wicked schemes are demonstrably redeemed from
him. The comic ending of the work, when seen in this way, is thus doubly
parodic and doubly ironic, for it simultaneously denies and enforces the
gestures of affirmation with which criminal narratives usually close. Society wins out in Fielding's hilarious parody, but the real lesson of the
ironic moral history of Jonathan Wild is that greatness leads to the
triumph of public disgrace, while goodness leads only to contentment. In
a final innovative maneuver, Fielding delays the moral climax until after
Wild himself has been disposed of on the gallows, and then presents it in
that quiet tableau showing the Heartfrees all together in loving compan-
ionship.

This richly parodic conclusion to the story brings to fulfillment the
moral, social, and political implications of the narrative as a whole. *Jonathan Wild* by no means belongs fully to the Heartfrees, but in an important
sense it is as much their moral history as Wild's, cast into the familiar
form of a fable of beleaguered virtue. Upon this fable Fielding superim-

poses his history of a rapacious "polite gentleman" who is a "true aristocrat" in vice, unmistakably reflecting the realities of contemporary class
conflict. At least some readers have even found *Jonathan Wild* a book of
advanced democratic tendencies.[25] Near the end, the speech of the "very
grave man" of Newgate (in 4.3) urges the weak and oppressed like Heartfree and himself not to "submit to the rapine of the *prig*," but, as he puts
it, to "separate from the *prigs*" and "enter into a closer alliance with one
another. Let us consider ourselves all as members of one community, to
the public good of which we are to sacrifice our private views; not to give
up the interest of the whole for every little pleasure or profit which shall
accrue to ourselves. Liberty is consistent with no degree of honesty inferior to this, and the community where this abounds no *prig* will have the
impudence or audaciousness to endeavor to enslave; or if he should, his
own destruction would be the only consequence of his attempt."

This statement represents an extreme denunciation of the leaders of
contemporary politics, while it also contains the seeds of a revolutionary
philosophy. These seeds are never allowed to grow in this work or indeed
anywhere else in all of Fielding's fiction. The author of *Jonathan Wild* was
not a political theorist, and he was certainly not a radical reformer. He
was instead a committed moralist who saw a need for human decency and
upright behavior among politicians—among all members of society—in
order to secure the welfare of the community. The grave man's description
of a moral alliance of interdependent people is only an unsentimental definition of the ideal of the family of love we see represented in the Heartfrees. Fielding returns again and again, almost obsessively, to this same
ideal in his other works, most obviously perhaps in *Amelia* but also in
Joseph Andrews and *Tom Jones*, which conclude with small communities of
devoted people coming together to bring order and repose to their world.
But, perhaps provoked in part by the many frivolous biographers of robbers and rapists and murderers who had preceded him with their sensational tales of disorder and violence and glorified villainy, he nowhere
pronounces more emphatically on the human need for harmonizing love
and Christian resolution than in his brilliantly ironic moral history of the
master criminal Jonathan Wild.

Roderick Random closely resembles *Jonathan Wild* in the intensity with
which it renders the world as seen from the underside, where it appears
to teem with scheming villains, and where ideal goodness inevitably looks

very weak and ineffectual indeed. Smollett's novel is, in fact, almost a *Jonathan Wild* divested of its ironic vision and the continuous, visible manipulations of a benevolent author. The story of Roderick Random unblinkingly explores the depths of degradation in contemporary life, relentlessly exposing its cruelty and heartlessness and criminality, and it does these things so energetically and with such ferocity that it comes very close to upsetting the moral balance Smollett means to display. We learn at last that the world of *Roderick Random*, like the world of *Jonathan Wild*, is governed providentially, and is comic. But for much of the novel the baseness and general perversions that Smollett's wayward adventurer sees and struggles with, and often participates in, define virtually all we know about the reality of his experience, and about what that reality means. Chance seems to rule; the erratic structure of the novel enforces this sense of things, as the hero is tossed violently about from one encounter with villainy and meanness to another. There is little if anything in the way of aesthetic distance between the reader and Roderick, who tells his story in an exceedingly strident voice of outrage at the sordidness and lawlessness of life. Indeed, it is almost as difficult for the reader as for Roderick to discover any ordering principle in the fictional world except the principle of disorder itself.

Roderick's morally confused response to his experience, understandable enough given the horrors he must endure, all but completely disorients him, and it probably reflects a certain ambivalence on his author's own part. The spectacle of evil was as deeply fascinating to Smollett as it was to Fielding or any of the authors of criminal and rogue biography, but they all expressed their commitment to the ideals of moral optimism, and yearned for a more stable order. Roderick may be a young man of "modest merit struggling with every difficulty to which a friendless orphan is exposed," as Smollett describes him in the preface, but for much of his life he is a rogue among rogues, seduced by the evil that surrounds him. Only in the end does he fully recognize—and then it is because the author's benevolent manipulations make such recognition possible—that the felt reality of disorder he has lived through is illusory, a texture of "dismal apparitions" which obscures the real, transcendent, and permanent moral order accessible through the redeeming power of faith and the practice of Christian love.

No one who has ever read *Roderick Random* needs to be reminded that it is a satiric novel, even darker in its vision than *Jonathan Wild*. It was in fact deliberately intended, Smollett wrote to his friend Alexander Carlyle (in December 1747), as "a Satire upon Mankind."[26] By the time he wrote *Roderick Random*, Smollett was already the author of two able satires in verse, *Advice* (1746) and *Reproof* (1747), but in the preface to his first novel he proclaimed his belief that of "all kinds of satire, there is none so entertaining, and universally improving, as that which is introduced, as it were, occasionally, in the course of an interesting story." Ronald Paulson has suggested, provocatively but I think unfairly, that Smollett did not make the transition from Augustan satirist to novelist very successfully, that *Roderick Random* represents a failed attempt to blend the conventions of picaresque realism with those of Juvenalian verse satire.[27] Actually, Smollett seems to have conceived his first novel in the form of a moralized picaresque, and to this end he exploited the conventions of all kinds of rogue narrative, including criminal biography. Roderick is of course not strictly a criminal, and he is a much more complicated character than Gilbert Langley or Roger Johnson. Basically good-natured, he begins his adventures armed with ideals which are the wellsprings of his indignation at the world's depravity, and which he never completely loses. He receives his reward partly because he learns to be faithful to the abiding image of Narcissa, a shadowy creation who nonetheless, from the time of her introduction about halfway through the novel, serves as the embodiment of all virtue, the promise of joy in life, the mirror reflection of Roderick's real but often hidden inner goodness. And yet, given his own rigorous standards of right conduct, his vigorously articulated code of benevolence, honesty, and justice in human affairs, Roderick's behavior is often no better than criminal—we may cite, for example, his barbarous treatment of Captain O'Donnell in chapter twenty, or his fortune-hunting schemes to extort money from unwitting heiresses—and it must have been understood in this way by Smollett's first readers.

In proclaiming *Gil Blas* as his avowed model, Smollett departed from the practice of most contemporary rogue biographers and offered his work as an imaginary moral history of a wayward adventurer. Nevertheless, as his preface declares, his story is grounded in familiar experience. "Every intelligent reader," he says, "will, at first sight, perceive I have not deviated from nature, in the facts, which are all true in the main, although the circumstances are altered and disguised to avoid personal satire." The private experience of the hero of *Roderick Random* is to have broad and sometimes specific public relevance, as this remark implies, but the author rather disingenuously suggests that no particular members of his audience should feel obliged to bear any of the sting of it. As a contemporary moralist and as a serious novelist interested in the complexities of human character, Smollett takes great pains to differentiate between his own method and vision and the conventions and satiric strategies of LeSage's work.[28] The conduct of Gil Blas, he says, "not only deviates from probability, but prevents that generous indignation, which ought to animate the reader, against the sordid and vicious disposition of the world." The incidents of cruelty and meanness exhibited in LeSage's story, Smollett seems to suggest, are not treated with sufficient seriousness and severity; they merely amuse or startle, and serve only as occasions for showing the protagonist's resourcefulness and mettle. In this context the "disgraces of Gil Blas, are for the most part, such as rather excite mirth than compassion; he himself laughs at them; and his transitions from distress to happiness, or at least ease, are so sudden, that neither the reader has time to pity him, nor himself to be acquainted with affliction." What Smollett appears to mean here is that the character of Gil Blas, unlike his own Roderick Random, is not to be taken seriously as a moral agent.[29]

The story of Smollett's wayward Scottish youth, on the other hand, is obviously as much intended to show the chastening effects of hard experience as it is to laugh at or scourge the moral grotesqueries of society. As an intensely personalized autobiographical tale of a quite ordinary fellow, it is in the most explicit sense a moral history of the interaction between a private character and a mystifying, even terrifying, public world. Smollett deepens the significance of his narrative beyond anything achieved in *Gil Blas* by implicating his hero so seriously in the sordidness and cruelties that beset him, and he far exceeds the reach of any contemporary criminal biographer (even Defoe, in so accomplished a work as *Moll Flanders*) in his portrayal of the violent and perversely seductive reality of low life. It is by no mistake that the inhabitants of Roderick's world so regularly respond to him through a kind of projection, seeing themselves mirrored in him; he is here a thief, there a dangerous mutineer, elsewhere a rascally fortune-hunter. His fundamental good nature belies the absolute validity of such projections, which often suggest, nonetheless, the degree to which his appearances and his occasionally vicious acts unite him with his surroundings.

Roderick is initially a virtuous character terribly isolated by his merit, but if we read Smollett's novel carefully we will recognize that he finally convicts his hero of the moral crime of consuming and even despairing cynicism, and then punishes him for it. This represents a significant reversal upon the traditions of picaresque, which is a form typically giving overt expression (as in *Lazarillo de Tormes* and even *Gil Blas*) to the cynicism of satirists who are transfixed by ideas of human inadequacy or moral deformity. Roderick's moral crime is one difficult not to commit in so nightmarishly horrid a world as his is: sadistic, ugly and smelly, grotesque, and almost conspiratorial in its thwarting of all expressions of individual will. From the beginning, Smollett's hero is the victim of overpowering circumstances. Before he was born, his mother dreamed prophetically that she was "delivered of a tennis-ball," which the devil "struck so forcibly with a racket, that it disappeared in an instant" (chap. 1). Dispossessed and tormented during his childhood, Roderick ripens into an indignant youth who learns to ascribe the natural benevolence of his kinsman Bowling to "the dictates of a heart as yet undebauched by a commerce with mankind" (chap. 6). His own heart is to be debauched, though not irretrievably; he remains continually capable of surprise at the depths to which human viciousness can sink. He is repeatedly "confounded," he says in chapter fifteen, at the "artifice and wickedness" of the human race. Knocked about like the tennis ball in his mother's dream, Roderick confronts a world that appears to make no sense, a world apparently without hope or meaning in which the pursuit of goodness seems, if not impossible, then downright whimsical.

Roderick must ultimately learn to harmonize his life with the ideals represented in characters like Bowling, Strap, Thomson, Mrs. Sagely, and Narcissa. They are all people of simple and perfect innocence—foils, really, to the more complex character of the hero. Dramatically, their role is to suggest the hope of Roderick's redemption from the buffetings of Fortune, or Chance. But for much of the story his awareness of what they signify—and our awareness too, since we must rely on Roderick for the representation of things—is simply overwhelmed by the frantic rush of threatening experience. Seen from Roderick's perspective, cruelty and villainy abound everywhere in the world: in his ancestral Scotland, in the Navy Office, at Bath, in the taverns and prisons of London, on board the *Thunder*. Smollett's exposés in the manner of the secret historians and the writers of spy fiction hint at his personal view of how broadly and how deeply the corruptions of life actually run, while the shipboard scenes place Roderick's experience in the conspicuously public context of a controversial war, at the same time concentrating and intensifying the helplessness of the solitary man in the midst of immediate and unimaginable cruelty. Roderick is justly outraged by what he witnesses and endures while aboard the *Thunder*. There, the approved method of dealing with the sick, when they become too many, is to put them to hard work, thereby expeditiously reducing their numbers. Roderick himself is subjected to horrors. In a deeply ludicrous and corrupt perversion of the law, the captain convicts him of the crime of mutiny on the basis of some harmless observations in the Greek language entered in his diary, which nobody but Roderick himself can read (chap. 30). Here, ironically, Roderick is judged a criminal, but is guilty of no crime. Even more terrifying is his experience while pinioned a prisoner on the poop-deck of the ship during a bombardment, when the explosion of human flesh all about him drives him into frenzied hysteria. Brave resignation gave way, he tells us, and "I could contain myself no longer, but began to bellow with all the strength of my lungs"; then, "finding myself disregarded, lost all patience and became frantick; vented my rage in oaths and execrations" (chap. 29).

The ship is, as so many of Smollett's readers have pointed out, a microcosm of the world at large, and like the macrocosm it is characterized not only by cruelties which are fiendishly calculated but also by an equally horrifying mindless brutality. Roderick is appalled by the hopeless plight of the "fifty miserable distempered wretches" thoughtlessly crowded into the ship's foul-smelling, vermin-infested sick-berth (chap. 25). Later, when he is shipwrecked, stripped, and beaten by his fellow survivors, Roderick himself is treated with equally cruel indifference at a succession of English village houses, where no one will take him in; he is bare human nature abandoned, and his forlorn state makes for a dark comment on the heartlessness of mankind. Interestingly enough it is at this moment, when he is reduced to nakedness, that Mrs. Sagely comes to his relief, he meets Narcissa, and the real course leading to his final happiness is actually begun—at almost the exact midpoint of the novel. The old lady and the beautiful young girl respond to what he naturally is, and though he afterward puts on the desperate appearance of a fortune-hunter, he can never forget what he found in this remote place, the representations of perfect benevolence and ideal goodness. From this point on, in Roderick's mind at least, the image of Narcissa serves as a powerful attraction to goodness.

The shipboard sick provide a poignantly suggestive analogue to Roderick's own experience, but not the only one. When a grateful Nancy Williams tells him the history of her victimization and degradation, he is touched by the unrelieved solitariness of her plight, and sees her misery as comparable to, but worse than, his own. Late in the novel, when his fellow Marshalsea inmate Melopoyn recounts his tale of woe at the hands of theatrical managers and proprietors, Roderick is moved by the misfortunes of the playwright. He especially responds to one of Melopoyn's elegies "in imitation of Tibullus," which gives such expression to the present hopelessness of his love for Narcissa, and of his life in general, that (as he says) he could not recover his tranquility: "I awaked in the horrors, and found my imagination haunted with such dismal apparitions, that I was ready to despair" (chap. 61).

Almost the entire course of Roderick's experience is a progress through a nightmare filled with "dismal apparitions" or worse. The ending of the novel is like an awakening into paradise from the hellish dream of the world, where everything bustles with terrific energy, is noisy and foul-smelling, and where fiendishly misshapen people move furtively and dangerously about. A majority of the characters in the fictional world are grotesques, and Smollett frequently represents them as bestial figures, so that Roderick's environment is rather like a zoo with no cages, where the animals look remotely like people, but are animals after all, deficient in the human qualities of thought and compassion. The reductive effect is Mandevillean. Captain Weazel, whom the hero meets inauspiciously in chapter eleven, seems a formidable great man when he is heard thundering from inside the wagon in which he is riding, but turns out to be a shrivelled-up fellow of "about five foot and three inches high, sixteen inches of which went to his face and long scraggy neck; his thighs were about six inches in length, his legs resembling spindles or drum-sticks, two feet and a half . . .; —so that on the whole, he appeared like a spider or grasshopper erect."

Very few more convincing grotesques are to be found anywhere in English fiction. But Weazel is only one among many subhuman creations in *Roderick Random*, and their presence partially defines the psychological reality of the hero's world as he sees it and transmits its apparent meaning. The episode of Ralpho the raven (chap. 13) only underscores the nightmarish quality of this world inhabited by grotesques, so many of whom seem to be half animal. This "terrible apparition," only a tame bird really, appears in the middle of the night, as in a dream, leaving Strap in a swoon and Roderick "almost petrified with fear" that some violent spirit may have come to haunt them. The episode is much more than just a gratuitous comic interlude, though comic interlude it is. The same chapter plays an ironic reversal upon the hero's perception of the world as populated by subhuman creatures when a tavern wag takes the red-haired Roderick for a silly little beast of the wild, a fox who could not have been long caught, for his "tail was not yet cut." In chapter fourteen the Scottish teacher mocks Roderick's awkward dress and his "carroty locks." "I wonder the dogs did not hunt you," he tells him; "you look like a cousin-german of Ouran Outang." These instances of projection represent cruel hits at Roderick, newly arrived from Scotland, but suggest darkly his own future as an archly superior, brawling, gambling, fortune-hunting swindler—as a participant, in other words, in the bestial wickedness of the world which torments him with such jibes.

Roderick's progress toward complete despair is made all the more convincing by the visual precision with which he renders horrid experience. The violence of his language, moreover, contributes powerfully to the intensity of the story's texture, and says something important about Roderick's response to the world, even about his complicity with its harshness. Words like *immediately, seized, bellowed, inflamed, cursed, vengeance, noisome stench, staggered,* and so forth spatter the pages of the novel. And, as Phillip Stevick has observed, "People say, tell, speak, and declare in Smollett, but at least as frequently they whisper, simper, sigh, cry, protest, assure, pronounce, profess, rave, blubber, and demand aloud."[30] The very names of the characters, especially the most foolish or villainous ones—Wagtail, Quiverwit, Oakum, Cringer, Banter, Weazel, Thicket, Lavement, Chatter, Straddle, and the rest—involve a species of linguistic eccentricity that surely derives in part from Smollett's participation in the tradition of comedy of humors, as Stevick suggests (p. 718). But they are also consistent with the function of hyperbolic language generally, and help to define Roderick's world as a dark apparitional place in which people are only partial human beings, their essence really their eccentricity or, sometimes, their grotesqueness. It is a technique that Dickens later would learn from Smollett.

The portrayal of roguery given in *Roderick Random* gains depth and richness by the way in which we are allowed to see a decent fellow degenerate into a reflection of the world that victimizes him and which he scourges. As the portrait is filled out, it becomes increasingly clear that Roderick lacks the self-knowledge necessary to moral survival. His scourging of the world is a natural response to what he must endure, but he grows so obsessive about it that he all but loses contact with everything but the empirical reality he represents in this way. Roderick fails to defeat the world by condemning it, and so he joins it. It is a fundamental irony of Smollett's rogue biography that the hero's roguery, as portrayed, arises not from depravity, the usual source of villainy in criminal narrative, but from impossible idealism. On Smollett's part, the portrait of Roderick is at once sympathetic and judgmental, and it demonstrates a penetrating understanding of the impact of environment upon the individual life quite beyond the reach of the criminal biographers of the day and quite foreign to the purely satirical purposes of picaresque writers like LeSage. In moral terms, Smollett allows Roderick to define his despair as a consequence of insufficient faith in the redemptive powers of human love and goodness, and in the miraculous ways of Providence. Narcissa, who is always in his mind and whom he adores, seems more and more remote from him as his life progresses. She remains the "amiable apparition" she was when he first saw her. Roderick's very real crimes of fortune-hunting increase the distance separating him from her, for they cynically pervert the ideal of harmonious love and marriage she represents into a matter of deceptive appearances and dishonest economic transactions. At last, he says, melancholy and despondence "took possession of my soul; and repining at that providence, which by acting the stepmother towards me, kept me from the fruition of my wishes, I determined, in a fit of despair, to risk all I had at the gaming-table" (chap. 60)—in other words, to cast his lot with Fortune. Following a series of losses at the tables, Roderick is thrown into the Marshalsea for the crime of swindling a tailor out of twenty-five guineas.

Gambling, in this novel as in so much other eighteenth-century literature, becomes a metaphor for the game of life as played by Fortune's indecipherable rules, which decree only that there is no such thing as certitude. Roderick's absolute surrender to the rule of Fortune, or Chance, represents his final guilty capitulation to the moral chaos of the world, the total and, it seems, inevitable collapse of any kind of meaningful idealism. Smollett never denies the very real provocations that have brought Roderick to this deplorable condition. But the penalty he imposes upon him for his crimes, and for his cynicism and submission to despair, is severe. The very harshness of the punishment makes it clear that it is the hero of the novel and not the author who is the cynic, the arrogant Juvenalian scourger of the world, blinded and defeated by his own rage. The story is, after all, told by Roderick. Smollett repeatedly denied that he attempted any kind of self-portrait in *Roderick Random*, and there is no reason to doubt his word, though many have done so in their confusion over the meaning of this seemingly ambivalent, often savagely satirical work. At the moment just before Tom Bowling's arrival to rescue him from prison, Roderick presents himself as the very picture of complete, suffering hopelessness: "I was neither washed, shifted nor shaved; so that my face rendered meagre with abstinence, was obscured with dirt, and overshadowed with hair, and my whole appearance squalid and even frightful" (chap. 64). Narcissa, meanwhile, does not share in his despair, but instead writes to him expressing her continued faith that heaven will "contrive some . . . unforeseen event in our behalf" (chap. 60). This, of course, is precisely what happens. Suffering, it appears, has a redemptive power. While in prison Roderick turns reflective, judges his past, and is "seized with a deep Melancholy" (chap. 64) signifying new self-knowledge. And then, punished enough, he is delivered by his author.

The final chapters of *Roderick Random* are, as Robert Alter has complained, "egregiously incongenial to the picaresque spirit."[31] The writers of picaresque tales typically reject all possibility of meaningful reconciliation between the picaro and his world, and in fact they question all a priori assumptions about the moral purposefulness of human life. Smollett's moralized version of the picaresque affirms the possibility of reconciliation; or rather, it works out an accommodation of the hero's character with an ideal conception of moral life, and it does so from the premises of just such a priori assumptions as those the picaresque mode so emphatically denies. The very first page of *Roderick Random* reveals that the author has in mind two patterns to be applied to the hero's experience in the development of his moral history. In the mother's dream, the tennis ball slammed out of sight by the devil was returned "with equal violence" and entered the earth "beneath her feet, whence immediately sprung up a goodly tree covered with blossoms." Smollett's fictional construct allows the forces of evil to set in motion an empirical pattern of harsh moral and physical experience carried forward in a progression of mercurial adventures. But the sudden return of the devil's volley announces that a moral pattern, to be imposed by the providential author through the manipulation of his comic fiction, will finally supersede the empirical. Roderick's own good nature and basic decency, the presence of Bowling, Thomson, Morgan, Mrs. Sagely, and Narcissa, the sentimental love story superimposed upon the dark chaos of human cruelty and lovelessness that characterizes Roderick's world: these all anchor the moral pattern and help to authenticate the novel's comic resolution.

It must be said that this moral pattern is often obscured and left awash in the horrid facts of Roderick's experience, which he renders with such violent intensity and furious indignation. The reader, as I suggested earlier, may have nearly as hard a time perceiving it as the hero himself. The providential maneuverings that come at the close of the novel do seem very sudden. Don Rodriguez's ecstatic words in chapter sixty-six— "Mysterious Providence!" he cries out, and "God be praised for this happy meeting"—supply the first overt and extended sign of anything like an inevitable providential ending to the story, and we do not hear them until the resolution is actually unfolding. It may be argued, and often has been argued by Smollett's critics, that the author of *Roderick Random* did not manage the materials of his fiction particularly well; that in the haste of his composition[32] he violated the novelistic principles of organic unity by awkwardly contriving such a conclusion to his hero's adventures. There is some justice in this argument. But we must not dismiss the final chapters of the novel too quickly as an instance of Smollett's ineptitude, or as a clumsy irrelevancy. Presumably they represent a deliberate feature in the design of his moralized rogue biography. The radical wrenching of the fictional world brought about in these chapters just possibly reflects Smollett's sense of the great distance separating the actual behavior of mankind from the humanitarian ideals of justice, love, and benevolent action that alone can make for social and moral harmony and for the happiness of the individual as a member of the human race. In a letter to David Garrick written some years after the publication of his first novel, Smollett expressed his personal conviction that in real life mankind is always destined to struggle toward happiness, or contentment, in the midst of cruelty, hardship, and exasperating uncertainty. "I am old enough," he mused, "to have seen and observed that we are all playthings of fortune."[33] But *Roderick Random* is art, not life, and it is comic art at that. It may be said to develop as an extended metaphor expressing another of Smollett's private beliefs: namely, as Thomas R. Preston has described it, that the Christian part of mankind, though subject to the turnings and tossings of Fortune and the weaknesses of human nature itself, is engaged in a "gradual but nevertheless certain moral progress to the utopian state of physical and moral harmony that, according to the Christian tradition, he once possessed in Eden."[34] It is something like this journey to Eden, rendered in the form of a comic novel, that Roderick completes at the end of his story when he travels to Scotland and settles tranquilly into his now happy ancestral estate together with his father and his bride.[35]

We may observe in conclusion that the comic and providential resolution of *Roderick Random* parallels the ending of Fielding's rogue biography of *Jonathan Wild*, though of course there is no playful irony in it, and though in the case of Smollett's novel the rogue himself is redeemed. Both works affirm the highest moral and social ideals of the culture that produced them, but without ever softening their attack on the real and darkly visible corruptions of those ideals. Roderick, like the Heartfrees, is brought by his author to personal happiness, but Smollett, like Fielding, leaves the world itself in a state of degeneracy. There will be other Oakums and Mackshanes and Potions and Lavements, just as there will be other "great men" like Jonathan Wild—notwithstanding Fielding's delightfully wry suggestion that few of these will be able to avoid owning themselves inferior to his hero.

Neither *Roderick Random* nor *Jonathan Wild* partakes of the simpleminded sentimentality or the self-righteous complacency characterizing so much of the sensational literature of roguery in the period, with its numerous tales of suddenly repentant swindlers and rapists and thieves. Fielding specifically mocks such sentimentality and complacency. Smollett, to be sure, by rescuing his guilty but penitent rogue from prison and despair, comes extremely close to repetition of the facile convention by which a good many criminal biographers wishfully proclaim society's great power over the minds and souls of its deviant members. He may have deliberately echoed this convention, and if he did, it was so that he might exploit its familiarity while transforming it in the expression of an alternative vision of things. Far from celebrating society for any kind of triumph over Roderick's threats to itself, Smollett actually convicts the world of grievous moral crimes and finally removes his hero from its crushing grasp. As benevolent author of a moralized picaresque novel he reserves his applause, and the rewards by which it is signified, for the genuine courage and resilience displayed by his errant young Scot, whom he raises to conspicuous moral eminence. Endowed only with natural liveliness and his allotted share of "modest merit"—the most, it seems, that ordinary mortals in a Smollett novel can ever hope for—Roderick suffers painfully through the chastening miseries brought on by his own frailty while he strives bravely against the overwhelming dangers of a depraved world which is determined to corrupt him, and which nearly succeeds in doing so. The author of *Roderick Random* judges his roguish hero, and punishes him convincingly for his very serious failings, but it is obvious that he nonetheless admires him for what he represents. Presumably the reader will understand the meaning of his experience and learn to admire him too.

CHAPTER V

Fiction as Contemporary
Biography: Records of Spiritual Life

HE PSEUDOBIOGRAPHIES of devoutly pious men and
women present a very sharp contrast to the stories of impious
criminals and rogues. Instead of spectacular murderers and
thieves and whores, these narratives usually take as their subjects otherwise unexceptional people whose stout Christian resolution represents a
special and very appealing kind of heroism. Readers of the period seem to
have been almost as eager to applaud these exemplary folk as they were to
despise the deviant types who so deeply troubled and fascinated them. At
any rate, one out of every ten or so memoirs and biographies (both genuine and feigned) published during the first half of the eighteenth century
relates the intensely personalized moral history of some amazingly resilient Christian man or woman who sturdily withstands the onslaughts of
the forces of evil and corruption, often after having suffered through the
painful but exhilarating experience of conversion from a life of wickedness
and debauchery. The audience for such stories had declined somewhat by
the 1740s, when only about a dozen new narratives in this mode appeared, possibly because the need they fulfilled was being met in part by
the immensely successful and even more compelling novels of Samuel
Richardson. But interest in them persisted, and pious lives were a staple
of numerous evangelical books, pamphlets, and magazines right into the
nineteenth century.

Despite their radical differences in subject matter, pious biography and
rogue narrative may be said to echo each other in that they share in the
qualities of a literature of affirmation. They are actually separate but
closely related manifestations of some of the same important contempo-

rary interests, as the author of *Clarissa* surely knew when he shrewdly joined features of the two kinds together in recounting the distresses of his saintly heroine at the hands of her criminal tormentor Lovelace. Both types of narrative offer the alluring drama of a fantasy life that plays out patterns of wish fulfillment, and they do so by presenting stories of people whose experience is accessible to anyone precisely because of its familiarity, but whose great accomplishments in impiety or piety give them a kind of universal importance.

The pious lives, of course, emphasize spiritual experience, the record of the inner lives of their characters, to a degree quite beyond anything achieved in criminal and rogue biography. In fact, this is a chief source of their appeal and the only apparent reason for their existence. After all, many other popular tales of all kinds routinely repeated the conventional fable of virtue tested and proven in physical confrontation with the world—memoirs, voyages, spy fictions, amatory novels, even secret histories and criminal biographies themselves. Naturally, the men and women whose courage is celebrated in the pious lives must all defend themselves against an environment of real texture, inhabited by real people. But these stories typically demote physical experience to a level of secondary importance, instead focusing imaginatively upon the interior armor of passionate faith which alone (as they try to show) can protect virtue. Meanwhile, they emphasize the actual responses in feeling with which their Christian heroes and heroines meet external reality. The relevance of their psychological interest in human character to the new fiction of the 1740s, and to the novels of Richardson in particular, is both real and important. Obviously, a major purpose of the writers practicing in this form of extremely didactic biographical narrative—like the author of *Pamela* himself—was to provide an alternative kind of emotional excitement. But, just as obviously, they intended to portray quite ordinary people whose extraordinary stories would inspire their readers, teach them the rigors and rewards of spiritual discipline, and help them to fortify themselves against the threats posed by the disorder and the degeneracy of the world in which they lived. The pious lives are indeed a literature of affirmation, but they may be described even more accurately as a literature of devotion.

Pious Heroes and Pious Heroines

The origins of the pious life as a species of fictionalized biography lay in seventeenth-century Puritan and Quaker theology, which had the great leveling effect of proclaiming the spiritual equality of all men and women as individual spirits standing before an interested Providence. The Puritans and Quakers vigorously stimulated the production of private records of religious experience, many of which were inevitably made public. These accounts of spiritual life often took a confessional form, as Bunyanesque spiritual autobiography or as intensely personalized journals or diaries. As G. A. Starr and J. Paul Hunter have shown, Daniel Defoe came powerfully under the influence of this confessional literature, and the "Providence tradition" of which it was a part, early in the eighteenth century.[1] Later, the Methodists would appropriate the same forms and give them increased popularity. Meanwhile didactic romances like Fénelon's *Télémaque* and Palafox's *New Odyssey* enjoyed their most enthusiastic following during roughly the same period that the pious biography was in its formative stages, and they surely exerted some influence upon the authors just beginning to work in the new mode of edifying popular narrative. Possibly their influence was joined by that of Christian epics like Cowley's *Davideis* (1656) and Sir Richard Blackmore's *Prince Arthur* (1693).

As early as the year 1649 Jeremy Taylor, that "Shakespeare of divines," as eighteenth-century admirers were fond of calling him, had translated the biblical epic into the form of prose narrative in his *Life of Our Blessed Savior Jesus Christ*, and the book reached its tenth edition in 1742. Though based on the scriptures, this perennially popular work should be classed as fictionalized biography, since much of it was the product of Taylor's vigorous imagination. The *Life of Christ* was followed by numerous similar biographies, two of which were announced in the *Gentleman's Magazine* for July and August of 1740: a translation from the French of François T. de Choisy called *The History of the Life and Death of David*, and an anonymous volume entitled *The History of Adam and Eve*. A steadily increasing majority of the pious biographies issued during these years, however, took their subjects from recent English history or from the contemporary scene itself. In such narratives the ordinary man or woman was raised to something like the stature of the biblical hero. The latitudinarian divines (among others) of the late seventeenth and early eighteenth centuries had called for just such productions as these—stories of ordinary, flawed people who might serve as inspirational models of Christian behavior to those who read of them. In the pious biographies, the treatment of the inner lives and private sufferings of the characters is almost inevitably very detailed, since an avowed purpose of such works is to render in a credible manner the importance of spiritual experience in a worldly context. From this effort contemporary novelists may well have learned a good deal. On the other hand, the attempts by biographers to dramatize spiritual experience and capture the hearts and imaginations of their readers inevitably brought them under a reciprocal influence; many works of this kind provide a rich fantasy life by injecting a goodly dose of narrative art into what is purportedly a literal presentation of the truth.

Among the pious lives on secular subjects written during this time, one of the most interesting is a work called *The Journal of Mr. John Nelson, Preacher of the Gospel.*[2] This is an authentic account of a successful Yorkshire stonemason saved from spiritual desperation by a sermon of John Wesley. Nelson's story may be genuine, but it is so intensely dreamlike, and so dominated by a personal religious experience, that it may be said to provide pleasures usually associated with imaginative narrative. At age thirty, Nelson had been tormented by a hell of doubt over his relationship with God. At the point of his most extreme distraction, he had heard Wesley preach, and conversion to an absolute faith had come to him in a blinding vision of Christ: "That moment Jesus Christ was as evidently set before the eye of my mind, as crucified for my sins, as if I had seen him with my bodily eyes: and in that instant my heart was set at liberty, from guilt and tormenting fear, and filled with a calm and serene peace."[3] The sudden intensity of Nelson's faith persuaded his skeptical wife to a like faith, and she subsequently gave him her moral support in his decision to renounce his successful trade and live a life of poverty as a Methodist preacher. Nelson is eventually persecuted for his faith and his preaching, is pressed for a soldier, imprisoned, and generally harassed. But as witness in the world, he triumphs over all adversity, and becomes an exemplary spiritual hero of the struggle between good and evil. And as a Christian visionary whose dreams give him access to holy truths ("I saw a great white Throne"; "O what a scene was opened to my mind"), he no longer feels the terror of the damned. Providence, having intervened in his life to save him, never fails to protect and inspire him. In *The Case of John Nelson* (1745), an earlier pamphlet describing the terrible consequences of his refusal to serve as a soldier, Nelson had cried out: "Glory be to God on high! He kept my Soul all this Time in perfect Peace, and I could say to him from my Heart,

> Whilst Thou, O my Lord, art nigh,
>   My Soul disdains to fear;
> Sin and Satan I defy
>   Still impotently near:
> Earth and Hell their Wars may wage,
>   Calm I mark their vain Design,
> Smile to see them idly rage
>   Against a Child of Thine. (p. 6)

The *Journal* itself preserves the same intensity of feeling and of faith, the same serenity in the face of all threats and persecutions.

Nelson's *Journal* is one of the earliest among a large group of mid-century Wesleyan lives, many of which were not published until later years. In his *Art of Biography* Donald Stauffer calls it "probably the most vital and simple of all the Methodist biographies" (p. 285). It stands out as the only narrative of its kind in the 1740s to employ the first-person journal form of earlier confessional literature, and in this respect it anticipates the wave of Methodist lives that was to sweep over England in the latter half of the eighteenth century. As a printer, Samuel Richardson was aware of the activity of writers like Nelson, and of the enduring popularity of this species of literature.[4] Certainly the method of Richardson's epistolary novels, especially *Clarissa*, results in an intensely rendered revelation of the protagonist's spiritual and emotional life, and *Pamela* itself is partly in journal form.

The publication of Richardson's novels overlaps with a handful of other pious biographies issued in the 1740s. One of these is particularly relevant to *Clarissa*, as its title hints. It is impressively called *The Power and Pleasure of the Divine Life: Exemplify'd in the Late Mrs. Housman, of Kidderminster, Worcestershire. . . . To Which Is Sub-Joined, An Account of Her Triumphant Death* (1744). This widely reprinted work, which is supposedly by the Reverend Richard Pearsall, is a very routine performance, and may therefore be taken as representative of its kind. The story of *Mrs. Housman* focuses on the inner life of an ordinary woman, an exemplary character who, strengthened and made inviolable by her faith, resists all the wicked attacks of the world. The heroine, in fact, like Clarissa Harlowe after her, embodies an unblemished ideal of piety, and her very existence in the microcosm of Pearsall's book implies a judgment on all the forces that threaten purity. For Mrs. Housman, as for Clarissa, final moral victory comes with death. But Pearsall's work is a crudely hortatory narrative whose author, immersed in his homiletic purpose, forgets that he is dealing with human frailty. The absolute perfection he imparts to his heroic lady is obviously a distortion of her real character and experience. In his preface Pearsall says that he has tried to "embalm this excellent Person, that you might have her in your Houses." Unfortunately, that is just what he succeeds in doing. His work suffers from a lack of dramatic tension and character interest, while Mrs. Housman's death is only the logical and on the whole welcome conclusion to a perfect and therefore uninteresting life. Mediocre as it is in quality, however, the book does anticipate *Clarissa* in some obvious ways. Richardson may never have read *Mrs. Housman*, but a number of the conventional devices and attitudes of pious biography that seem so superficial in Pearsall's narrative are repeated later in *Clarissa*, which expands and invests them with the power of its author's imagination, and makes of them the instruments of conflict and compelling drama. In Richardson's novel, the heroine's death is truly a "triumph."

Among the pious lives published in the 1740s, unquestionably the most subtle and convincing is Dr. Philip Doddridge's *Some Remarkable Passages in the Life of the Honourable Col. James Gardiner* (1747). Gardiner was a real hero of the 'Forty-Five, and Doddridge's biography displays considerable fidelity to its subject's actual career. The documentation is impressive; there are frequent quotations from Gardiner's letters, and all sources are scrupulously authenticated. Yet this life, one of the fairly large group of early eighteenth-century works treating pious military heroes, must be described as fiction, since it yields ample evidence of a shaping and heightening imagination. The strategic center of the book is a religious experience, a moment of spiritual illumination. From the earliest pages, Doddridge prepares for this moment. For years prior to his conversion, we are shown, Gardiner had lived an exclusively physical existence. Born to an affluent middle-class family in 1688, the year of the Glorious Revolution, he had seemed destined to be a soldier; he fought valiantly and almost died on the battlefield at Ramilles during the War of the Spanish Succession. Subsequently, as the ward of the expatriate Earl of Stair, he lived as a gallant young courtier at Versailles. During this eleven-year period in his career, Gardiner's thoughtless passion for the active life and its pleasures led him into a series of illicit love affairs, earning him the dubious epithet of "the happy rake." It was in the midst of one of these affairs that he suddenly read a hortatory work called *The Christian Soldier*, by the sixteenth-century English sonneteer and Christian humanist Thomas Watson. Immediately Gardiner had a painful vision of Christ, as a result of which he pronounced his own damnation. Later, he perceived the effects of grace, emerged from his despair, and was saved. His sense of relief was profound and almost overwhelming.

Gardiner's conversion is passionately detailed over the course of many pages. So private and momentous an experience could only be understood by an effort of the imagination, and the dramatic power of Doddridge's narrated version of that experience can thus be ascribed to his capacity to feel and transmit its intensity. But there are other signs of a creative intellect at work. Doddridge, a celebrated Nonconformist clergyman and hymn-writer, could have had no more than secondhand knowledge concerning the widely varied scenes of Gardiner's early life, yet he treated them with an almost Fieldingesque energy, and imparted to them a vividness that would do honor to Defoe himself. Most of Gardiner's later life was less dramatic and exciting than his youth, but in handling it Doddridge preserved his gusto while detailing the events with skill and Richardsonian compassion. We see the hero as a wholly reformed character, yet we believe in him; we endure with him the loss of his children, and admire him for the sincerity of his religious enthusiasm and benevolent conduct in the domestic sphere. Finally, we share the horror of the devoted servant who recounts the heroic death of this exemplary Christian soldier on the battlefield at Preston-Pans.

Col. James Gardiner is impressive in many ways. Part of its power as a story derives naturally from the drama of its subject's actual life, just as its neatly balanced structure arises from the symmetry of his career. But it is the strength of the Reverend Doddridge's imagination, together with the singlemindedness of his didactic purpose, that gives the work its unity of tone and hence its dramatic impact. How much Doddridge may have added to the actual biography of the hero is impossible to say, but the narrative often reads like a historical romance, and we may be certain that pure invention plays a large role in transforming mere facts. In *Col. James Gardiner* the protagonist emerges as a figure almost larger than life. Chiefly through the influence of Doddridge's biography, he came to be widely regarded as an all but legendary embodiment of the ideal of the pious hero—an ideal toward which Richardson was to turn in his history of Sir Charles Grandison. Succeeding generations of readers recognized the merits of Doddridge's early story of the colonel, which went through no less than eight editions over the latter half of the eighteenth century, and several more in the nineteenth. In 1814, Walter Scott paid a high tribute to Gardiner's character by enshrining him in *Waverley* as the young hero's brave, compassionate commanding officer.

The pattern of experience recorded in the stories of Colonel Gardiner and the preacher John Nelson expresses their authors' real optimism that the individual life can be redeemed from the welter of the world's circumstances, that a new richness of spiritual experience may be purchased by faith, which in turn holds the promise that anyone possessing it will be able to approach hardship, sorrow, even death, with serenity. The trauma of conversion, with its terrifying prospects of hell followed by equally dramatic but comforting visions of things heavenly, signifies the possibilities of personal renewal that these works are intended to proclaim. The story of Mrs. Housman is simply a variation upon the same pattern, showing from page one until the end how the resolute man or woman can, through the daily practice of piety—prayer and meditation, devoted study of the scriptures, regular attendance at church, meaningful commitment to the ideals of Christian benevolence, constant reflection and self-examination—withstand all manner of evil, from the seductive threats of would-be abductors to the temptations of self-indulgent melancholy and despair.

All of these works seek to stir the emotions of their readers to an unusual kind of thrill deriving from a close personal identification with the trials of their heroes and heroines, whose innermost thoughts are exposed for all the world to see in their diaries, journals, and letters. Sometimes the stories seem deliberately contrived along the lines of the appealing and inspiring biblical tale of Job. But the spiritual adventurers they celebrate are also projected by their authors almost as objects to be contemplated; this is what the Reverend Pearsall means when he says that his story is an attempt to "embalm" his heroine so that readers might always have her before them. Almost in the manner of a biblical character like Ruth, or

Esther, or Job himself, Mrs. Housman is portrayed as a person worthy of reverent attention, and, perhaps even more importantly, worthy of the reader's emulation. Presumably her example will strengthen the resolve of the already faithful, and will have the force to convert the unbelieving. The same homiletic purposes may be attributed to the other contemporary works of pious biography, though the lives of John Nelson, and of Colonel Gardiner especially, are much more eventful and thus may be said to possess somewhat broader interest and appeal. The enviable success of all of these heroic men and women in the enterprise of meeting life's severest trials is achieved as a consequence of their discipline in their faith, and so their stories, like the very different tale of *The Pilgrim's Progress*, could be suitably read and even studied as exercises in private devotion. It would be foolish to suppose that all readers used or for that matter understood them in this way. But certainly it is how they were offered.

In this connection the now-famous anecdote of how Dr. Benjamin Slocock stood in his pulpit and recommended the calculatedly pious epistolary tale of *Pamela; or, Virtue Rewarded* as a book of devotion takes on new interest.[5] The best of the pious biographies published in the 1740s came out after the sudden explosion of excitement over Richardson's first novel, their accomplishments as pure narrative possibly reflecting the influence of that celebrated work. But they were only the latest and most able examples in a long succession of such stories. There can be no doubt that the interests appealed to in the closely drawn portrait of Richardson's heroically virtuous serving maid directly coincided with, and perhaps intentionally duplicated, some of the most important attractions of the many biographical accounts of saintly men and women that preceded its appearance on the scene.

※※※

Pamela and *Clarissa:*
Fiction as Devotional Literature

Samuel Richardson thought of himself as a conscious innovator, the deliberate creator of a "new species of writing," and so it would be much too limiting to suggest that he contrived his novels as nothing more than fictional works of devotional literature, or as conduct books for the practice of Christian faith. Something like this, however, formed a part of his purpose in *Pamela* at least, if his own words may be believed. "I thought the story," he declared to Aaron Hill in a letter of January 1741, "if written in an easy and natural manner, . . . might tend to promote the cause of religion and virtue."[6] It is revealing that a good many of *Pamela*'s first readers responded directly to its hortatory and inspirational powers. An anonymous congratulatory epistle to the *Weekly Miscellany,* included by Richardson in his introduction to the novel, prophesied that *Pamela* would "reclaim the Vicious, and mend the Age in general." One reader, Knightley Chetwood, seriously proposed that "if all the Books in England were to be burnt, this Book, next the Bible, ought to be preserved." Richardson's acquaintance the Reverend Smyth Loftus wrote him to say that the story of *Pamela* afforded "a beautiful simplicity which I never knew excelled except in the Bible."[7]

It is not difficult to understand how at least some members of Richardson's audience might have responded to his book in this way, especially given the currency and familiarity of pious biography. The flawless maiden Pamela Andrews displays very fervent religious feelings through her regular devotional habits, pious verses, naive self-scrutiny, and constant spiritual reflections on the threats and temptations that confront her in a fallen world complete with its own "Lucifer" in the form of Mr. B. In many respects Pamela's reactions to experience coincide with those of writers like the exemplary John Nelson. Later, in *Clarissa*, Richardson would pursue resemblances to confessional literature in even more striking ways by lavishly detailing the heroine's prayers and her regular attendance at church, her tormenting self-doubts, and her agonies over the extent of her guilt in her relations with Lovelace. Devotional meditations of the kind Clarissa assiduously composes were a regular feature of pious biography. Very often in such works these meditations powerfully affected the lives of characters who read them, as they were intended to do, and as Clarissa's affected the life of Belford.

We may pause to observe that, in general, the pious lives are much more immediately relevant to the novels of Richardson than of Fielding and Smollett. It is worth mentioning, however, that the Reverend Philip Doddridge's popular life of Colonel James Gardiner in some ways anticipates Fielding's treatment of Captain Billy Booth in *Amelia*. Both heroes are soldiers, and both begin as imprudent, irresponsible men too much concerned with the ways of the world and not enough with the state of their souls. In each case a conversion occurs suddenly and with finality, as though by an interposition of Providence. Gardiner reads Watson's *Christian Soldier*, and Booth, while in prison, succumbs to the power of Isaac Barrow's sermons. The conversion experience strikingly alters the life of each character. Once a loving, good-natured, but profligate husband who brought little but pain and hardship to his adored wife and children, Booth now becomes—as does Gardiner late in his life—the perfect husband and father. Each character, too, after his conversion, attains the highest kind of heroism, that of the Christian man functioning resolutely in a hostile, secular world. I have already made the point that in *Amelia*, Fielding effectually turns the conventions of the military biography inside out, and he appears to have done so in a manner closely resembling that of the Reverend Doddridge, who accomplishes much the same thing in his pious life of Gardiner. There is no evidence to suggest that Fielding was at all influenced by Doddridge's book, or that he was even aware of it. The resemblances between *Col. Gardiner* and the much finer story of *Amelia* are very real, but they are probably mere coincidental occurrences of a kind common enough in literary history. Yet one is tempted at least to think that Doddridge's distinguished account of a famous Christian warrior may in some way have helped to prepare the contemporary audience for Fielding's portrait of the repentant soldier Billy Booth.

The remainder of Fielding's fiction, and Smollett's *Roderick Random* as well, relates to the pious lives in less specific ways. Instead it registers the influence of a prevailing climate in popular literature to which all kinds of didactic writing contributed, and which found two of its leading influences in didactic romance and pious biography. Fielding and Smollett, like Richardson, urge upon their readers the recognition that only through the pursuit of Christian virtue may the human character impose any kind of order upon a troubled existence. Certainly this is the lesson of the histories of Tom Jones and Roderick Random, both of whom undergo the severest trials, sink into a terrible nadir of ill fortune and misery, and finally undergo a transformation of character which, like Colonel Gardiner's, changes their lives for the better and ensures their happiness. Neither Fielding nor Smollett really portrays the inner realities of spiritual experience, but their first readers would easily have seen that their general didactic strategy parallels that of pious biographers like Philip Doddridge.

The amazingly enthusiastic reception enjoyed by Richardson's *Pamela* reveals how very nearly this pious book touched the hearts and minds of the contemporary audience with its intensely rendered story of private virtue persecuted and triumphant.[8] No doubt part of the novel's appeal may be attributed to its reflection of unresolved contemporary social conflict, as described by William M. Sale, Jr., and others.[9] Pamela Andrews, a servant girl representing a kind of native nobility in virtue, is pursued by an aristocratic seducer who, along with his coequals in the world of the novel, gives dramatic embodiment to what Richardson obviously viewed as a decaying, shiftless, morally bankrupt class now being superseded in public esteem by sober, industrious, pious middle-class folk. Richardson's own ambivalence on the subject of the aristocracy—often discussed, and sometimes smugly—reflects an important preoccupation of his time. Pamela's resilience, and her meteoric rise through marriage to Mr. B., play out an exercise in wish fulfillment as old as the Cinderella legend and the romances of dispossessed moral nobility, but as current as Hogarth's *Industrious Apprentice*.

Henry Fielding, like many readers after him, denounced the social vision of *Pamela* as false and naive if not downright dangerous. Some of those who, like Fielding, parodied or adapted or continued *Pamela* were very severe in their criticisms. But Richardson's most authoritative biographers argue convincingly that he had no intention of projecting his heroine's social experience as part of the usual order of things.[10] Actually, he seems to have had in mind the kind of meritocracy represented in the legend of Cinderella and in later comic fictions like *Evelina* and *Pride and Prejudice*. Richardson's social vision in *Pamela*, in other words, cannot be understood apart from his moral vision. His most able and prolific predecessor in the enterprise of pious novel writing, Mrs. Penelope Aubin, had articulated a similar meritocratic pattern in detailing the widely varied moral adventures of her dispossessed Christian heroes and heroines, whom she frequently confronts with threats and temptations on a worldwide scale before at last bringing them to rest in an exalted state of happiness and tranquility. Mrs. Aubin's novels and *Pamela* are moral fables, biographical in form, designed to display personal piety in action and to proclaim the hope of meaningful personal reward with which, in the view of their authors, the faithful Christian may approach the challenge of living in a deeply vexing world.[11] This very serious homiletic purpose, so richly fulfilled in Richardson's first novel, subsumes all other purposes and unquestionably constituted an extremely important part—perhaps the most important part—of its appeal to the contemporary audience.

Mrs. Aubin, in stories like *The Life and Amorous Adventures of Lucinda* (1722) and *The Life of Charlotta Du Pont* (1723), allegorized her familiar heroines into figures larger than life itself, very much in the manner of the writers of pious biography. The characters featured in all of these works, both novelistic and pseudobiographical, transcend ordinary reality, though their authors unfailingly insist on the genuine moral reliability of the stories they tell. Mrs. Aubin offers her works as avowed fictions, but contrives them as allegorical moral histories possessing a special kind of imaginative truth. Richardson, by posing as editor of his heroine's letters, and by approximating some of the strategies of spy fiction and the secret history in his exposures of country life, proclaims the authenticity of Pamela's experience, but we have already seen how he adapts romance conventions in projecting her as an almost archetypal figure of innocence and goodness. As a surreptitious novelist dealing with imaginary reality, Richardson greatly exceeds the pious biographers in his attempts to portray the depths of private character and the spiritual life. He endows Pamela with much finer sensibilities, drawn lavishly in the details of her many letters and her journal entries recording her innermost responses to the particular circumstances of Mr. B.'s advances against her. Pamela has been justly accused of lacking self-knowledge, but her often anguished correspondence may be trusted in its display of her feeling—her fears, confusions, anxieties, and strengths. Every serious and sympathetic reader of Richardson has observed that the epistolary method as he practiced it, despite its many limitations, has the effect of intensifying the reader's experience of the fictional world while commanding direct and very close reaction to the writer or writers of the letters themselves as they dramatize and reflect upon their experience. To put the matter more cynically: epistolary narrative encourages a kind of emotional voyeurism, which is sometimes precisely what an author desires as he seeks to manipulate the sensibilities and the judgment of his audience. No novelist before or after Richardson has ever equaled his success as a storyteller in the epistolary mode. And this mode suited his didactic purposes perfectly, since he obviously intended both *Pamela* and *Clarissa* as expressions of the highest possibilities of Christian idealism, calculated to inspire his readers in the most deeply personal way.

That *Pamela* succeeds as a work of literary art revealing its author's consciousness of a meaningful relationship between form, purpose, and content is a point no longer in need of arguing, thanks to the contributions of sensitive commentators like A. M. Kearney, Elizabeth Brophy, and Margaret Anne Doody.[12] It is Richardson the artist as much as Richardson the moralist who, anxious to certify the significance of his heroine's experience, actually places it in a carefully suggestive biblical context, thus imparting to it a kind of cosmic importance and, in an almost literal way, taking his own work far beyond the territories of moral life usually explored by the writers of pious narrative in his day. "O Sir!" Pamela writes to Parson Williams early in the novel, her words freighted with social as well as moral suggestiveness, "my Soul is of equal Importance with the Soul of a Princess; though my Quality is inferior to that of the meanest Slave" (p. 141). This outburst, which comes after one of her more desperate encounters with Mr. B., expresses Pamela's resolve as well as her conviction of her own worth. It is followed much later by a scene in the chapel at the B. family's Lincolnshire estate, just prior to the marriage, when the heroine interprets her experience in much more than just personal or even social terms. "*My Soul doth magnify the Lord,*" she says, repeating words from the Magnificat (Luke 1:46–55), "*for he hath regarded the low Estate of his Handmaiden—and exalted one of low Degree.*" Mr. B., meanwhile, attributes his miraculous reformation and his sudden discovery of transcendent happiness to the effects of grace. "I owe all this to the Grace of God," he remarks, and it is clear that Pamela has been the instrument of that grace. As the newly betrothed couple stand in the chapel together with Goodman Andrews, Mr. B. places his own moral history in a biblical context. "*There is more Joy in Heaven over one Sinner that repenteth,*" he declares, paraphrasing Luke 15:7, "*than over Ninety-nine just Persons that need not Repentance.*" Pamela's father, deeply moved, solemnly draws a comparison between his daughter's story and "the Book of *Ruth*" (pp. 261–63).

The effect of Richardson's strategy of biblical allusiveness is to sanctify the private experience of an ordinary girl, to suggest that in moral life

139

there can be no meaningful distinction between the sacred and the secular. Pamela is of course drawn to Mr. B., despite her genuine terror at the moral as well as physical threat he poses to her. But this temptation, far from making her a hypocrite, only deepens her trouble. In Richardson's orthodox view temptation is not temptation unless it is tempting, and so the real attraction Pamela feels for her tormentor greatly increases the danger she faces. The Christian determination and daily piety with which she meets this danger provides an example of how the individual life may be redeemed from the threat of evil and the bondage of sin. In contemporary terms at least, Pamela's story is therefore worthy of study and emulation.

The mildly racy titillations of the scenes of attempted rape in no real way detract from, much less contradict, the homiletic function of the narrative. In fact they have been exaggerated out of all proportionate importance by smug readers anxious to convict Richardson of unacknowledged fixations and neuroses. The representation of the novel's conflict in sexual terms does not simply grow unbidden out of the author's prurience. In the Puritan tradition that Richardson inherited, the knowledge of evil is carnal knowledge. Sexual conflict in *Pamela* actually reflects mythic associations between goodness and sexual purity, evil and sexual promiscuity. Dramatically and metaphorically, Richardson makes his heroine equate sexual violation with the direst of all threats, the ultimate invasion of personal integrity, or, to use Pamela's own rather conventional term, "honesty": "I dread of all things to be seduced," she exclaims in a letter to her parents, "and would rather lose my Life than my Honesty!" (p. 112).

The particular way in which Richardson represents Mr. B.'s sexual advances upon Pamela further defines his conception of the importance of his heroine's moral experience. At the very beginning, the novel establishes itself as a version of Christian pastoral narrative. The story deliberately follows a rhythmic movement from the Arcadian innocence of the opening pages, to the episodes of attempted rape (significantly, the first of these occurs in the Summer-house, in the Bedfordshire garden), to the terrifying abduction and confinement at Lincolnshire, finally to the restoration of paradisal bliss at the end. There is a quality of Edenic, prelapsarian tranquility about the world of *Pamela* as it is represented in the earliest letters, but it is disrupted by the new master of the estate, who is projected as a serpentine tempter; he is, says the heroine, "as cunning as

Lucifer" (p. 61). No reasonably alert contemporary reader would have missed Richardson's echoes of the Genesis story, which he actually adapts in his novel and re-creates into a New Testament fable of redemption and renewal.

Throughout all of her trials at her master's hands, Pamela repeatedly characterizes him as the devil incarnate until at last he responds to the force of her virtuous example and repents.[13] Only a day or two before the process of their reconciliation begins, on the occasion of his last attempt against her virtue in the Lincolnshire garden, she upbraids Mr. B. directly as a demonic villain. You are *"Lucifer* himself in the Shape of my Master," she cries to him, "or you could not use me thus" (p. 181). When eventually he is transformed by the effects of grace he becomes, in Pamela's new and final estimation, "all Goodness" (p. 244), a "good Angel" (p. 316). Now, instead of sexual threats signifying disturbance in the order of Pamela's moral universe, there is to be fertile marriage, which the heroine characterizes as her true "happiness"—the highest possible state of earthly bliss[14]—and which is sanctified by "GOD, the All-gracious, the All-good, the All-bountiful, the All-mighty" (p. 407). Colbrand, Mrs. Jewkes, and the others who had hardened themselves against Pamela's earlier pleas for help are, like Mr. B. himself, completely won over by her goodness. Even lecherous old Sir Simon Darnford cries out to Mr. B., "I believe there is something in Virtue, that we had not well considered. On my Soul, there has been but one Angel come down for these thousand Years, and you have got her" (p. 339). Lady Davers is finally reconciled too, following that remarkable theatrical scene in which Pamela (who is by now Mrs. B.), shrewdly mixing deference with proud resilience, is made to prove her mettle in yet another way. "Thou'rt almost got into Fool's Paradise, I doubt!" says Mr. B.'s haughty sister (p. 318), and the delicious irony of the remark only underscores what the reader has already come to understand about the heroine's effect on this world once so dominated by the likes of Mr. B. and his sister.

The paradise established at the conclusion of the conflict between Pamela and Mr. B. is comprehensive, deep in its significance, something to be celebrated. This paradise is real and permanent, unlike that projected in the earliest scenes of the book, where the vision of Eden is an illusion, preserved by the good Lady B. as long as she lived, but fragile and unstable, the reality of evil merely lying in wait in the person of her son,

141

who puts on all the airs of graciousness and goodness: "I thought he look'd like an Angel," says Pamela (p. 31). For much of the narrative, Pamela is a heroine cruelly isolated by her own merit in a world which denies the value of what she is. Her isolation becomes most menacingly real and terrifying during her imprisonment at Lincolnshire, where she is driven to despair and to the brink of suicide—in Christian terms an unforgivable act of prideful self-indulgence. But she preserves her courage as well as her virtue. And in the end, when she has triumphed over all adversity, her victory extends outward to all the world, which miraculously appears to have no evils left in it. Richardson devotes many (and sometimes tedious) pages to showing how the happiness Pamela has achieved spreads itself everywhere, partly through the deliberately benevolent actions by which the heroine herself endeavors to share the "Ease, Pleasure and Tranquillity" (p. 311) that gladden her own heart. She wants, she declares, to make "the whole Creation, so far as is in the Circle of my Power, happy!" (p. 303). The latter half of the novel, following Mr. B.'s proposal of honorable marriage, is dramatically weaker than the first half, but it is consistent with Richardson's didactic purpose, which is to demonstrate the power of goodness to redeem a fallen, wicked world.

Pamela's story, with its pattern of dire conflict between good and evil resolved into a perfected order affirming the complete supremacy of the good, has about it the definite air of the moral fable. Certainly it is not a strictly realistic representation of human life, in either moral or social terms.[15] The novel is actually an allegorical moral history, in the sense that, like many other biographical narratives of its period, it draws from the walks of ordinary contemporary life a representative personage who embodies collective private experience and gives it public visibility and significance. By his whole pattern of biblical allusiveness, Richardson elevates his heroine to the status of a historical character of the first magnitude while preserving her familiarity and accessibility through the minutest detailing of her particular experiences and her innermost responses to them. More specifically, *Pamela* possesses all the most appealing attributes of a pious biography. It is deliberately intended to teach the methods and the ultimate pleasure of spiritual discipline, and to enforce the ideals of "religion and virtue" upon its audience. Pamela herself is a model to be followed, and a source of inspiration. We cannot read Richardson's novel quite properly unless we recognize how serious he was about his didactic purposes, which hardly differ at all from those of the Reverends Pearsall and Doddridge, or for that matter from those of the pious novelist Penelope Aubin. Within the world of the novel Pamela's letters, meditations, and journal entries have upon Mr. B. precisely the effect that Isaac Barrow and John Tillotson had claimed for lives and histories of familiar Christian heroes and heroines, and presumably they are to have similar effects upon the reader.

Given what he actually does in *Pamela*, it would be foolish to suppose Richardson unaware of a tradition of pseudobiography whose aims and methods so closely matched his own impulses as a writer. It seems very likely indeed that he consciously exploited the devices of the pious life as a means of placing his first novel firmly in a context of popular didactic narrative, partly to counter the usual run of frivolous and, in Richardson's view, dangerous novels and romances, no doubt partly to improve his own book's chances of success with the contemporary audience. Richardson certainly wished *Pamela* to be read, and read widely. To say this is not to demean his motives or his accomplishment. He surely yearned for fame, but it is more important to note that his ambitions as a serious Christian moralist required an audience if they were to be fulfilled. And besides, we still remember and read *Pamela*, whereas no one reads John Nelson's *Journal* or the story of Mrs. Housman. To state the obvious: Richardson was an artist of great talent, blessed with unusual powers of human understanding and inspired by a deep Christian faith. His first effort in the vein of pious fiction is richer, more ambitious, more complex and rewarding, than any other work of its kind published during his lifetime, with the exception of his own *Clarissa*. Not even *Sir Charles Grandison* sustains the same unity and intensity of tone and feeling as *Pamela*.

To look at *Pamela* as it appears in relief against the background of minor pious fiction is simply to recognize anew its profound relevance to eighteenth-century life and to illuminate its purposes and its excellences in a fresh way. What Richardson may have borrowed from lesser works of this kind he changed, developed, refined, and made his own. In this connection it is particularly revealing to notice that *Pamela* is actually a deliberately comic transformation upon the mode of pious biography. The Christian vision, as dramatized, is hopeful; the fictional world is at last reconciled completely to everything that the heroine represents, and the broad idealism expressed gains further force by the work's association with a pastoral tradition which includes Sidney's *Arcadia*, the greatest of English pastoral romances in prose and the probable source of the heroine's name. Margaret Anne Doody has justly called *Pamela* a pastoral comedy,[16] her epithet interestingly suggesting the degree to which the author brought the devices of art to bear upon his telling of the simple story of a courageous country girl whose life becomes a celebration of the highest principles of Christian virtue. It is often said that the villagers at Slough rang the church bells on Pamela's wedding day because Richardson convinced them that she was real, or that she could be real. That does not seem motivation enough. We may imagine that they sounded the bells because Pamela's story, as the astonishingly fresh, compelling, and enriched achievement of an accomplished artist in the vein of pious moral history, actually inspired and excited them beyond any other tale of contemporary sainthood they knew. It must have taught them deeply to value her for what she was and to enjoy her triumph as though it were their own.

Clarissa; or, The History of a Young Lady began to appear in December 1747, when Samuel Richardson issued the first two volumes of his new novel. Four months later, in April 1748, volumes three and four were published. By the fall of that same year the final three volumes were almost ready to go to the booksellers' stalls, and copies apparently were sent out to some of Richardson's friends and fellow writers for advance reading before the publication date in December. Henry Fielding was one of those to receive an advance copy of volume five, and on October 15 he wrote to Richardson praising the new novel most extravagantly. In the *Jacobite's Journal* (for January 2 and March 5, 1748) he had already expressed his warm admiration for *Clarissa*'s powerful "Simplicity," its "deep Penetration into Nature," its command over the reader's passions, and the masterful "Witchcraft" of its suspenseful plot, which was just unfolding in the initial two volumes.[17] In the October letter Fielding dropped the manner of the public man, the critic, and wrote in extremely personal terms of his enchantment with Richardson's heroine and of his susceptibility to the emotional power of her story. It is an amazingly generous letter, especially considering Fielding's rough treatment of Richardson in *Shamela* only a few years earlier, and it is even more remarkable in that Fielding and Richardson were, in Fielding's words, "Rivals for that coy Mrs. Fame."

"Can I tell you what I think of the latter part of your Volume [five]?" Fielding asks. "Let the Overflowings of a Heart which you have filled brimfull speak for me." Fielding is alternately shocked and terrified by Lovelace's vile machinations, he is melted "into Compassion" for the "poor betrayed Creature" Clarissa, he is "thunderstruck" by Lovelace's terse announcement of the rape, nor can "many Lines explain" what he is made to feel "from Two." "Here my Terror ends," he continues, and "my Grief begins which the Cause of all my tumultuous Passions soon changes into Raptures of Admiration and Astonishment." He sincerely congratulates Richardson for a "wonderfull Art," which compels "both Terror and Compassion" on the heroine's account.[18] The real enthusiasm of Fielding's response to the "wonderfull Art" of *Clarissa*, to the "Witchcraft" of its management of suspense and of the reader's emotions, proclaims the respect he felt for the craftsmanship of his rival's second novel. But his words also register the impact of *Clarissa* as a dilated and greatly intensified study in pious biography. What the "thunderstruck" author of *Shamela* and *Joseph Andrews* feels for the wicked Lovelace's miserable but resolute victim—awe, genuine compassion, admiration—is precisely what the reader of an exemplary work like Richardson's, or like the Reverend Pearsall's tale of Mrs. Housman, is expected to feel. The immensely varied, intimate, and moving story of *Clarissa* obsessively pursues a homiletic purpose, following its author's powerful didactic impulses, so as to erect its familiar heroine as a triumphant monument to the ideals of piety and Christian virtue. "Indeed I *did*" mean Clarissa as an exemplary figure, Richardson wrote to Aaron Hill, and "that in the most trying and arduous Cases, or I would not have set Pen to Paper."[19] Even more successfully than he had done in *Pamela*, Richardson allegorized his new heroine into an almost mythic figure of goodness whom the villain of the novel must himself recognize as "angel" and who is, as Dorothy Van Ghent has aptly put it, "more than an individual character"; she is "a fabulous creature of epic stature, clothed with the ideals of a culture and a race."[20]

Fielding's warm praise of *Clarissa* for its art and its power was echoed in other contemporary reactions to the novel. Richardson had his detractors, of course, and it is a fact (a fact that disappointed Richardson himself) that *Clarissa* never sold as well as *Pamela*. But the novel was still greatly admired and widely read. Dr. Johnson, among his many remarks on Richardson's masterpiece, is known to have proclaimed that it was "not only the first *novel*, but perhaps the first *work* in our language, splendid in point of genius, and calculated to promote the dearest interests of religion and virtue."[21] Sarah Fielding, in her anonymously published *Remarks on Clarissa* (1749), resumed her brother's applause for the novel, but commented in much greater detail on both its moral and its literary value; she especially appreciated the author's achievement as a tragic moral historian. *Clarissa* was expensive (3s. per volume in the first edition), but its four editions in just over three years (three in duodecimo volumes and a fourth, slightly more expensive, in octavo) suggest a considerable measure of popularity. If we take as evidence nothing more than the many letters Richardson received from readers and admirers, it would appear that his affecting story was on everybody's mind and in everybody's conversation. One woman, Richardson's biographers tell us, wrote to the author of *Clarissa* to upbraid him for revealing to the world the most closely guarded secrets of her own life. Richardson reacted smugly by noting on the letter that this lady flattered herself.[22] Yet that she wrote to him at all shows how nearly he had touched the common facts of everyday experience, and how important he had made those facts seem.

Like *Pamela*, *Clarissa* was doubtless appealing in large measure because of the way it reflected the tensions of contemporary class conflict, which many people also viewed as a moral conflict of the highest order. The heroine herself, as Christopher Hill and William M. Sale, Jr., have argued so convincingly, represents an idealized version of the most important middle-class virtues of honesty, chastity, humble dutifulness, and piety as they undergo threats from an attractive libertine who bodies forth the dazzling but finally pernicious characteristics of a promiscuous, arrogant, impious, and decaying aristocracy.[23] Hill, Sale, and Dorothy Van Ghent have said almost the last word on the subject of Richardson's success in capturing and mythologizing the social realities of his day, and so I need not pursue the matter here. But it is worth emphasizing that in this novel Richardson reveals an even more profound sense of the relations between social and moral reality than he does in *Pamela*. From the time of Lovelace's introduction to the Harlowes and the duel with James, Clarissa writes, "Our family has indeed been strangely discomposed.—*Discomposed!*—It has been in *tumults* ever since the unhappy transaction; and I have borne all the blame" (1:3–4). What is to become a crucial fact of the heroine's experience is thus established at the outset: she is trapped in the midst of the social and moral discomposition of everything around her—family, community, society. Eventually her very self will be threatened with fragmentation by the forces contending for her soul, for the satisfaction that would come with the violation of her integrity and with the possession of her being. In the battle over the heroine, the Harlowes and Lovelace actually take the same ground, entrapping and confining Clarissa in a situation that is both perverse and deeply paradoxical. The father's curse upon his disobedient daughter unites him with the diabolical villain who fulfills it. Mr. Harlowe and his family, in fact, prove just as ready as the hated libertine to impose their will upon Clarissa's. Their whole approach to her, like Lovelace's, engages them in an attempt to enclose her within the bars of their own desires and to use her for their own gratification; Lovelace wants to possess her sexually, while her ambitious "friends" wish to improve their estate by marrying her off to Solmes.

Clarissa herself is always the center of everyone's moral attention in the novel, and the whole world, it seems, goes to war over her—aristocracy versus middle class, old order versus new; it is a war without hope of conclusion unless one side adopts the values the heroine represents, and that is not to be. Much has been written to demonstrate Richardson's own troubled ambivalence over the social tensions suggested by the angry resentment between Lovelace and the Harlowes. The novel actually dramatizes that ambivalence very deliberately, with a crystalline clarity of purpose. The Harlowes yearn for the position, power, and elegance that accrue to members of the aristocracy, but in so doing inevitably make a mockery of the virtues supposed to reside in their class, virtues which Clarissa herself possesses in abundance. Lovelace already is what the Harlowes wish to be, but he is spoiled and arrogant, he uses his power and position irresponsibly, and his elegance is a sham because it has no substance in goodness and decency—it is all ornament, as even the stylized extravagance of his language attests. Lovelace and the Harlowes are the chief vehicles by which Richardson conveys his social vision, and it is an unhopeful vision of almost complete disarray. He may have been ambivalent, but he seems to have understood one thing easily: if reconciliation between the classes as represented could be achieved, it would not even be desirable. This is one of the darkest and most pervasively apparent facts about *Clarissa's* world, and it helps to define the general context within which the "discomposition" of moral life and the threatened disintegration of individual integrity take place.

Most modern readers seem to agree that, because of the nature of the moral and social conflicts projected in the novel, Clarissa and Lovelace could never marry; there is no joining the two sets of values they represent. Richardson's decision to end the story with Clarissa's death was morally, socially, and dramatically right, although many of the people who advised him during the composition of his novel urged him to end it in a conventionally happy way; Fielding was among these, according to Richardson himself.[24] As the story of Clarissa Harlowe unfolded with the gradual appearance of its first five volumes, it must have struck its readers as a remarkably sensitive, intensely compassionate record of the inner life of an admirable heroine, destined, Cinderella-like (or, more probably, Pamela-like) to establish personal supremacy over the fleshly world and reconcile its wickedness to her goodness. One can easily imagine a typical contemporary reader reacting in sympathetic identification with Anna Howe as she begs Clarissa to be content with her triumph of spirit and will, to marry Lovelace (who is developing the appearances of a reformed rake), and to make the best of an imperfect world. The hideous episode of the rape itself occurs in the fifth volume, and with the publication of the concluding pair of volumes the author signified his resolute refusal to echo the conclusion of *Pamela* and a host of other contemporary narratives. In his new novel, Richardson resisted what must have been a strong temptation to play out in a routine way the conventional pattern of wish fulfillment. Unlike *Pamela*, *Clarissa* looks hard at the world, refuses to allegorize it as susceptible to goodness, and finds it finally depraved almost beyond redemption. Lovelace cries out at his death, "LET THIS EXPIATE!"; but it is clear that his dying, though it may be understood as a sacrifice on the altar of the martyred divine Clarissa, does not and cannot redeem him any more than it undoes or compensates for the moral horrors he has wrought. In a world largely defined by the character of Lovelace, the only safe place for the goodness of a Clarissa is heaven itself, where she goes to meet her bridegroom, Christ, in a union signifying the beginning of eternal and unthreatened bliss.

Clarissa actually repeats the formula of Pearsall's *Mrs. Housman*, which also ends with a triumphant death. And Richardson's story, like Pearsall's, is sprinkled with the heroine's devotional meditations, while it also emphasizes her almost obsessive attention to the discipline of daily piety—prayer, study, reading, resolute resistance to the world's most hostile advances against her. Clarissa's letters have a powerfully confessional quality about them, and, together with her meditations and the actual physical example of her beauty and her hard experience, they have the effect of reforming Lovelace's onetime accomplice, Belford, who then unites with Clarissa in the cause of Christian goodness. But Richardson transcends the usual restrictions of pious biography as he had done in his pastoral comedy of *Pamela*, only this time he projects his work as a fully developed Christian tragedy.

We know from the postscript to the final volume of *Clarissa* that the author designed his novel in this mode, though he hedged his claims about with some important qualifications. Richardson was not a learned man, and while in the postscript he quotes Addison and Rapin on Aristotle, his notion of tragedy as applied to *Clarissa* seems to have been improvised. Probably it derived largely from the plays he had seen and admired, among them the domestic tragedies of George Lillo and Charles Johnson, the she-tragedies of Nicholas Rowe, Addison's *Cato*, and the various "improvements" of Shakespeare by Nahum Tate and others.[25] Richardson did, of course, reject the neo-Aristotelian doctrine of poetic justice as espoused by so many post-Restoration tragedians and critics. Karl Jaspers has said that "*there is no tragedy without transcendence*"[26]—without the kind of ennobling self-knowledge brought about by the suffering of such awesome but flawed tragic figures as Oedipus, Antigone, Hamlet, Lear, Marlowe's Doctor Faustus. Richardson would have agreed with Jaspers, but he resisted the theoretical principle by which Tate, for example, had foolishly made Lear's arrival at transcendent self-knowledge the justification for earthly rewards in a happy ending.

And yet, of course, the author of *Clarissa* actually designed to have the matter both ways. For "the notion of poetical justice," he says in the postscript, "founded on the modern rules, has hardly ever been more strictly observed" by the writers of histories "than in the present performance" (4:557). Who, asks Richardson (again in the postscript), that "are in earnest" as Christian believers, would not rather "envy than regret the triumphant death of CLARISSA; whose piety, from her early childhood, whose diffusive charity; whose steady virtue; whose Christian humility; whose forgiving spirit; whose meekness, and resignation, Heaven *only* could reward?" (4:558). In a footnote to this passage Richardson reminds the reader that Clarissa's death and reward come from the "dispensations of Providence." Divine law, in other words, and not critical precept or authorial whim, determines the outcome of the heroine's story. And insofar as the author himself is concerned in the actual management of his narrative, he is "well justified by the Christian system, in deferring to extricate suffering virtue to the time in which it will meet with the completion of its reward" (4:554).

The real but postponed bliss accruing to Clarissa has led some critics, most notably Dorothy Van Ghent, to think of the novel as a comedy, and more specifically as a "divine comedy." It must be regarded as such, argues Van Ghent, "if we use as the generic distinction between comedy and tragedy the happy and the unhappy ending." *Clarissa* "has a 'happy ending,' the good are rewarded, the evil are punished."[27] Of course, this distinction is inadequate to separate comedy and tragedy; by such a measure, *Don Quixote* would not be a comedy at all. Richardson certainly thought *Clarissa* was no comedy, and it is best to credit him with full knowledge of what he was about in devising his pious moral history of Clarissa Harlowe. The postscript makes it clear that he meant to "attempt something that never yet had been done." He "considered that the tragic poets have as seldom made their heroes true objects of pity, as the comic theirs laudable ones of imitation; and still more rarely have made them in their deaths look forward to a future hope." When these heroes die, they seem "totally to perish," and for them death must thus appear "terrible," "the greatest evil" (4:553–54). No so with *Clarissa*. Richardson had a clear sense of his novel's newness, and he obviously saw it as a work whose freshness arose at least in part from the effort to fuse the formal properties of tragedy with his own version of Christian orthodoxy. In other words, he thought he had written a Christian tragedy which would truly ennoble all who read it, and inspire their faith in a final reward which could be theirs no matter what hardship life itself might bring. In a letter to his friend Aaron Hill, written before the first volumes of *Clarissa* were published, Richardson remarked that the "prosperous and *rewarded Virtue*" of *Pamela* had recommended that book to the world, and he worried just a bit that the "tragical" or "*triumphant*" ending of the new novel might make it unpopular. But, as he says of *Pamela* and *Clarissa* respectively, "In the one I looked principally to Happiness with respect to the Enjoyments of this Life; in the other, beyond them, and to which all should aspire, and the more for their Calamities."[28]

The depth and intensity Richardson imparts to the tragic story of his Christian heroine is achieved largely through his triumphant use of the epistolary mode, which ensures just the kind of emotional and moral impact that the homiletic purpose of the novel requires. In both *Pamela* and *Clarissa*, as Margaret Anne Doody has suggested, epistolary narration actually becomes an image of the material world translated into consciousness.[29] The world *is* what the letter writers understand it to be, and in the case of *Clarissa* this is especially important to recognize, for the novel is finally about the heroine's spiritual life; in other words, it is about her growth into the painful but exhilarating knowledge that she is not of this world. In the comic story of *Pamela*, what is represented is a world capable of being reconciled to the heroine's conception of it; no other correspondents register contradictory versions of reality, and so the resolution grows naturally out of Pamela's singleminded pursuit of the highest personal and moral good. The tragic novel of *Clarissa*, on the other hand, portrays a reality that rejects the ideals represented by the heroine and defined in the letters recording her feelings and her actions. Clarissa's example certainly does help to effect the reformation of Belford, and the presence of Mrs. Smith and Mrs. Lovick in the later episodes of the novel likewise suggests that the world is not entirely bereft of all possibility of redemption. But Belford's early correspondence with Lovelace, Lovelace's own letters and actions, the exchanges of the Harlowe family with Clarissa after the elopement, even the letters of the virtuous pragmatist Anna Howe, all image forth a corrupted moral environment that is out of harmony with the heroine's superior conception of ideal reality. That this is irretrievably so determines her fate. Like Mackenzie's Harley (in *The Man of Feeling*, 1771), Clarissa is disqualified by her very perfections for happiness in the imperfect here and now. If the world of *Clarissa* is what the letter writers perceive it to be, and it is, then the heroine must not survive. The meaning of the novel, then, and its method of rendering reality through the revelation of human consciousness of experience, complement one another perfectly and are in fact inseparable.

Clarissa's intensive spiritual experience is easily accessible to anyone through her letters, and it is obviously Richardson's intention to seduce and even overpower the emotions of his readers so as to draw them into that experience for their edification and inspiration. The world is hideously evil and thus hostile to virtue, and all who would leave it well must hearken to the lesson that the tragedy of Clarissa's life teaches. If they do, the story reveals, they will at last find the tranquility and fulfillment that she achieves upon her ascension to heaven. This novel, we may say, like *Pamela* before it, articulates the promise of the Christian's final release from the threat of evil. Its vision is both personal and cosmic. Richardson himself declared as much in his defense of the work as a Christian tragedy. But the story is most immediately about the actual circumstances in which the heroine must live and, finally, die. The author heightens the moral power of his narrative, and deepens the significance of the experience it dramatizes, by some of the same maneuvers he had used in *Pamela*. Clarissa, a divine creature, embodies all native innocence and goodness; Lovelace, much more menacingly than the Mr. B. of Richardson's first novel, is a devil, a serpentine arch-villain whose very "*rattle*," Clarissa says, "warns me of the *snake*" (2:53). The terms of moral conflict in the novel are most familiar, but clarified by the allusive manner of their delineation. Richardson's contemporaries would surely have caught the many references to the biblical fable of Eden throughout the story, and would just as surely have felt the way in which they unite Clarissa and Lovelace with the history of Christian religious experience.

Lovelace, moreover, is a criminal who possesses a "plotting villain of a heart" which rejoices "when any roguery is going forward" (2:186). I have already observed that Richardson greatly intensified the moral drama of his history of *Clarissa*, and furthered his didactic purposes, by bringing together some of the interests of pious biography and criminal narrative in a unified story. Lovelace, as criminal, is grandly drawn, unredeemed, and profoundly attractive—a kind of Jonathan Wild the Great, one might say, treated without any irony whatsoever. Eternal punishment is reserved for him while his victim Clarissa goes to heaven, and this proper conclusion justifies and compensates for any fascination he may have compelled from readers. But until this point Lovelace, in all his restless demonic energy, is a powerful force who dominates the fictional world, turns apparent order into a state of "discomposition," and causes all the dark confusion of illusion and reality that converts the heroine's life into a nightmare existence. By sheer invention he transforms a brothel into a respectable lodging house, whores into a family, and all sorts of rabble into messengers and gentlemen acquaintances with trustworthy names and military titles. He is a superb actor who takes perverse pleasure in clever disguise, and can play with apparent conviction the role of reformed rake.[30] His triumphant performance comes on the night of the rape, and features a considerable cast of false relations all engaged in assisting him to fulfill his designs upon the virginal heroine—to destroy the only vestige of purity that remains in this world of his making. Lovelace is obsessively and consistently a scheming deceiver and player of roles. It almost seems true that, rather like Milton's Satan, he *is* by nature exactly what he *does*.

And yet, he is divided, for there is a real tension within him between his overpowering desire to possess Clarissa's body and soul—to "reduce such a goddess as this to a standard unworthy of her excellence" (1:514)— and his genuine admiration, even reverence, for her purity of mind and spirit. Clarissa herself, as so many critics have observed, is not exempt from such fragmentation as this. Her infatuation with Lovelace, by her own admission, engendered a weakness which made it easier for him to carry her away from her father's house. This recognition notifies her of a division within herself, and since it parallels Lovelace's fragmentation it makes for a kind of *doppelgänger* relationship which actually unites them in a certain paradoxical togetherness of spirit. That is to say, the dramatic tension between Clarissa and Lovelace and the ideals they represent— tension between good and evil, spirit and flesh—gives external form to the inner conflict that threatens to rend each of them, while emotionally they come to depend utterly upon each other for the working out of a definition of moral identity.

Eventually all of the inner as well as external turmoil of the nightmare that Lovelace inflicts upon her drives Clarissa to the edges of madness. "Alas!" she writes to Lovelace, "you have killed my head among you. . . . I shall never be myself again. . . . So let me be carried out of this house, and out of your sight; and let me be put into that Bedlam privately, which I once saw: but it was a sad sight to me then! Little as I thought what I should come to *myself!*" (3:211–12). Clarissa regains her equilibrium when she realizes that since her will has never been violated, her soul remains pure. But she has already revealed her frailty. However grandly mythologized a Christian heroine she may be, she is deeply human. Her "fall" at the hands of Lovelace makes Clarissa acknowledge that she has been proud, too ready to assume that her own superior virtue was perfect proof against the world. In a letter to Arabella she admits that her sister's long-held jealous view of her may have been correct after all. The admission touchingly reveals the cruel ironies of Clarissa's plight. She is a "humbled creature," she tells Arabella, "whose foolish heart you used to say you beheld through the thin veil of humility which covered it. It must have been so! My fall had not else been permitted" (3:206–7). In the end she arrives at full self-knowledge—the transcendence that Karl Jaspers mentions as an essential element of tragic experience—and places her trust where she knows it belongs. "GOD ALMIGHTY," she says to Belford, "WOULD NOT LET ME DEPEND FOR COMFORT UPON ANY BUT HIMSELF" (4:339).

Clarissa's new and complete understanding, and only that, releases her from Lovelace and from a world he has so evilly made over into his own image. The serenity of her long approach to death—it is not morbidity, despite the presence of her coffin in her bedchamber—signifies the complete reintegration of her spiritual self, for she now knows with complete conviction who she is and is able to envision with hope a harmonious future world ordered by divine love where she can be at home. "And what, after all, *is* death?" she quizzes Anna Howe. "'Tis but a cessation from mortal life: 'tis but the finishing of an appointed course: the refreshing inn after a fatiguing journey: the end of a life of cares and troubles; and, if happy, the beginning of a life of immortal happiness" (3:521). Significantly, as Clarissa progresses through her illness toward death, Lovelace likewise sickens with frustration over his loss and remorse over his perfidious use of her. His moral identity is in the end illuminated and defined by the light of her goodness, just as her brightness is framed by the darkness that he represents. Each has emerged from the abrasive conflict of their tormented relationship having remained finally true to an original self; and Clarissa is exalted, while Lovelace, unredeemed, is brought low.

The story of Clarissa Harlowe and her triumph most richly fulfills all the requirements of a pious biographical fiction of heroic Christian virtue in action. No doubt Richardson wished his second novel, like *Pamela*, to be read in a context of popular didactic narrative. *Clarissa* makes an orthodox statement about the profound importance and the eternal promise of human goodness, while it celebrates an exemplary character from ordinary life whose courageous resistance to a corrupt world exalts her to the status of a contemporary saint worthy of the worshipful attention of readers, who also learn from her the discipline of the Christian life. The familiar homiletic purpose of Richardson's great novel is clear, genuine, and insistently carried out. *Clarissa* is, in the fullest possible contemporary sense, a work of devotional literature cast into the form of a fictional narrative.

To describe Richardson's vast and complicated novel in this way is not to diminish it; *Clarissa* is obviously much more than such a description, if taken too narrowly as a kind of precise taxonomical label, would imply. Rather, it is to illuminate the author's goals as an artist while underscoring the real nature of his achievement. *Clarissa* possesses enduring qualities as Christian myth, and these qualities could have only deepened its contemporary relevance as a valuable story dramatizing the spiritual experience of a remarkable young woman. The novel is actually a surpassing accomplishment in the mode of pious moral history. Certainly there is no other work among the popular didactic fictions of Richardson's day that can match the raw emotional appeal of the Christian tragedy of *Clarissa*, or the range and complexity of its portrayal of human conflict and moral dilemmas. In writing this novel, we may say, Richardson greatly expanded the boundaries of the routine pious life and, in his own imaginative identification with his suffering heroine, he established at least the outlines of the modern mode of psychological fiction.

Dr. Johnson seems to have recognized both the immediate power of *Clarissa* and its boldness as an innovative work, and he reserved his highest praise for Richardson's consummate ability to move the passions. Richardson's achievement as an innovator, as the founder of psychological realism in prose fiction, as myth-maker, has been warmly praised ever since *Clarissa* first appeared, more than two centuries ago, to astonish, delight, and instruct its audience. Presumably his work will continue to be praised on just these same grounds. But it is useful to remember that the instincts of this great novelist were those of a Christian moralist, that he was above all things a deliberate didactic writer, his aims exactly coinciding with those of the many lesser pious biographers and storytellers whose works were as current as his own. It was surely these instincts and these aims, so skillfully and so sensitively followed in *Clarissa*, that made Richardson's novel what it was and is: a complex, rich, and deeply rewarding work still capable of causing its readers to respond very directly and very personally to its drama, as the thunderstruck Henry Fielding did so many years ago.

CHAPTER VI

"Novelistic" Fiction in the 1740s

ABOUT A MONTH AFTER Richardson published the first two volumes of *Pamela* in 1740, the Earl of Chesterfield posted the following exercise in literary taxonomy to his novel-reading natural son, Philip Stanhope:

> I am in doubt whether you know what a Novel is: it is a little gallant history, which must contain a great deal of love, and not exceed one or two small volumes. The subject must be a love affair; the lovers are to meet with many difficulties and obstacles to oppose the accomplishment of their wishes, but at last overcome them all; and the conclusion or catastrophe must leave them happy. A Novel is a kind of abbreviation of a Romance; for a Romance generally consists of twelve volumes, all filled with insipid love nonsense, and most incredible adventures.[1]

Chesterfield's definition, imprecise as it is, renders with fair accuracy the early eighteenth century's understanding of the term *novel*. Judging from the works themselves, when a reader picked up a narrative labeled "novel," he did so with only certain rudimentary expectations. Most novels were brief. As Chesterfield says, they were mostly about love, but not too long about it, and they were often mildly erotic. The stories usually turned upon intrigue or some form of surprise, and they were frequently cynical about the formalities of courtship and marriage. The lovely ladies of novels, who sometimes panted with love, were likely to be impeded in the fulfillment of their wishes by aging husbands or cruel guardians who thought only of money or the disadvantages of cuckoldry. The original novella had emerged as a kind of antidote to romance, and in the eighteenth century many novels still preserved a certain bias against romance, although their language could be as stilted as that of any of the grand stories of La Calprenède or the Scudérys, and their subjects fully as stereotyped. In general, however, their characters and settings tended to be taken from contemporary life.

Any work of fiction that called itself a novel was also avowedly an invented tale, designed to give the kind of pleasure associated with imaginative narrative. For this reason, among others, novels suffered the particular abhorrence of pious readers, and were frequently denounced in the eighteenth century as trivial and immoral. Many of them fully deserved this opprobrium, although they frequently professed to have a moral intention, even when freighted with erotic scenes and overheated sentiments. A great many novels are not labeled as such, despite numerous signs of their origin. Instead, they offer themselves as histories, lives, memoirs, collections of letters, and so on, partly no doubt as a means of avoiding the stigma that was widely attached to this breed of fiction, partly as a strategy of authentication in the general move toward what Ian Watt calls formal realism. This mannerism was not entirely a matter of mere strategy. Most novels, including those actually identifying themselves by that name, take the form of some factual or pseudofactual mode, from which they sometimes differ only in that they are acknowledged fictions. At any rate, it is this enlarged class of works that is here termed novelistic, even though only a minority actually carry the label of "novel."

Fiction as Fiction: The Novelistic Mode

The origins of the novel in English were very old, and may be traced to several Continental sources—the Italian *novella*, of which Boccaccio was the most distinguished practitioner; the French *nouvelle;* and the Spanish *novela exemplare*, with which the popular *Exemplary Novels* of Cervantes were identified. Each of these Continental types possessed a certain national character, but the tales in all three kinds share the qualities of brev-

ity and a certain superficial realism of tone and manner; they are antiromances of a sort, even though they frequently deal with the emotion of
exalted love. Translations of works in Continental modes virtually dominated the considerable English market for novelistic fiction in the last
years of the seventeenth century and the first two decades of the eighteenth. Thus native readers became accustomed very early to little tales
that appealed mainly by the mild sensationalism of amorous anecdotes
pitting virtuous characters against adversities posed by lechers, tempters,
evil persecutors, and sometimes their own uncontrollable passions. The
journalistic terseness and moral neutrality of the novella, in its treatment
of love in Court and high life, found a ready reception in England. So did
the light sentimentality and mild didacticism of the more complex Cervantean exemplary novel of domestic amours, and the French *nouvelle's*
sentimental depiction of aristocratic characters torn by the conflict between duty and Racinean passion. These European forms, particularly
the Italian and the Spanish, were fixtures in the marketplace, so familiar
that they must have seemed almost borrowed culture. The French *nouvelle*
was perhaps less popular than its Italian and Spanish equivalents. Mme
de Lafayette's *La Princesse de Clèves* (1678), the one real masterpiece in the
French mode, did not achieve a single separate English edition between
1680 and 1762. But *nouvelles*, along with novellas and *novelas exemplares*,
were gathered in popular anthologies such as Samuel Croxall's *Select Collection of Novels* (1720).[2] Furthermore, their formulae were broadly
adapted in numerous "assembly" collections like the popular *Lady's Drawing Room* (1744; with a Dublin edition in 1746 and a second London edition in 1748), which employed a *Decameron*-like frame-tale into which they
wove a great variety of novelistic stories.

The popularity of the original novellas and *novelas exemplares* continued
into the 1740s. A translation of the Italian Bandello's *Novelliere* (1554) was
announced in 1740, to be followed a year later by an edition of *The Decameron*. Meanwhile the fortunes of Cervantes's original collection of *Novelas
ejemplares* (1613), long favored in England, continued to prosper. Thomas
Shelton's early translation called *Novelas exemplares* was reprinted three
times, once in 1743 and twice more in 1746 and 1747.[3] Two other miscellaneous collections from the Spanish also came out, both trading obviously on the popularity of Cervantes's book.[4] In addition, a collection of
stories by one of Cervantes's early Spanish adapters, Alonso de Castillo,

was promised under the title *Spanish Amusements: Being a Curious Collection of Fifteen Novels* (1741). Alonso had expanded upon his great model's example, loosening the formula of the exemplary novel to cover extended travels away from the domestic background. His object was apparently to vary the adventures and heighten the entertainment value of his amorous tales. The effect was to broaden the exemplary novel's moral perspective by giving it a range of reference encompassing mankind the world over—Barbary pirates on the high seas, slavery in North Africa, and so on.

These Continental modes found only a few exact imitators among eighteenth-century English novelists, but the number of native adaptations was legion. The tendency of early English writers of amatory fiction was toward "novels" that merged the strains of the novella, the *novela exemplare*, and the *nouvelle* in stories of contemporary English or European life. In short, they diffused and naturalized the forms upon which they drew. The typical result was a work that treated native—or at least familiar—subjects, and in so doing joined the mild titillations of the novella to a love story of allegedly exemplary characters who might well be rent by stormy (often very inflated) passions that set them against their Christian duty. The seven "novels" collected in Mrs. Delarivière Manley's *Power of Love* (1720, 1741) illustrate this practice. All but two of the tales gathered in this volume were derived from Bandello through William Painter's very successful sixteenth-century collection of Italian novellas, *The Palace of Pleasure* (1566–67). But Mrs. Manley deliberately reshaped the tales she borrowed. She extended their length to about that of a modern short story, charged them with at least a superficial exemplary morality, and provided the appeal of a mild emotionalism worked out through the display of conflicting passions.

The pair of novels not drawn from Bandello through Painter provide the same attractions, and are the more interesting because original with Mrs. Manley. One of these new pieces, "The Physician's Strategem," gives us a sense of what its author tried to achieve throughout *The Power of Love*. The narrative tells the extremely complicated story of one Mariana, an ambitious but virtuous young girl who lives in Richelieu's France. Daughter of a count and loved by a marquis, she falls into the clutches of a hypocritical young libertine doctor named Fauxgarde. Having gotten Mariana's maid pregnant, Fauxgarde designs with the help of his adoring victim (who is secretly Mariana's enemy) to drug and rape the heroine, and thus, without her knowing it, to get her pregnant too. This accomplished, Fauxgarde treacherously sells the maid into slavery, and then awaits his opportunity to trap the wealthy Mariana into marriage. He succeeds again. The marquis righteously denounces the heroine, and shortly Fauxgarde appears and is accepted—though reluctantly all round—as a husband for the mother-to-be. The count and his wife die reconciled to the alliance, believing that their daughter had earlier eloped with the doctor. Mariana goes on not knowing how she became pregnant. The couple lives for awhile in peace, but the braggart physician finally reveals his secret to some drunken friends who spread it everywhere. Mariana's anger is unbounded, and she starts legal proceedings immediately. The marquis reappears, however, and, impatient of a trial, murders Fauxgarde and renews his offer of marriage to the heroine. But she cannot accept; though she still loves him, her virtue and the future honor of her children (she now has several) will not permit her to do so. As the story closes, Mariana retires to a nunnery, the marquis to a monastery.

This lively tale unashamedly offers sensational violence, sadism, and bizarre eroticism without much qualification or open moral judgment. Throughout, Mrs. Manley employs an objective, almost journalistic perspective, and she reveals little apparent interest in anything beyond the most visible motivations of her characters. In all these respects, "The Physician's Strategem" is very close to the example of the novella. But its moral ideology receives emphatic articulation through the "exemplary" status accorded a heroine who, like the virtuous women of Cervantes's *novelas exemplares*, resigns herself to life's misfortunes and, by her strength, survives them morally and even triumphs over the agents who bring them upon her. The latter episodes of the story exhibit in a mildly sentimental way the tension that arises when Mariana's passion for the marquis clashes with her sense of painful duty. In the manner of the *nouvelle*, Mrs. Manley's narrative closes with a display of its heroine's brave commitment to moral choice. "The Physician's Strategem" is less complex, much less a story of character than *La Princesse de Clèves*. But the fidelity of its resolution to the example set by the French work is nonetheless obvious. Mariana's final retreat to a convent even repeats the conclusion of Mme de Lafayette's tale.

Samuel Richardson would surely have been offended by the frankness of a story like "The Physician's Strategem," but it offers precisely the kinds of situations that the pious moral history of *Clarissa* transforms and expands into a fully dilated novel. Clearly, an important part of the background for *Clarissa* may be traced to novelistic works which, like Mrs. Manley's, "naturalize" and merge the three Continental modes of amatory fiction. The most important and prolific of the early native novelists following this practice was Eliza Haywood. In the 1720s Mrs. Haywood produced an astonishing number of frankly titillating little novels about "tender passions" and ranting, superficially exemplary heroes and heroines of elevated station. She seems to have reasoned that among readers who enjoyed the popular *chroniques scandaleuses*, the heroic romances, and a variety of imported Continental narratives of love and intrigue, there was potentially a large market for sentimental novels that would exploit all these varied tastes at once. And so she wrote *Love in Excess* (1719).

Mrs. Haywood's little book was enormously successful.[5] It became the advance guard of a virtual army of similar Haywoodian productions like *Idalia* (1723), *The Injur'd Husband* (1724), *Lasselia* (1724), *Philodore and Placentia* (1727), and *The Irish Artifice* (1728). In these years it was Eliza Haywood, more than any other native fiction writer, whose name was identified with the novel. She inspired scores of imitators. Her efforts probably did more than those of any other single author to stimulate the production of *native* novels. Therefore, although the vogue for Mrs. Haywood's tales of passion had declined by the time *Pamela* appeared, they figure very importantly in the background of Richardson's love stories and are also historically relevant to the amatory aspects of the novels of Fielding and Smollett.[6] At the same time, however, frothy tales like *Love in Excess*, by their very popularity, justified the critical scorn with which the novel was so often treated. By some, Mrs. Haywood's narratives were regarded as a real threat to public taste and literary values. By others, they were taken as a corrupting, demoralizing influence on their many readers. In book two of the *Dunciad* (1728) Pope heaped all his wrath upon Eliza for her "secret histories" and "novels" (the two types were, as she practiced them, not very different). Pope's assault wrecked Mrs. Haywood's literary reputation, and registered a powerful and lasting condemnation of the kind of fiction associated with her name.

Eliza Haywood's period of triumph as a novel writer was therefore brief, but so complete that during her reign superior works like the epistolary *Lindamira* and Mrs. Davys's avowed novels *The Reform'd Coquet; or,*

Memoirs of Amoranda (1724) and *The Accomplish'd Rake; or, Modern Fine Gentleman* (1727) almost escaped the notice of the English public. These breezy, unpretentious, judiciously conceived stories of love and intrigue were only sporadically reprinted in subsequent years.[7] But some of Mrs. Haywood's other contemporaries were extremely popular, and the moral emphasis of their works, combined with the attacks of the literary establishment, helped to dethrone the author of *Love in Excess*. The works of pious reformers like Penelope Aubin, Elizabeth Rowe, and a few other novelists appear to have been deliberately conceived as didactic reactions to the trivial, "corrupting," insidiously "immoral" novels of the redoubtable Eliza.

Mrs. Rowe was a celebrated woman of exemplary virtue, the author of numerous hymns and pious poems, the admired friend of contemporaries as different as Isaac Watts, Matthew Prior, Alexander Pope, and Samuel Richardson. She published only two pieces of novelistic fiction—the combined *Friendship in Death* and *Letters Moral and Entertaining* (1728–32)—but their popularity reached huge proportions. The late 1720s and 1730s witnessed at least five editions of these works, and four more appeared in the 1740s.[8] Both are gatherings of short epistolary sketches in which stout-hearted Christian heroes and heroines report to their correspondents the trials by which they have recognized the world's folly, overcome its temptations, and thus achieved their exemplary status; in the *Friendship*, which is Mrs. Rowe's version of the *Dialogues of the Dead*, the characters write from the perspective of the afterlife. The letters of Mrs. Rowe deal chiefly with stories of love, and they all celebrate pure, exalting marriage, which they define as the earthly condition nearest to heavenly paradise. The correspondents exhibit a sincere piety not to be found anywhere in Mrs. Haywood's amatory novels, and there is a genuineness in the passion with which they tell of their troubles in life. Occasionally, there is even a touch of real psychological penetration as the writers reveal themselves, though it is offered not for its intrinsic interest but as a means of furthering Mrs. Rowe's didactic purpose. In fact, the epistles really function as pious polemics: their explicit aim, wrote Mrs. Rowe in the preface to the *Friendship*, was partly to entertain but mainly to "impress the Notion of the Soul's Immortality; without which all Virtue and Religion, with their temporal and eternal good Consequences, must fall to the Ground."

Penelope Aubin was likewise a serious moralist and, late in life, a Dissenting preacher. Her novels appeared earlier than Mrs. Rowe's, and they are more expansive, but their piety is no less fervent. The first, *The Life of Madam de Beaumont* (1721), came in the wake of Mrs. Haywood's earliest success. In an attempt to entertain her readers so as to capture their moral attention, Mrs. Aubin actually modified and combined the appeal of Mrs. Haywood's sentimental love stories and Defoe's adventurous voyage narratives. To this combination she added elements from such distended *novelas exemplares* as those of Alonso de Castillo. We have already seen that *The Life of Madam de Beaumont, The Life of Charlotta Du Pont* (1723), and Mrs. Aubin's other biographical novels are actually pious moral histories exhibiting perfectly virtuous heroines and heroes as they progress through domestic trials, tumultuous travels, world-wide temptations and persecutions, finally to scenes of moral triumph. As in Mrs. Rowe's work, true love and marriage become metaphors for the highest state of earthly happiness, a state accessible only to the feeling heart and the purified soul. Mrs. Aubin's expressed desire, as described in the preface to *Madam de Beaumont*, was that her readers should identify with her Christian heroes and heroines and take inspiration from the message that, even in a real world peopled with monsters of evil, there can exist moral wonders and indestructible moral values. To this end she frequently approaches the troubled thoughts and feelings of her characters very closely, revealing certain real though limited powers of psychological observation. Mrs. Aubin's gestures in this direction are much less convincing and impressive than Richardson's fine achievements in his later creations of Pamela Andrews and Clarissa Harlowe, but they give her pious tales a richness and depth and breadth of moral relevance—it is actually at once global and internal—quite unmatched in native novelistic fiction before *Pamela*. Much more completely than Delarivière Manley or Eliza Haywood, or even the circumspect Mary Davys, Mrs. Aubin places the moral experience of her heroes and heroines firmly in a worldly context and then interprets that experience meaningfully from the perspective of their interior lives. Along with the stories of Mrs. Rowe, her works contributed importantly to the expansion of the boundaries of novelistic writing into the realm of the most private human experience.

Mrs. Aubin's novels of sentimental piety avoid even the slightest touch of eroticism. Their moralism, in fact, is occasionally almost overwhelming. Furthermore, they unfortunately suffer from what William H.

McBurney has described as an "excessive and unintegrated variety."[9] Their popularity, though hardly equal to that of Mrs. Haywood's novels in the 1720s, was nonetheless very considerable and more enduring. *Charlotta du Pont* alone achieved four separate editions between 1723 and 1739, three of them in the 1730s. *Madam de Beaumont* survived even longer, and enjoyed a new edition in 1749. Just one year before the arrival of *Pamela*, these two pious novels were gathered with the rest of Mrs. Aubin's narratives into a three-volume set called *A Collection of Entertaining Histories and Novels, Design'd to Promote the Cause of Virtue and Honour*. The contemporary popularity of Mrs. Aubin's books, and Mrs. Rowe's as well, makes them highly important precedents for the pious novels of Richardson.

As avowed novelists Mrs. Aubin and Mrs. Rowe brought a new seriousness to novel writing; in some important ways, they were conscious innovators. The impact of their fervidly moral works coincided with the currency of numerous pious lives, the perennial popularity of Bunyan's *Pilgrim's Progress*, and the warm reception accorded didactic romances like *Télémaque* and Palafox's *New Odyssey*. The type of influence exerted by Mrs. Aubin and Mrs. Rowe is illustrated by two works that appeared early in 1740, almost simultaneously with the publication of *Pamela* in November of the same year. One is a piece of pious polemics called *Injur'd Innocence; or, The Lives and Surprizing Adventures of Amicorus and Amicana*. This narrative, despite its author's vigorous prefatory protestations of a mimetic aim, offers a very conventional love tale about characters whose delineation is only slightly more plausible than their names. The work has no depth whatever, and is neither dramatically nor thematically convincing. But its almost strident moral tone echoes the strenuous homiletics of Mrs. Aubin and Mrs. Rowe, while it anticipates the conspicuous piety of Richardson's first novel. Much the same may be said of a sentimental "exemplary" narrative entitled *The Freaks of Fortune; or, Memoirs of Captain George Conyers. A Novel*, which also appeared in 1740. This book differs very little in texture from *Injur'd Innocence*, except that its characters have familiar names. Its first sentence bears a vague resemblance to Richardson's introductory remarks to *Pamela*. "Let not the mind," cautions the author, "which either age or nature has rendered callous to the misfortunes of mankind, seek for amusement in the following pages; they are written but for those who can feel for the distress of virtue; for innocence oppressed."

Works like *Injur'd Innocence* and *The Freaks of Fortune*, crude as they are, reveal that by 1740, when Richardson, Fielding, and Smollett were poised on the threshold of their great careers, a new sobriety of moral—if not aesthetic—purpose had come to characterize the productions of avowed novelists. The "novel" as a species of popular narrative may have had no reputation, but it was now possible for a native writer to offer a work of nonallegorical fiction openly as a worthwhile story of human experience in a familiar context, and to be credible about it, as the early Eliza Haywood never was. Novelistic writers of the early eighteenth century were always eclectic, borrowing their materials from other, supposedly factual modes of history, biography, and voyage literature as well as from the various kinds of perennially popular Continental novelistic fiction. In their eclecticism they were sometimes merely opportunistic and most often awkward, but they did make it serve their interests as the authors of invented narratives written for an audience of people many of whom professed to scorn stories that were not somehow demonstrably true. Mrs. Aubin and Mrs. Rowe in particular managed to verify the imagination as a potential source of moral and emotional truth, proving by their example that prose fiction, acknowledged as such, might be as reliable a record of human life—and particularly of its meaning—as the most conspicuously authenticated biographies and voyage narratives, many of which were themselves surreptitious fictions.

By thus licensing the author's invention to play freely over its subject, the best of the early eighteenth-century novelistic writers helped in important ways to prepare for the astonishing achievements of the 1740s. At least tentatively, their works confirmed new possibilities of form, range, and seriousness in contemporary novelistic fiction, and encouraged broad inquiry into moral and social life of a kind not normally attempted in the more limiting pseudofactual modes of popular storytelling. Many novelists of the mid-century years followed their lead: Samuel Richardson, Henry Fielding, Tobias Smollett, Sarah Fielding, Mary Collyer, a reformed Eliza Haywood. Richardson and Smollett triumphantly exploited the new possibilities of novelistic narrative in works that preserved the circumstantial illusion of a specific historical reality while affirming their fictionality through the sheer imaginative power of their authors' transmission of private experience. Smollett, of course, went a step further than Richardson; he acknowledged that the reality he projected was only a fabrication by announcing the title of his model, *Gil Blas*, which everybody knew to be a work of the imagination. Fielding departed significantly from the circumstantial method of both of his great contemporaries, dropping entirely the illusion that his works were anything but artifice, deliberate and elaborate contrivances from the truth of his own wide observation of life, and boldly proclaiming once and for all the high value of prose fiction as a noble form of artistic expression.

Fiction as Fiction: "I confess the Characters are of my own Invention"

Richardson's first novel took the world by surprise in 1740, but as the example of Mrs. Aubin and Mrs. Rowe alone proves, *Pamela* was not entirely *sui generis*. Even before Richardson had begun to write, a conspicuous new moral emphasis in prose fiction was visible, together with a tendency to produce longer books encompassing a wider range of characters and moral choices traditionally associated with the English novel. Some of these, as we have seen, were pseudohistorical or pseudobiographical narratives of one kind or another. Several dozen new English works that can be loosely described as novelistic were published in the decade of the 1740s, among which, of course, must be included the stories of Richardson, Fielding, and Smollett. Putting aside these justly celebrated works, the many remaining novels may be said to be extremely miscellaneous in character and uneven in quality. Only a very few are at all remembered today. Sarah Fielding's *David Simple*, *The Fortunate Foundlings* by Eliza Haywood, and one or two other titles are now and again mentioned by historians of the novel. Some of the new novelistic works are quite brief, as in an earlier period most novels were, but others are very lengthy indeed; the anonymous *Leonora; or, Characters Drawn from Real Life* (1745) totals eight hundred pages. Richardson's *Clarissa* has been called the longest novel in the English language, but its coming was partially prepared for by *Leonora* and others. Love is still a presiding concern of the lesser novelists, but there is a very wide range of approaches. A few of these works are undisguisedly prurient, while others lean toward scandal and the titillations of *Love in Excess*. But many exude the new airs of moral sobriety made fashionable by Mrs. Aubin and Mrs. Rowe.

The direction of the lesser novels of the 1740s, of course, was deflected by two phenomena which in time deeply changed the course of events. The first was the growing presence of the major novelists; the second, the gathering influence of French fiction in translation. If Richardson, Fielding, and Smollett were an inevitable part of a larger community of English fiction writers sharing similar subjects, themes, and narrative procedures, then in turn their lesser contemporaries could not fail to be aware of the extraordinary interest created by *Pamela, Joseph Andrews*, and *Clarissa*. Predictably, they attempted to accommodate themselves in some degree to new conditions in the rapidly expanding world of prose fiction. Beginning in 1740 the works of many lesser novelists visibly display a pronounced feedback from the success of Richardson, and later Fielding. Meanwhile the extremely sophisticated novels of Marivaux and Prévost had crossed the Channel and were providing further evidence of the kind of artistic achievement possible in the realm of domestic narrative. The writings of several minor French imitators, notably Charles de Fieux, Chevalier de Mouhy, also appeared in English and lent support to their example. The excellence of French fiction was not lost on the authors of *Clarissa, Joseph Andrews*, and *Roderick Random*, whose many interesting relations to contemporary French novelists have already been fully explored in modern scholarship, and do not need recapitulation here.[10] What is worth pausing over is the important fact that French fiction also influenced the lesser native novelists, and after 1740 this begins to be an increasingly generative force among run-of-the-mill storytellers, as illustrated by the work of Mrs. Mary Collyer.

Mrs. Collyer, significantly, was most active as a translator of French fiction, especially the work of Marivaux. But in 1744 she published the first volume of her own novel, formidably titled *Felicia to Charlotte: Being Letters from a Young Lady in the Country, to Her Friend in Town. Containing a Series of the Most Interesting Events, Interspersed with Moral Reflections; Chiefly Tending to Prove, That the Seeds of Virtue Are Implanted in the Mind of Every Reasonable Being*. This work is one of the most ambitious and most competent of the lesser novels of the 1740s. The initial volume created something of a stir, and was probably in its third edition when Mrs. Collyer finally joined to it a second installment in 1749. The *réclame* achieved by the work is clearly registered by an entry in the *Monthly Review* for January 1750 (vol. 2): "The first volume of these letters was published about four years ago [*sic*], and met with so favorable a reception from the public, as not only to occasion a new edition in a short time, but to encourage the ingenious author to publish a second volume; which, in our opinion, is not inferior to the first; and will, we doubt not, be as well received" (p. 229).

Felicia to Charlotte, as one might expect from its title, possesses considerable feminist appeal. It gained the notice of a select group of bluestockings, including Mary Wortley Montagu and Richardson's friends Miss Catherine Talbot and Miss Elizabeth Carter. It is not difficult to understand why the work interested these and other readers. Volume one at least is an engaging, if sometimes erratic, narrative. Felicia, the letter writing heroine, proves to be a sprightly, well-rounded character whose correspondence tells a very conventional, very sentimental but lively domestic love story detailing the trials and adventures leading up to her joyous marriage to Lucius, a poor Shaftesburean moralist. Tears of Richardsonian sensibility flow throughout the narrative, but they are countered by a number of attractive comic scenes. The most delightful of these scenes occur during the episodes when the heroine, momentarily hopeless of ever gaining her proud father's approval of Lucius, is diverted by the suit of a fashionable buffoon called Mellifont. Mellifont is an amusing fellow whom Felicia likes but cannot love, and their "affair" becomes a kind of Cervantean game in which she plays the romantic heroine and he the chivalrous hero. In a particularly witty letter, Felicia reports how Mellifont came to her one day in transports of mock-passion and

> threw himself upon his knee, and taking one of my hands, which he tenderly pressed in his, See, my dear, said he, as great a conquest as ever love has made. In vain I have struggled to regain my liberty. All my wishes center in you; I love you with all the passionate softness that can fill a human breast: as tenderly as—as—Nay, Madam, for heaven's sake don't laugh at me, continued he seeing me smile; but tell me sincerely now, don't I look very silly. I sigh like the fam'd

knight-errants of old, and like them bending before the divine
object of my sublimest wishes, beg, O thou adorable fair. . . .
(1:163)

Suddenly he slips and crashes to the floor, from where he hears Felicia
charge him to "lie there, . . . thou unworthy knight, nor ever more appear
before me, till thou bringest me the heads of those savage monsters that
infest the woods, the trophies of thy prowess and renown" (1:164). In the
very next scene Mellifont, bearing an old lance and sporting a battered
helmet, rushes in and lays at his "fair princess's" feet a heap of badger
pelts. The irony of this episode is transparent, and taken with others in
Mrs. Collyer's novel, it defines the work as an antiromance in the manner
of Fielding and Cervantes. Felicia is fully aware of the difference between
romance and reality in her own experience. Of Lucius she says: "He is
too good a christian to deify his mistress, and has too good an opinion of
me to think I should be pleased with such senseless homages. In short, in
spight of his humility his love was incapable of blinding him so far as to
make him forget that I was a very woman still" (1:69).

The story shadows contemporary class conflicts in its display of the
social obstacles the impoverished hero must pass before he can be
awarded Felicia's hand, and other issues get an even fuller airing. For
example, the work's glorified country setting exploits the eighteenth-century myth of rural innocence, a myth also exploited by the major novels,
but given much fuller substance by their complex treatment of the moral
tensions aroused by the invasions of evil (often urban) forces. In effect
Felicia to Charlotte, as *Clarissa* was later to do, exposes to view the inner
workings of a country family, but finds almost total harmony instead of
bitter discord. Moreover, coincident with the attractions of its rural setting, its love story, and the cluster of unblemished principals on whom it
centers, Mrs. Collyer's narrative emphatically articulates an orthodox
moral ideology extolling the virtues of chastity, sensibility, and benevolence. Felicia and Lucius are the familiar Christian heroine and hero,
whose passionate love for one another derives from, and is sanctified by,
a mutual, almost reverential esteem. "I feel the force of your charms,"
says Lucius to Felicia; "they run thro' my heart, and captivate every
thought; but chief that amiable virtue, that sanctity of manners, and all
those dear unutterable graces which perpetually blossom with fresh beau-

ties and undecaying charms, fill my ravish'd soul, and inspire a tender admiration and awe." With characteristic humility, Felicia reflects silently as, she writes to Charlotte, a "sweet enthusiasm possessed all my soul, and I could not help thinking how much better this dear man deserved a compliment of this kind than myself" (1:153–54).

To the orthodoxy of Christian heroism, the story clearly engrafts a modified Shaftesburean deism, thereby entering the arena of current religious controversy. Lucius, who is incidentally one of the earliest "men of feeling" as well as one of the first avowed and practicing lovers of nature in eighteenth-century English fiction,[11] plays the role of Mrs. Collyer's chief homiletician. At many moments the narrative is interrupted so that we may overhear him pontificating on the "moral sense," or on the natural beauty of virtue and benevolence, and the happiness they bring. Principally through these lengthy speeches, which so endear Lucius to the less pompous Felicia, the book really attacks all formalist theologies, offering instead a "religion of nature." For the Methodists it reserves a special scorn, which it humorously dramatizes with constant ironic strokes at the aptly named caricature Prudilla, a hypocritical female whose sneaking dishonesty anticipates that of Fielding's Blifil and provides most of the difficulties in the way to the heroine's marriage. Prudilla is actually a kind of criminal, whose threats, however, are minimized by the liberating irony with which she is treated. Her deathbed confession late in volume two is cleverly handled so as to draw connections with criminal biography. The scene furthermore achieves an ironic reversal upon the strategy of confessional literature and, because Prudilla exposes all her past misdeeds (including some amatory slips) in a little history, the account of her perfidies is also a small *chronique scandaleuse*.

The love story proper concludes with a triumphant wedding that occasions many joyous speeches on the pleasures of virtue and true love, and brings forth countless happy tears. The ecstatic description of the preparations for this event fills the last letters of volume one, and the wedding day itself is lovingly detailed at the outset of the sequel. This done, the balance of volume two of the work develops as a dull superfluity, the *Monthly* reviewer's praise notwithstanding. Like part two of *Pamela* (the comparison is inescapable), it exists primarily to continue discussion of the moral subjects started dramatically in the first installment, and to underscore the moral significance of the love story itself. Volume two is a monotonous series of episodes displaying the exemplary married couple in endless scenes of connubial bliss and innumerable acts of charity and general beneficence. These are frequently halted long enough for Lucius (now more windy than ever) to elaborate upon his various philosophical and religious convictions. Only one new subject is even introduced. When their child is born, Felicia and Lucius suddenly become educational theorists. From the background of their Shaftesburean attitudes, they formulate some surprisingly advanced ideas on the theory of learning that actually adumbrate Rousseau's doctrines of natural education.

It should be clear from this brief analysis that *Felicia to Charlotte* has an immediate relevance to the work of Fielding and Richardson. Its sentimentalism probably came directly from Marivaux, whose *Marianne* Mrs. Collyer very competently translated. Its epistolary method, too, perhaps mirrors the influence of the French novelist, but the sprightly letter writing heroine and the two-part format reflect even more the immense popularity of *Pamela*. Felicia's ironic sense of humor, meanwhile, is in the vein of *Joseph Andrews*. In short, Mrs. Collyer's book deploys the same subjects, techniques, and thematic strategies as the decade's first two major novels. The current vogue for *Don Quixote* also figured powerfully in the conception of this work, as is revealed in the charming scenes with Mellifont. Yet *Felicia to Charlotte* is fresh and original enough in its idea and its treatment of character to stand on its own merits. If we ignore its second volume (as most modern readers have elected to ignore part two of *Pamela*), the work is also a skillfully sustained narrative, the quality of which anticipates *Clarissa* and *Tom Jones*. Mrs. Collyer's novel is one of the very few minor works of early eighteenth-century English fiction that have been unjustly neglected.

By contrast, Charlotte McCarthy's novel *The Fair Moralist; or, Love and Virtue* (1745) is a rather plodding tale that no one would wish to rescue from the oblivion into which it fell after the publication of its second edition in 1746. It is the kind of work which makes established conventions seem stale. And yet it may be said to possess a certain historical interest for the unvarnished way in which it reveals some of the usual practices and the attitudes of contemporary novelistic storytellers. The plot line more than faintly echoes *Pamela,* suggesting the impact of Richardson's famous work upon the most minor of minor novelists. The chief characters include the matchless heroine Emelia and her spotless friends

Melissa and Theodore, who bear relatively familiar names deliberately and obviously tinged by associations with romance; a few characters are improbably called by names like Philemon and Philander. The work's aim clearly was to paint ordinary people and familiar events in heightened colors, and to idealize them in moral terms. This was the aim of Richardson and Fielding too, but Mrs. McCarthy's ineptness allows the dual purpose to divide instead of strengthen her work. She seems to have been partly aware of the difficulties of her task. The preface to the second edition makes the following admission: "I confess the Characters are of my own Invention, for I fear I might have search'd in History long enough, before I could have found a Maid to have resembled Emelia, or a Youth so honourable as Philander; however, it is not impossible that there may have been such, tho' their story is not made publick; . . . it is not my Business here to describe both Sex [*sic*], as they really are, but as they ought to be."

Mrs. McCarthy's timid maneuvers in her preface are typical of most novelistic writers of her period. There is an apologetic quality about the acknowledgment that her work is a fiction, as though she was conscious of herself as a writer at work in a climate generally unsympathetic to what she was doing and therefore felt a strong need to proceed very cautiously. Mary Collyer, Sarah Fielding, Eliza Haywood, and indeed even Samuel Richardson and Tobias Smollett proceed with much the same caution, but in differing degrees. Their works all deliberately avoid any self-conscious display of specifically aesthetic value, though the novels of Richardson and Smollett are conspicuously ingenious contrivances. They thus fall short of proclaiming the integrity of prose fiction as a mode of narrative art. Some of these writers, like the author of *Pamela*, only tacitly admit that their stories are the products of their own invention. Others are more forthright, but seem to say with Charlotte McCarthy, "Yes, I admit the whole is my invention, but behold what truths of nature I have uncovered, and see what a moral is here!" Even Smollett joins this chorus in the preface to *Roderick Random*, though he adds a discordant note by characterizing his work as a moralized picaresque, thereby all but directly proclaiming his role as an artist deliberately imposing a particular vision upon the facts of reality as they are recorded in his narrative. Most novelistic writers of this period, just as surely as Smollett or even Fielding, impose their personal vision as they re-create the material world in the forms of their works—Charlotte McCarthy says that it is not her business to "describe both Sex, as they really are, but as they ought to be"; but few are willing to identify this practice as a proper function of the artist as creator, and so their works are projected as alternative species of homiletic writing, or biography, or history.

The author of *The Fair Moralist* was very possibly unaware of the aesthetic issues raised—or, perhaps more accurately, disguised—by the words of her preface. She appears to have been too preoccupied with her homiletic purpose to have noticed much of anything else. It must be said that she pursues this purpose with a vigorous single-mindedness that gives her book a kind of moral energy, or centrality of emphasis, that overcomes some of the crudities of the composition. The story assigns a very large role to a third-person moralizing narrator, whose insistent pomposity of manner and turgidity of language sorely try the reader's endurance. The characters themselves are at least mildly energetic figures acting out a complicated, potentially intriguing story of virtue tried and tested in a myriad of domestic circumstances. There is a certain woodenness about them, however, and the language they speak sometimes falls annoyingly into the rhythms of blank verse, echoing the irritating histrionic mannerisms of the narrator. At one point, for example, the hero Philander, a toned-down version of the conventional theatrical rake, says of his intentions toward the spotless heroine Emelia:

> I'll make her Queen of all my Wealth and Wishes,
> the Sun shall not be more ador'd than she;
> her Virtue shall protect where e'er we tread,
> and be our Shield, if we shou'd meet a Foe. (p. 58)

No reader of the 1740s could have failed to notice the sincere piety of this novel, which is essentially, like its model *Pamela*, a moralized Cinderella story. The exemplary Emelia, a poor girl, has been orphaned by the death of her excellent father Philemon. She encounters, resists, and, in the manner of Richardson's heroine, finally reforms the libertine Philander. As a Christian heroine, Emelia always acts decisively and courageously, with little but her faith and the pious admonitions of her dead father to guide her. Shortly after her first unwilling confrontation with the notorious aristocratic seducer, she learns that he had once debauched her best friend and confidante Melissa. These initial episodes unmistakably exploit contemporary class tensions. Later Emelia escapes Philander's clutches and, in clever disguise, wanders over the countryside. Here begins another stage of what is now explicitly defined as the heroine's moral journey through life's entanglements. Comforted in a moment of despair by an apparition of Christ reminiscent of the experience of the pious John Nelson, she assumes the name Vileria, dons the clothes of a page boy, and goes into service as footman to a young country squire. Again, her virtue is tested and outraged. The squire, saddled with an old, ugly wife whom he had married for money, is carrying on an illicit affair with the aged local parson's pretty young bride. Meanwhile, like Fielding's Lady Booby, the squire's hideous wife makes advances upon Vileria/Emelia herself. In these episodes Mrs. McCarthy, in the manner of Richardson, provides a closeup view of a country family. The virtuous heroine's alien status under these conditions, and her indignant flight, pass judgment on the family's moral infirmities, while her behavior extends her function to offer an example of male virtue as explicit as Fielding's similar example in *Joseph Andrews*. In the midst of her turmoil over this unfortunate incident, Emelia suddenly meets Philander again. It is clearly a providential accident, contrived by a benevolent author. Emelia learns from Philander that he has wounded Melissa's brother Theodore in a duel, and, her identity concealed by her disguise, she extracts from the young rake (who now repines for his crimes and adores his "lost" Emelia) a promise of reformation and a declaration of love for herself. Upon hearing that Theodore is recovered, Emelia forgives Philander, and the two return to Melissa's house, where the heroine joyfully tells him who she is. During their wedding preparations Emelia, in an interesting departure from the example of Pamela Andrews (possibly this is a direct response to Richardson's novel), decides that Philander should redeem Melissa's spotted honor by marrying her instead. This courageous act, a final measure of the heroine's integrity, is rewarded when Theodore discloses a long-nursed love for Emelia and takes her as his own bride. Both couples live happily ever after, says the author,

> Whose fair Examples still this Truth record,
> Virtue, and Love, must meet their just Reward.

This novel's genuine moral fervor links it directly to the work of Mrs. Aubin and Mrs. Rowe, while its several resemblances to *Pamela* make clear Mrs. McCarthy's intense awareness of Richardson's novel. *The Fair Moralist* is not a full-blown imitation of *Pamela*, however. Emelia's sacrificial Christian heroism, in fact, is closer to the example of Clarissa Harlowe, whose story was still to be published. Because he is an idealized, aristocratic seducer, Philander resembles Richardson's criminal Lovelace, although like *Pamela*'s hero he arrives at a good end through the influence of his beloved's shining virtue and inviolable spirit. In a sense, then, *The Fair Moralist* both reenacts and passes beyond the morality of *Pamela*. Moreover, like *Felicia to Charlotte*, its popularity, though short-lived, probably helped to cultivate the public attitudes that would receive *Clarissa* so warmly only a few months hence.

The most productive of the successful minor novelistic writers of the 1740s was that adaptable author Eliza Haywood. The year 1741 marked an end to more than a decade of very low activity for this normally energetic writer. Since Pope's blast in the *Dunciad*, her output had been virtually limited to the oriental political romance *The Adventures of Eovaai* (1736) and a sporadic series of miscellaneous letters, essays, and translations.[12] The publication of *Pamela* prompted Mrs. Haywood's return to the novelistic scene, and to her old prolific habits. Beginning with her own lively *Anti-Pamela* (1741), an imitation of Fielding's recent *Shamela*, she produced at least six new novelistic works (none of which is signed) before her death in 1756.[13]

Mrs. Haywood's new work preserves certain generic resemblances to the little amorous tales with which she began her career, but greatly subdued. The reformed Eliza was not the sly female rake who amazed and captivated the public with the hot-blooded *Love in Excess*. In fact her most popular production in the 1740s, a sober work called *The Fortunate Foundlings: Being the Genuine History of Col. M——rs, and his Sister, Madam du P——y* (1744; "third" edition, 1748), is closer to the example of Mrs. Aubin than to her own earlier novels. *The Fortunate Foundlings* narrates the adventures of virtuous twins named Horatio and Louisa, who, having been abandoned as infants, rise heroically through an extended series of separate trials to happy marriages, great wealth, and the discovery of their truly genteel lineage. As *Tom Jones* was later to do, the work capitalizes on the extraordinary popular interest in Captain Coram's royally chartered Foundling Hospital; this was part of its topical appeal. The novel offers an ingeniously contrived story line which is worth detailing, partly because in both manner and tone it registers the influence of Richardson and Fielding.

Born and left for dead in the portentous year 1688, the twins are found and taken in by a kind, wealthy gentleman named Dorilaus, who raises them to be unblemished exemplars of Christian virtue. Dorilaus falls below his own ideals, however. He finds the mature young lady Louisa irresistible, and his incestuous advances drive her from his house. Following a stint as an apprentice milliner in the corrupt back streets of London, the heroine journeys to Europe, where she acquires considerable knowledge of the polite world and bravely resists repeated threats upon her virtue. Louisa's courage is adequate to every moral danger, but her strength is not. At one point she has to be rescued from a ravisher. She falls in love with her gallant savior, but refuses to marry him because of her obscure origins, her poverty, and her low rank in life. She retires sadly to a convent, where her shining virtue soon makes the abbess plot her conversion to Catholicism. At once Louisa flees and is at last reunited with Dorilaus. In stock romance fashion, her true identity is revealed and her happiness secured. The rich old gentleman claims her as his real daughter, thus paving the way for her marriage to the lover she had earlier turned away. Meanwhile Horatio has a set of equivalent adventures, though more military than amorous. He leaves his school at Westminster to serve bravely under Marlborough, and then after a period as a prisoner of the French, he enlists with the Chevalier for the first Jacobite Rebellion of 1715. Along the way, he becomes entranced with a beautiful, spotless virgin named Charlotta de Palfoy. In hopes of gaining a fortune that will make him her eligible suitor, he joins the rampaging army of Charles XII of Sweden. After very brief service he is captured by the Russians, and languishes in a St. Petersburg prison. Many other difficulties both physical and moral beset Horatio before he, like Louisa, is welcomed as the child of Dorilaus and rewarded with the hand of his beloved.

The moral ideology of *The Fortunate Foundlings* is obvious and familiar; the story is a serious account of Christian heroism rewarded. Its characters are projected as exemplary figures whose adventures, as Mrs. Haywood (in her transparent guise as editor) claims in her preface, were published only "to encourage Virtue in both Sexes, by shewing the Amiableness of it in real characters. And if it be true (as certainly it is) that Example has more Efficacy than Precept, we may be bold to say there are few fairer, or more worthy Imitation." The broad geographical scope, as in the work of Mrs. Aubin and later of Fielding and Smollett, is designed to give the book's moral emphasis a wide significance. Considering its author, however, what is remarkable is that this narrative in no way undercuts its didactic purpose by including gratuitously erotic displays of seduction and amorous dalliance. It is less cloistered than, say, *Madam de Beaumont;* at its most extreme moments (some of them are comic) it is guilty of about the same degree of looseness as the Molly Seagrim scenes in *Tom Jones.* But all this is quite distant from the titillations of *Love in Excess.* Mrs. Haywood's very earnestness appears to have secured her renewed success with readers who had abandoned her in favor of Mrs. Rowe, Mrs. Aubin, and Richardson.

Mrs. Haywood's novel held other attractions, of course. Its eclectic method, combining the interests of romance, travel literature, and popular biography, she carried over from her old fiction, which had always reached out in as many directions as possible. But *The Fortunate Foundlings* is more insistently and authoritatively "familiar" than Mrs. Haywood's early novels. The preface makes a routine claim to authenticity, but attempts to secure that claim by negative reference to exactly the kind of thing for which the author had previously been known and maligned:

> The many Fictions which have lately been imposed upon the World, under the specious Titles of Secret Histories, Memoirs, &c. &c. have given but too much room to question the Veracity of every Thing that has the least Tendency that way: We therefore think it highly necessary to assure the Reader, that he will find nothing in the following Sheets, but what has been collected from Original Letters, private Memorandums, and the Accounts we have been favoured with from the Mouths of Persons too deeply concerned in many of the chief Transactions not to be perfectly acquainted with the Truth, and of too much Honour and Integrity to put any false Colours upon it.

Here Mrs. Haywood affirms the value of her work, not as art but as moral history. In her preface she actually approximates Richardson's pose in *Pamela,* and the narrative that follows more nearly justifies such prefatory gesturing than anything the author had written earlier. The descriptions of English and European geography, the passages of history, the pictures of life in a nunnery, even the uncharacteristic borrowings from the mode of military memoirs Mrs. Haywood handles with considerable circumstantial precision. The extensive topical references to the almost legendary Marlborough and the rapacious Swedish monarch, to Catholicism and to Jacobite political maneuvers, must thus have seemed very interesting to Mrs. Haywood's readers, because so authoritative. The characters themselves, though little more than stereotypes, have at least descended from the ridiculous heights of pretentious passion typical of the author's earlier personages. Louisa and Horatio display a more judicious sentimentality, influenced, no doubt, by the example of Marivaux and Richardson. They are slightly idealized, ordinary people (at least until the end) instead of glorified figures of high life.

The heroic twins are uneven creations, just as the book as a whole is uneven and fragmented. *The Fortunate Foundlings* tries to be technically sophisticated, but erratically mixes rant and plain-style in its theatrical dialogue and badly fumbles the complexities of the kind of dual plot that Fielding was soon to employ so skillfully in *Tom Jones*. The degree of foreshadowing is surprising nevertheless. Even though she failed, Mrs. Haywood appears to have been seeking a formula that could satisfy the tastes of a new generation of novel readers. As part of this endeavor she seems to have responded very directly to the success of Richardson's story of a heroically virtuous, ordinary maiden, and Fielding's more expansive tale of Pamela's brother and male counterpart in Christian heroism, Joseph Andrews.

In April 1748, Mrs. Haywood published a new book called *Life's Progress through the Passions; or, The Adventures of Natura*, in which she confirmed the reformation wrought upon her new novelistic habits, and explored further some of the possibilities she had opened up. The titular hero of the work she makes the son of a good family (though neither rich nor noble), and promulgates the doctrine that his ordinariness is what makes him most remarkable. Fielding was to make the same claim for Tom Jones less than a year later. Mrs. Haywood's narrative strategy is simple. It exposes the hero, a good-natured but lusty young adventurer, to all of the various passions possible in human experience. Natura's travels take him about England and Europe, where he entangles himself with predatory whores, lusty nuns, rapacious French soldiers (the War of the Austrian Succession is raging at the time), treacherous Roman priests, and so on. He marries happily and prosperously, but is suddenly widowed, and his grief propels him wildly and progressively into the consuming passions of despair, melancholy, revenge, pride, ambition, and lust. In the declining years of a miserable life he meets, falls in love with, and marries a virtuous matron whose example steadies him and leads him to peace and the rewards of quiet happiness. This novel, which is surprisingly fresh in its systematic enunciation of psychological tensions, exalts prudence—the product of the reasoning faculty—as the governing principle of human behavior: "Every one will acknowledge, because he knows it by experience, that while he is possessed of *passions*, his *reason* alone has the power of keeping them within the bounds of moderation" (p. 227). It is a sentiment worthy of Johnson's Imlac, and it is not very distant from the principle Tom Jones must learn to accept and live by.

The various emotional turns and starts of this story actually occasion a good deal of rudimentary psychological analysis, which marks a new development in the career of the author. There is no deep penetration into the motives or various mental states of her hero, but it seems that Mrs. Haywood had read attentively not only Marivaux and Richardson, but also Prévost—especially the currently popular translation of the memoirs of the endlessly wandering, passionate Man of Quality. Natura, a kind of Everyman whose name signifies only his failure to control his natural passions, really appears to be a picaroon of sorts. The degree to which Mrs. Haywood was attuned to contemporary trends is indicated by the fact that in January 1748, only four months before Natura made his entrance in the world, Smollett published his adaptation from the picaresque mode, *Roderick Random*. While *Life's Progress through the Passions* is a less sophisticated work than *The Fortunate Foundlings*, it was a timely and well-written story, though for some reason a commercial failure. In the next decade Mrs. Haywood would publish her best and longest-lived novels, *The History of Miss Betsy Thoughtless* (1751), *The History of Jemmy and Jenny Jessamy* (1753), and *The Invisible Spy* (1755). Even in these quasi-domestic tales she did not reach what she seems to have been groping for throughout the latter years of her career: a species of didactic novel fusing Richardsonian minuteness of detail with Fieldingesque panorama and comic vision.

One other minor novelistic writer of the 1740s, Henry Fielding's sister Sarah, attempted the same kind of fusion in *The Adventures of David Simple* (1744), though she was not much more successful than Mrs. Haywood. Miss Fielding's instincts were those of a moral allegorist, as may best be seen in the impressive sequel (1753) to *David Simple*. The sequel, which is beyond the scope of this study, may be briefly described as an uncluttered story in which the allegorical effects are concentrated and the ambiguities of moral "simplicity"—that is, goodness and purity qualified by naiveté, in the manner of Henry Fielding's Heartfree and Parson Adams—are fully worked out. In the original two volumes, however, Miss Fielding's sporadic attempts to pursue her friend Richardson's technique of scrupulous circumstantiality on the one hand, and her brother's strategy of sweeping social commentary on the other, diffuse the impact of her moral allegory. When we look beyond these failures, we find the substantive essence of her narrative, which resides in the Bunyanesque tactic of embodying moral ideals in lifelike characters and then bringing them together in abstract, as well as dramatic, confrontations. The "psychological penetration" for which Miss Fielding was so often applauded is thus not the kind of probing into the human psyche's moral reactions to objective events characteristic of Richardson and Marivaux. Rather it is the intellectualized display of general principles.

After the fashion of her brother Henry's novels, Miss Fielding divides her work into books. She calls her hero a Don Quixote, but he hardly fits the description; he is really her version of Heartfree. David, an ordinary character, stands as a one-dimensional representation of moral simplicity; that is, he is unvarnished, uncomplicated, open, true. Early in life, a usurping brother Daniel, with the help of scheming servants, strips the hero of his birthright and small fortune. This experience disillusions him almost irretrievably, whereupon he sets out on a journey (the metaphor is obvious in its purpose) through Westminster "in Search of a Friend." Along the way he meets a whole array of unsympathetic moral types. They include a devious female named Nancy Johnson, whom David courts and drops after discovering her purely mercenary motives, as well as the excessively proud Mr. Orgueil, the nonsensical, thoughtless, unfeeling Mr. Banter, the vicious slanderer Mr. Splatter, and the complacent Mr. Varnish.

The world Sarah Fielding depicts through David's slow motions is morally dark, and her grimly ironic exposure of its deceptive appearances is appropriate. In the second volume the hero finally meets a truly estimable person, the young, beautiful, and virtuous maiden Cynthia, whom he kindly rescues from her unhappy station as "toad-eater" to a fine lady. For a while he courts her unsuccessfully, and loses her when she journeys to the country to find a missing friend. David then relieves the admirable sister and brother, Camilla and Valentine, who are in desperate circumstances. Unknown to him, Camilla is really Cynthia's lost friend, and Valentine her beloved. The two have been driven into misery and poverty by the cruelty of their hypocritical stepmother—a distress that is echoed in the opening pages of *Roderick Random*, and virtually duplicated in Henry Fielding's *Amelia*. David becomes their companion and support. At this point, the work settles into a diffuseness that obscures its allegorical purpose. The grim plight of Camilla and Valentine could have been used for further exploration of the moral issues already raised. But Miss Fielding chose neither to use it that way nor to dramatize the complex moral relationships inevitably involved in the friendship David, Camilla, and Valentine profess for one another. Instead she takes refuge in a flabby succession of satirical episodes from high life, probably inspired by her brother's fiction. These are punctuated by a group of interwoven moral histories and travel adventures that attempt to stretch the work's moral purview to include European characters and scenes. By the end, *David Simple* has descended from Bunyanesque moral allegory to the easy options of romance and conventional providential maneuvering. David's dying, repentant brother delivers up the hero's stolen fortune; Cynthia reappears, and David suddenly discovers a love for Camilla. He has all along been searching not just for a friend, but, like one of Mrs. Aubin's lovers, for a marriage partner whose own virtues could match his Christian heroism. Shortly, his new beloved's father turns up and once again bestows his unclouded affection (and his fortune) on his children. David marries Camilla, Valentine weds Cynthia, and the tale ends with all the virtuous characters duly compensated for their goodness.

David Simple is the only one of the minor novels of the 1740s regularly mentioned by historians of English fiction as a significant work. Recently, it has even been honored with a new edition published in the series of Oxford English Novels.[14] Miss Fielding's book is apparently safe forever from the virtual oblivion enshrouding *Felicia to Charlotte* and *The Fortunate*

Foundlings. Its contemporary success, as well as its survival, may be partly attributed to the luster attaching to it from the name of the author's brother, who gave the book the benefit of his reading and wrote in his own name a preface for the second edition in which he denominated it a "comic-epic-poem in prose." But the work has definite merits, which must have recommended it to early readers, among them its partial character as a kind of secularized *Pilgrim's Progress*. *David Simple* does, of course, move beyond the boundaries of Bunyanesque fiction and, perhaps paradoxically, its appeal may have been strengthened because supported by those explicitly topical London references that to a modern reader seem to undermine its integrity as moral allegory. Probably most compelling was the story's consistent seriousness of purpose. It directly addresses the age's fascination with ideals of "simple" moral purity in triumphant contention with hostile forces.

In the preface that Henry Fielding contributed to *David Simple* he describes his sister's novel in terms that show his excited awareness of the possibilities that lay before practitioners of the expanding art of prose fiction in the 1740s. The beauties of the present work (he says) need little recommendation,

> tho' I will not say but they may sometimes stand in need of being pointed out to the generality of Readers. For as the Merit of this Work consists in a vast Penetration into human Nature, a deep and profound Discernment of all the Mazes, Windings and Labyrinths, which perplex the Heart of Man to such a degree, that he is himself often incapable of seeing through them; and as this is the greatest, noblest, and rarest of all the Talents which constitute a Genius; so a much larger Share of this Talent is necessary, even to recognize these Discoveries, when they are laid before us, than falls to the share of a common Reader.

During much of his preface Fielding is engaged in bringing the book in line with his own theories of comic romance. But in this praise of the fine strokes of character in *David Simple*, its natural incidents, the perfect credibility of its action, and the author's acute understanding of the world, he places it by implication squarely in the tradition of the novel from Boccaccio and Cervantes to Samuel Richardson and himself.

CHAPTER VII

Fiction as Artifice: The Achievement of Henry Fielding

I N THE PREFACE he wrote for the second edition of *The Adventures of David Simple*, Henry Fielding seems to impose upon his sister's novel a definition of its function as art, as the contrived product of a lively imagination which observes, interprets, and gives new and meaningful form to human experience according to the author's own thoughtfully considered vision of life. The imposition is just, though one doubts Fielding's wisdom in calling *David Simple* a "comic-epic-poem." It is significant that it was Henry Fielding, and not his sister Sarah, who was so bold as to characterize the book in this way, as a deliberate work of art. Of all the fiction writers so busily at work in the early years of the eighteenth century, only the author of *Joseph Andrews* and *Tom Jones* seriously undertook to articulate any aesthetic of the novel, or to identify and defend prose fiction as a new literary form—an assorted collection of literary possibilities, we should say—deserving to be recognized along with the traditional forms of the drama and the various kinds of poetic expression.

This is a commonplace, the sort of fact that always draws an obligatory casual mention from historians of the novel, but little more. To be sure, many scholarly books and articles have discussed the details of Fielding's theoretical posturing, his terminology of comic-prose-epic as he applied it to his fiction, his borrowings from the theater and from satire, and so forth. These are all serious subjects, and those who have studied them have shown their importance to anyone who cares about Fielding or about the early development of the novel. But it has not been sufficiently understood how radical and daring an innovator Fielding really was; indeed there is no way to understand this important aspect of his achievement unless we are able to place his work against the entire background of fiction writing in his period. Other novelistic writers, not to mention the many pseudobiographers and pseudohistorians, project their narratives as paradigms' of some moral reality, but unlike Fielding they articulate no meaningful connection between moral and aesthetic values. These paradigms presumably coincide with possibilities inherent in the real world, or at least their authors claim insistently that they do, and this is their only apparent importance. They may be to a certain extent composed on the principles of verisimilitude, but actually they serve as surreptitiously contrived substitutes for empirical reality—as disguised interpretations of real life, usually for some ostensible homiletic purpose, but projected as its mirror reflections. This practice was made familiar early in the century by Mrs. Aubin, Mrs. Haywood, Jane Barker, and others. Richardson continued it in the 1740s, as did Smollett and such lesser writers as Mary Collyer, Sarah Fielding, Charlotte McCarthy, and the rejuvenated Eliza Haywood herself. Their achievement collectively, and in some very obvious cases individually, was enormous—hugely important, we may say, to the emergence of the novel as we know it.

But for these writers, it appears, fiction had to be justified by association with other forms; hence the obviousness of their eclectic method, which verified the imaginative truthfulness of their stories by drawing easily recognized parallels to other, usually factual or pseudofactual, modes of narrative, without conspicuous reflection upon their own achieved or potential aesthetic value. For the novel to be established separately and authoritatively as a distinctive literary form of intrinsic interest and worth, it remained only for some committed writer of visible powers and convincing artistic integrity to proclaim it as such. This is of course precisely what Henry Fielding, himself an eclectic epical historian of contemporary life and of the world in general, set out to do in his comic tales of *Joseph Andrews* and *Tom Jones*. The unabashed artfulness, the conspicuous fictionality, of Fielding's works may be properly understood as a kind of novelist's manifesto which directly prepared the way for later affirmations of fiction as self-conscious art by such writers as Sterne, Burney, Austen, Dickens, and Thackeray—not to mention important twentieth-century figures like Joyce and Barth. If Richardson, Smollett, and the more accomplished of their lesser contemporaries in the novelistic mode managed to show what the imagination could do in the line of exposing, exploring, and interpreting the depths of human reality, Fielding certified the endeavor as a legitimate and exciting artistic enterprise.

Robert Alter has described the importance of Fielding's achievement as advocate for prose fiction in a most precise way. The author of *Tom Jones* is, in Alter's phrase, a "conscious artificer," the "first of the great intellectual novelists" who "theorizes about what he writes as he writes it."[1] Fielding possessed a finely analogical intelligence which made him able to see at once the absurdities of things, particularly the literary absurdities of much popular art, and their potential as the targets of his wit and the catalysts of his own constantly developing artistic consciousness. We have already observed, in brief glances at least, how he exploited the conventions of various kinds of popular narrative: *Tom Jones* is an ironic criminal biography in the form of a comic moral history, *Joseph Andrews* (in its early pages) is a secret history of the household of a fine lady, and so on. Fielding was surely the most alertly responsive of all contemporary novelists to the inherent and immensely varied possibilities of the form in which he practiced, which is perhaps why he so scorned all the silly "Authors of immense Romances" and the "modern Novel and *Atalantis* Writers" (*Joseph Andrews*, 3.1) whose works he answered with his own. In this connection it is worth emphasizing that his theorizing in the various prefaces to the books of his novels is rarely abstract, and it is never mere idle chatter, despite the frequent playfulness of his narrator. Very often the theoretical comments address directly the shallow conventions of popular romance, or the perversions of inept biographers, or the limitations of most historical writers, while they express Fielding's own lively and refined sense of what ought to be inside the world of a fiction, and what principles ought to govern it.

From the beginning of his literary career Fielding was a kind of pathological critic and moralist, deeply affected by classical and neoclassical traditions, his apparent preoccupation with ideal forms frequently finding its vent in farce or burlesque or parody. By the time he had completed the transition from dramatic *farceur* to novelist he was a seasoned, serious critic and theorist who moreover believed profoundly in the unity of art and morality. The conspicuously orchestrated intricacies of his works of fiction furnish ample evidence of his conviction that the artist's responsibility to moral purpose and his responsibility to form were indistinguishable, that the homiletic and aesthetic functions of a novel ought to mirror one another as reflections of the author's own ordered vision of life. It was on just such grounds as these that he raised objections to the works of other storytellers of his day, including Richardson, and it was surely these very objections as much as anything else that prompted him to devise his own alternative kind of deliberately artful novel.

Fielding's understanding of the role of the novelist is in no particular way better than Richardson's or Smollett's. Certainly many novelists after him took a different view of things, to the great delight of strict representationalist critics like Henry James, Percy Lubbock, F. R. Leavis, and even Ian Watt, who believe that the novelist's highest calling is to create a form capable of sustaining an illusion that the fiction is not fiction at all, but reality. This is what Richardson achieved with his "realism of presentation," to use Watt's phrase. But Fielding's forthright affirmation of the novelist as artificer and artist was undeniably a great event in the early history of the new form. It is worth a brief journey over some familiar ground in order to locate this particular accomplishment more firmly in a contemporary context, where its importance may be most fully appreciated and understood.

With the publication of *Shamela* in April 1741, Fielding completed his apprenticeship in fiction writing, which had begun with the early drafts of *The Life of Mr. Jonathan Wild the Great*. Both of these parodic works give signs of what we find in *Joseph Andrews* and *Tom Jones*, though both, in very different degrees, depend fundamentally for life and full effect on the author's (and the reader's) awareness of things outside their fictional worlds, things which Fielding did not create but which he did exploit. Without Richardson's *Pamela*, obviously, *Shamela* would not exist at all. The ordering principle for the narrative surface of *Jonathan Wild* is drawn primarily from the conventions of criminal biography. These two apprenticeship works are derivative performances, but of course they are fresh and original also, partly because they served the budding novelist as occasions to formulate some of his own most important new attitudes toward the art of fiction and the role of the fiction writer as artist.

We have already seen how, in the parody of *Jonathan Wild*, Fielding reacted to the supposed formal and moral perversions of criminal biographers in developing and articulating his own high ideals of life writing as a kind of literary expression. *Shamela*, in its function as explicit and precise parody, reveals the author's deep distrust of the limiting circumstantial method of Richardson's novel, with its restricted point of view and seeming lack of aesthetic distance, with its unqualified introspection and its apparent tendency to allow the emotional experience of one self-serving character to determine both the distended form and the blurred meaning of the work. The jabs at Colley Cibber and Conyers Middleton so plainly indicated on the title page of Fielding's little book—*An Apology for the Life of Mrs. Shamela Andrews*, "By Mr. Conny Keyber"—underscore his broad concern with the moral and artistic shabbiness of all kinds of contemporary biographical writing.[2] *Pamela*, it seems, was the object of particular scorn in *Shamela* because it was a work so celebrated as to be especially pernicious. To Fielding's mind, the manner of this book notoriously sanctioned a kind of artistic anarchy in the service of moral stupidity. The lesson of *Shamela* is that the author of *Pamela* possessed neither control over his material nor any valid and substantiated vision of life.

It was once a matter of routine in discussions of *Joseph Andrews* to say that Fielding's first novel was the accidental product of his irresistible impulse to write another and more elaborate spoof of Richardson. The narrative got away from its author, so the old argument went, upon the introduction of the character of Parson Adams. It is probably true that the modest success earned by *Shamela*, abetted by his abiding disapproval of Richardson's enormously popular work, encouraged Fielding to try his hand at a full-sized novel of his own. But the notion of a runaway parody is wholly inadequate to account for the genesis or the composition of *Joseph Andrews* as we have it, and it no longer has any currency. This is not to say that the question of Fielding's parodic intention is irrelevant to our understanding of his novel, or that his maneuvers against *Pamela* are merely playful gestures in a spirit of good fun. Within the last dozen years or so at least two important critics, Robert Alan Donovan and J. Paul Hunter, have shown in fresh ways how deliberate *Joseph Andrews* is in its responses to *Pamela*, but they have emphasized that Fielding's purposes are more complicated than those of the usual parodist.[3] Both Donovan and Hunter, though they start from different premises, show how Fielding uses *Pamela* as a backdrop for the display of an alternative moral vision which rejects the apparent simplicities of Richardson's moral absolutes and attempts a more substantial representation of the ideals and the difficult practice of Christian virtue and personal heroism.[4]

After Donovan and Hunter, nothing very worthwhile remains to be said about the specific parodic devices and maneuvers of *Joseph Andrews* as a calculated reaction to *Pamela*. But it may be useful to place the whole matter in a slightly broader context of literary history. Richardson's novel, as Fielding sat down to write his own new book, was still the best known example of a large and diverse class of biographical moral histories being enjoyed by the public. To a very real extent, as *Shamela* had already proclaimed, the supposed failures of vision and performance Fielding found so objectionable in *Pamela* were also typical of other popular works of its general kind. In the introductory chapter of the first book of *Joseph Andrews*, the author heaps high praise upon the biographer and his calling, but summons up Cibber's self-serving *Apology* and Richardson's story of virtue rewarded as particular instances of the shameful and ridiculous perversion of that calling. In other words, the objects of Fielding's scorn are not two but many. He uses the *Apology* and especially *Pamela* as very conveniently familiar butts of his ironic wit and as direct and easily recognizable examples of a version of biographical writing precisely antithetical to his own. Though one work is presumably true and the other a novelistic fiction, they are both false—the effusions of writers whose stories have little relation to observed reality; their authors are, as Fielding puts the matter later, but two among the multitude whose "Heroes are of their own Creation, and their Brains the Chaos whence all their Materials are collected" (3.1). It is not only the presumed stupidity but the transparent artlessness of such authors that troubles Fielding so, for in their ineptitude and lack of real moral and aesthetic values they reduce the vast complexities of life to minute and often trivial particulars, from which no meaningful principle of universal order can be extracted. In Fielding's Aristotelian view, it is the artist's function to affirm such order, which is why (in 3.1) he praises *Don Quixote* even above such respectable examples of authentic historical writing as Juan de Mariana's *Historia general de España* (1601).

Fielding himself avoids the seemingly undifferentiated minutia of a *Pamela*, but of course indulges in a special kind of particularizing habit, especially when he is at his most topical. The cowardly Man of Courage descants bravely to Parson Adams upon the mettle he would have displayed at Carthagena had he been there, but is too timorous to respond to Fanny Goodwill's sudden cries of distress. This extended episode (3.7–

10) obviously refers both to a recent controversial naval battle and to the shift of power from Walpole to the Carteret coalition—Fanny wonders whether her rescuer, Parson Adams, whom she does not at first recognize as he approaches her in the darkness, might not ravish her himself. We know that Fielding, in the manner of the secret historian, took aim at such real people as Peter Walter and Lord Hervey in his characterizations of many of the rogues who populate the world of *Joseph Andrews*. But his intention, obviously, is to universalize such references. Like Swift in *Gulliver's Travels*, Fielding straddles two purposes: *Joseph Andrews* offers instances of personal and topical satire, despite the narrator's several disclaimers to the contrary, but is projected finally as a broad commentary on human nature. No reader needs to understand the specifics of the many allusions to real people and current events in order to enjoy this novel, or fathom its meaning. To use Fielding's own words as applied to *Don Quixote*, *Joseph Andrews* is a "History of the World in general" (3.1).

It is the many and obvious signs of artifice in Fielding's fiction—the divisions into books, the epic similes, the stylized language, the often playfully ironic tone, the mannerisms and maneuvering of the narrator—that transform his story into a universal moral history designed to make visible the author's imposition of a comprehensive, ordered vision of life upon the disordered facts of real human experience. In his role of comic writer, Fielding assumes certain prerogatives as manipulator of the fictional world, as benevolent controller of the fate of his characters, whom he actually raises from their ordinariness to the elevated status of Christian heroes before rewarding them for their heroism. Unlike so many of his contemporaries, who disguise their manipulations and leave the impression that the patterns of wish fulfillment they typically develop are reflections of what is, Fielding certifies his manipulations for what *they* are. *Joseph Andrews*, like his other novels, is an elaborate, intricate design, an extended metaphor really, and the author as artist is projected into a role analogous to that played by God in the universe.[5] The narrator in *Tom Jones* speaks of his story as a "great Creation of our own," and dares any "little Reptile of a Critic" to "presume" to fault its perfection (10.1). The tone of this remark is playful, but the purpose is utterly serious, as is hinted by the amusing equation of the imaginary doubting critic with the serpent who arrogantly challenged the harmonious perfection of the original creation. *Tom Jones*, even more than *Joseph Andrews* before it, al-

most obsessively pursues the aim of keeping before the reader an awareness that the fiction is a deliberate contrivance whose internal harmonies
are intended to reflect—in fact, to merge with and even become—the
author's articulated vision of ideal order. No other fiction writer of Fielding's time, not even Richardson in his defense of *Clarissa* as a Christian
prose tragedy, reveals such an attitude of artistic self-consciousness.

In the comedy of *Joseph Andrews* Fielding actually represents two patterns, one empirical and the other moral. Eventually the moral pattern
supersedes the empirical in a radical transformation of the fictional world,
and this transformation is itself a conspicuous sign of the author's determined control over the material of his fiction. The two patterns do not
coincide naturally, and if the author's vision and his intentions for his
characters are to be fulfilled, wrenching must occur. The transformation
that comes at the end is not merely arbitrary, however. By allowing his
narrator and not the action to dominate the world he has created, Fielding
maintains tonal control throughout the narrative, so that no threat to the
safety and integrity of his virtuous characters is ever allowed to seem too
serious. Nevertheless, it appears that good people, no matter how resolute
they may be as they journey through the chaos of human life, are doomed
to be tricked, swindled, insulted, assaulted, abducted, and generally
abused by the wicked. Figures like Mrs. Tow-wouse, Parsons Barnabas
and Trulliber, Lady Booby, Peter Pounce, Beau Didapper, the roasting
squire, and their fellow rogues may be the objects of ridicule in the book,
but they are also thoughtfully projected as forces determining to a very
large extent the quality of the physical and moral environment through
which Joseph, Parson Adams, and Fanny must move. Deprived of the
presence of the garrulous comic author, the world of *Joseph Andrews* would
be as dark as that of *Jonathan Wild*. It is the narrator, after all, who softens
the real horror of, say, the "battle of the hounds" (3.6) by a mock-epic
rendering. The difficulties of life in this violent, anarchic, and potentially
destructive fictional world are real, and they constitute the empirical pattern as it is developed in the plot of the novel.

The alternative moral pattern imposed by the author as a kind of sub-
suming superstructure is really a constant in the fictional world, though
it is not fulfilled until the end. It is made manifest by the voice of the
narrator and, actually, by the admirable Christian heroism of the main
characters as they are carried along by the movement of the story on a

kind of pilgrimage to happiness. Fielding enforces this pattern in a manner that sometimes exploits the devices of farce, the delights as well as the limitations of which he well understood from his work in the theater. The episode of the night adventures at Booby Hall (in book 4), for example, is often accurately described as farcical, and its tonal and structural resemblances to some of the popular theatrical interludes of Fielding's day are real. But this episode, as reductive farce, actually serves as an extreme—and hilarious—exposition of the manipulative method of the author throughout the work. It is at once funny business and serious business, as Mark Spilka demonstrated in an important essay of some years ago.[6] Farce frequently works to such ends in *Joseph Andrews;* Mrs. Slipslop's predatory advances upon Joseph come to mind, and the wonderful battle of the chamber pot (3.9). It is as though by indulging in the most sportive and outrageous kinds of manipulations, which seek to provoke his reader into laughing acquiescence, Fielding hoped to enforce the value of his other, more circumspect and comprehensive contrivance of the fictional world as a comic whole.

The strategy works, if that is what it is, for Fielding knew what he was about. That is, he understood the important relationship between farce and comedy, and used the one to illuminate the other. The manipulations of farce are blatant, themselves a source of delight at the simplest level of pure fun. The manipulations of comedy parallel those of farce, and they are often no less blatant, but they are the source of a different and much deeper kind of delight, or satisfaction. Since a comic fiction has greater relevance to the real world than does a farcical one, its manipulations must, as Roger L. Cox has put it in one of the best recent studies of comic structure, be based solidly upon "some belief or conception which both author and audience regard as being effective" when applied to the realities of social and moral life.[7] Fielding the man shared with many of his readers a belief in the design of Providence which ensures that goodness will have its immediate rewards in personal satisfaction and contentment, in a kind of morally substantial happiness and tranquility, and its eternal rewards in paradise. It was upon the foundation of this common belief that Fielding the artist based his comic manipulations of the world of *Joseph Andrews,* whose story celebrates, even replicates the providential design for human happiness but without ever suggesting in any way that the celebration is a circumstantially realistic representation of life itself.

The novel actually expresses, through the overt formalities of an obviously *made* work of art, a hopeful Christian vision both personal and cosmic in its application. Like much comic writing, it is more a philosophic than a mimetic statement. To put this in proper literary and historical perspective: Fielding, in *Joseph Andrews*, is no less emphatically didactic a writer than Richardson in his pastoral comedy of *Pamela*, but he is much more openly and deliberately an artificer in the pursuit of his homiletic purpose.

The author of *Joseph Andrews* repeatedly underscores his roles as artist and moralist by all the conspicuous maneuverings of his narrator, but in one revealing episode he causes his characters to make the unity of the two purposes explicit. Chapter eleven of book three repeats a conversation between Parson Adams and Joseph, who is currently in a state of despair because his beloved Fanny, recently abducted, seems lost to him forever. Parson Adams energetically admonishes his young friend to trust in Providence, for "no Accident happens to us without the Divine Permission," and "it is the duty of a Man, much more of a Christian, to submit. We did not make ourselves; but the same Power which made us, rules over us, and we are absolutely at his Disposal." As we cannot know future events, he continues, "so neither can we tell to what Purpose any Accident tends; and that which at first threatens us with Evil, may in the end produce our Good." This statement may be, as Robert Alan Donovan suggests, a parodic response to Richardson in the form of an "ironic commentary on Pamela's dramatization of her own pathetic innocence."[8] And it is certainly true, as no reader can fail to notice, that Parson Adams later finds it hard to follow his own advice when his adored son is thought to be drowned—Fielding frequently spoofs Adams's amusing version of Christian stoicism. But the statement is double-edged, and especially the latter part may also be understood as a straightforward comment—like Mrs. Heartfree's pronouncement in *Jonathan Wild*—on the actions of Providence in the world of men and women. It is likewise a comment, oblique but unmistakable, on the role of the novelist in the world of his fiction: Fielding subjects his characters to accidents and threats which test them, but in the end, as benevolent manipulator, he procures for them the good they deserve. Parson Adams's speech actually foreshadows the way in which the conclusion of the novel will bring about reconciliation of the moral and empirical patterns it develops, and it is plain that the reconciliation is to be something deliberately wrought, and overtly so. Just as there is no pretense in Fielding's novel that the fictional world itself is anything but imaginary, so also there is no pretense that the completed form of the novel, and of the world it portrays and interprets, is anything but contrived.

The moral pattern begun with Joseph's spurning of Lady Booby's earliest advances upon him, and kept continually before us by the Christian travelers as their heroic resilience proves them superior to all that threatens them during their journey, concludes with rewards both tangible and spiritual. All threats cease. The sudden and surprising arrival of the pedlar and Mr. Wilson (and the discovery of the strawberry birthmark) straightens out the farcical confusion of identities, removes the last obstacle to the marriage of Joseph and Fanny, and brings order to the hilarious chaos of the final episodes. Joseph does not marry his seductress, Lady Booby, although he would thereby have achieved wealth and position—the jab at *Pamela*, one of several Fielding indulges in during the course of the final chapters, is obvious and telling. But, like a hero of romance, he gains his birthright as Mr. Wilson's son, is united to the virtuous woman he both loves and deserves, and he does advance a notch or two up the social ladder. He retires, with Fanny, to a life of serenity on a plot of land in the country near his father's utopian retreat. Parson Adams, for his reward, gets a living worth 130 pounds a year. What Joseph, Fanny, and Parson Adams really enjoy as the result of their heroic persistence in Christian virtue is happiness in a "family of love," to borrow Fielding's own phrase from *Jonathan Wild*. "Joseph remains blest with his *Fanny*," we are told in the last paragraph of the novel, "whom he doats on with the utmost Tenderness, which is all returned on her side. The Happiness of this Couple is a perpetual Fountain of Pleasure to their fond Parents" (4.16). It is a joy to the old patriarch Adams as well. Earlier in the tale, upon the travelers' departure from their visit to Mr. Wilson's house, Parson Adams had said of his kind hosts that "this was the Manner in which the People had lived in the Golden Age" (3.4). It is a Golden Age existence, a kind of prelapsarian world of love and harmonious human relationships, that is established at the end.

The moral reality of a Golden Age renewed, as expressed in Fielding's pictures of a loving family, gives final, definable shape to the ideals of order expressed throughout *Joseph Andrews*. What has threatened to be a

loveless and therefore disordered world of rogues and quarrelsome or dis-
solving families—the Tow-wouses, the Trullibers, the family in the fable
of Leonard and Paul, and so on—is now transformed. The romantic history of Leonora contains a passage that clearly reveals the conception on
which the notion of the family of love as an ideal of personal happiness
actually rests. "O, *Horatio!*" writes Leonora to her adoring lover—and
her insincerity does not at all diminish the truth of what she says: "What
a Life that must be, where the meanest domestick Cares are sweetened by
the pleasing Consideration that the Man on Earth who best deserves, and
to whom you are most inclined to give your Affections, is to reap either
Profit or Pleasure from all you do! In such a case, Toils must be turned
into Diversions, and nothing but the Inconveniences of Life can make us
remember that we are mortal" (2.4). Mr. Wilson, from the perspective of
his experience as a former rake, is able to be more convincing. He gives
concrete solidity to the sentiments expressed in Leonora's frothy letter.
He and his wife, Wilson says, found complete fulfillment in their deep
feeling for each other, and so, with only a very small fortune to sustain
them, they retired "from a World full of Bustle, Noise, Hatred, Envy,
and Ingratitude" to their private but complete haven of "Ease, Quiet, and
Love" (3.3).

The whole tendency of Fielding's comic novel has been to bring about
the happy marriage of Joseph and Fanny. All of the coincidences, temptations, unlucky accidents, abductions, and attempted seductions have led
in this direction. The singlemindedness with which Fielding pursues and
amplifies this conventional device of plot gives both unity and significance
to the experience of his irrepressible characters as they progress toward
their repose in a permanent, idyllic reality founded on Christian love and
characterized by social harmony and moral stability. But it is not a simple
unity; the tensions between the moral and empirical patterns are real,
though there is never any doubt that they will be happily resolved in this
comic fiction. Nor is the idea of the family itself a simple one as Fielding
uses it. In *Joseph Andrews*, as in *Jonathan Wild*, *Tom Jones*, and *Amelia*, the
family of love represents metaphorically the comprehensive fulfillment of
the possibilities of perfected order in all the dimensions of human life—
social, domestic, moral, personal.

The real world may not encourage or even permit such fulfillment, but
then *Joseph Andrews* is after all a novel; and its author, as artist, is at liberty

to re-create the sprawling and resistant facts of life so as to give them some meaningful moral and aesthetic configuration. Indeed, according to Fielding's lights, the novelist is obliged to undertake such a design, to carry it out forthrightly, to call attention to it as artifice; in other words, to present his imagined creation not only as fiction paralleling reality (or pretending to) but as art defining truth. By this conviction, publicly proclaimed in the form of his first novel, Fielding boldly differentiated himself from other fiction writers of his day, including his rival, Samuel Richardson, and gave the novel a new and significant identity. It would be hard to overestimate the historical importance of this achievement.

Tom Jones, like *Joseph Andrews*, is a festive comic fiction that proclaims its author's high valuation of the novelist's calling, but is obviously more ambitious about it. This novel is indeed one of the great examples of self-conscious art in the entire history of English fiction, and certainly the greatest of its age. The technical brilliance of the work, so often praised in our own time, was also appreciated by a good many of Fielding's contemporaries; not all serious-minded people of the day agreed with Richardson and Dr. Johnson that the author of *Tom Jones* was a low, immoral writer, or a "blockhead." The magnitude of Fielding's achievement as the artificer who celebrated his contrivance of the imaginary comic history of *Joseph Andrews* may have gone largely unrecognized by an audience accustomed to all kinds of claims to newness and originality from the authors of popular fiction. But *Tom Jones* brought home, to some at least, the lesson of what Fielding's work thus far had accomplished for the new form of the novel.

The anonymous author of a review essay on *Tom Jones* in the *London Magazine* for February 1749 spoke of the ingenuity of Fielding's arrangement of incidents and episodes, "all which arise naturally from the subject, and contribute towards carrying on the chief plot or design" (p. 51). Francis Coventry, in his *Essay on the New Species of Writing Founded by Mr. Fielding* (1751), called *Tom Jones* "the most lively Book ever publish'd" (pp. 43–44). Through its art, Coventry maintained, Fielding's novel had displaced the former run of "Romances, or Novels, Tales, &c. fill'd with any thing which the wildest Imagination could suggest," and it had also shown the world that "pure Nature could furnish out as agreeable Entertainment, as those airy non-entical Forms they had long ador'd" (pp. 13, 15). A popular and rather able imitation of *Tom Jones* called *The History of*

Charlotte Summers, the Fortunate Parish Girl (1749? 1750?) certified Fielding's attainment to the rank of artist, and argued the high value to be placed upon his work, by claiming to be the "first Begotten, of the poetical Issue, of the much celebrated Biographer of *Joseph Andrews*, and *Tom Jones*" (p. 3). *Tom Jones* was by no means so universally praised as *Clarissa*, but the terms of the praise it did receive are important for us to notice. And what is more, despite the controversy with which some people wished to surround Fielding's book, it was more widely read than any other native novel of its time.[9]

Once again, Fielding seems to have offered his own work as a reaction to popular biographical and historical writing, and perhaps most of all to the celebrated new story by his rival, Samuel Richardson. Fielding's sincere admiration for *Clarissa*, whose final pages were still warm from the presses when *Tom Jones* came out, was apparently hedged by some important qualifications. *Tom Jones* gives several signs, many of them probably added during the last hurried stages of revision just before publication, that it is intended partly as an alternative, on both moral and aesthetic grounds, to the melancholy tale of Richardson's heroine.[10] Fielding's exuberant and optimistic Christianity causes him to reject the fate of a Clarissa Harlowe for his own heroine, who suffers some of the same torments from family and suitors. Blifil is clearly Sophie's Solmes, and the machinations of Squire Western and his sister, though ludicrous, are hardly less threatening to her welfare than the sinister maneuverings of the Harlowes against Clarissa. But Sophie Western is projected as stronger than Richardson's heroine, tougher, more resilient in her Christian resolution and thus more sufficient as a model of female virtue. She is very convincing when she tells Lady Bellaston that she would never under any circumstances "run away with any Man" (15.3), not even Tom Jones himself, whom she loves. The ironic echo of Clarissa's indecisiveness, which leads to her abduction by the rakish villain of Richardson's novel, is unmistakable. Tom, meanwhile, emerges as a kind of inverted Lovelace, low-born and good-natured, and he is hated by the Westerns as the supposed cause of Sophie's escape from their domination.

There are other echoes of *Clarissa*, one of the most important of which raises the aesthetic issues that separate the two novels and their authors while it also comments quite directly on what Fielding thought of as the most deplorable tendencies of all popular biographical and historical writing. *Clarissa*, a purported collection of letters, is almost a disguised fiction on the order of so many familiar narratives of the day, whereas *Tom Jones* extols its own artfulness as much as it does the good fortunes of its characters and the ideals of Christian virtue they are intended to promote. In the introductory chapter of book two, Fielding pauses and carefully differentiates his own art of selection and shaping from the ineptitude, or at least the misguided practice, of the "painful and voluminous Historian, who to preserve the Regularity of his Series thinks himself obliged to fill up as much Paper with the Detail of Months and Years in which nothing remarkable happened, as he employs upon those notable Æras when the greatest Scenes have been transacted on the human Stage." The implication is that the ordering, interpretive faculty of such a "painful and voluminous Historian" is diminished below what the artist ought to possess, that the sometimes erratic and often trivial facts of the life rendered have gained power over the author's own intelligence; and there is the further hint that, as Howard Anderson has observed, the "apparent inclusiveness of such a work as Richardson's" is only "an illusion" anyway[11]—a naive illusion, and perhaps even a falsifying one. The reader of *Tom Jones* will be subjected to no falsifying and trivializing mannerisms such as those typifying the works of Richardson and other historical writers. He will find "some Chapters very short, and others altogether as long; some that contain only the Time of a single Day, and others that comprise Years"; he should not be surprised, says the narrator, if the history "sometimes seems to stand still, and sometimes to fly." And he will always know that the materials of the narrative are under the complete control of the author, instead of the other way around.

The references to *Clarissa*, along with Fielding's transformations of conventions assimilated from many modes of popular narrative, are all intended to distinguish *Tom Jones* as an alternative form of novelistic writing. Fielding's narrative is at once a comic romance, an ironic criminal biography, a record of domestic travels, a history of soldiering adventures, a novelistic love story, an account of the conversion of a wayward roguish fellow to the pious knowledge of his true Christian duty. It is an amazingly eclectic work which, however, purposefully subsumes all that it borrows as elements in an independent and original, deliberately artificial construction. Sometimes, as in the case of the playful projection of Tom as a "criminal" hero or the exaggerated complications of the love story, the allusions to familiar narrative conventions become contrastive devices assisting in the overt display of Fielding's thoughtful ingenuity of design. In other words, the author of *Tom Jones* turns the modes of popular narrative upon themselves in the enterprise of proclaiming his formalistic version of fiction as self-conscious art. It was not simply the label "comic-epic-poem in prose" which declared the newness, the importance, or the aesthetic pretensions of his work.

Fielding is, indeed, at greater pains in *Tom Jones* to affirm the supremacy of art than he is in *Joseph Andrews*. Much has been written about the many deliberate artifices of his second novel, so much in fact that the discussion of such subjects has become redundant. Critics have been particularly fond of exploring the intricacies of the most conspicuous instances of Fielding's technical brilliance: the multiple roles of his narrator as moralist, as critic and literary theorist, and as manipulative storyteller; the contrapuntal playing of character against character; the neat symmetries of his balanced design, with its dual plotting; the perfect turning of the arches of his novel's structure as they are exposed in the movement from the Paradise Hall episodes of the first six books to the adventures on the road occupying the middle section of the narrative to the sequence of Tom's experiences in London as detailed in books thirteen to eighteen. The list could go on. Possibly no other early work of English fiction has been so thoroughly dissected, analyzed, and speculated about by serious readers seeking to explain the accessible facts as well as the elusive magic of its achievement as art. What still needs emphasizing, however, as a way of underscoring the remarkable originality of what Fielding achieved in his time, is the absolute harmony of what we might call the intellectual or outer form of his novel with its emotional or inner form; that is, the integral relationship between the superstructure of authorial commentary, especially as it figures in the prefatory chapters, and the complexly plotted love story by which the author reveals and at last fulfills his comic vision.

The whole novel of *Tom Jones* is, one might say, all about love. If the hero is to have happiness, he must learn the value of prudence; he must, as Martin C. Battestin has put it, understand that true wisdom, or *sophia*, is something as much to be seen, desired, and possessed as the girl he adores.[12] It is in turn the person of Sophia Western, who actually embodies an unblemished ideal of beauty, wisdom, and moral perfection, that Tom loves and then learns to pursue through the extraordinarily complicated series of adventures the author devises for him; every reader is familiar with the pattern of coincidences and reversals by which Fielding both frustrates and advances his hero's desire for the heroine. The story eventually concludes when Tom, chastened by his experience, arrives at true wisdom, whereupon his good nature and new moral maturity are rewarded with the hand of Sophia and together they retire to wedded bliss in the country.

The entire movement of the plot of *Tom Jones* is an elaborate contrivance which expresses the author's affection for his characters and his admiration for what they represent. The resolution fulfills both his affection and his admiration, simultaneously giving festive celebration to the perfected harmony of his own fond creation. If we grant that Fielding is providential author and manipulator of the world of his novel, then his role may be understood (like that of the narrator in *Joseph Andrews*) as analogous to that of God in the real world, and his act of creation as an act of love comparable to Divine love. The form that the story takes, as an organic whole, is an emblematic expression of the author's own benevolent vision of an ordered moral universe with intricate and inextricably related parts and an intelligible system of rewards and punishments. Story and author, creation and creator, are united, merged, synonymous. The fact that Fielding's narrator is at once part of his story in the progressive unfolding of its development, and removed from it into a position of omniscience, certifies the perfect unity of conception he means to project. The author's moral vision of the fulfillment of Christian love, and his artistic vision of harmonious order in a fictional world, are one.

The narrator himself repeatedly emphasizes the essential connections between his story as creation and his own function as artist-creator. The most deeply revealing of such gestures may be found in the discourse "Of Love" (6.1), which comes at a strategic place in the carefully arched structure of the novel, shortly after the introduction of Sophie and her antithesis, Molly Seagrim (in book 4). The chapter begins by dismissing the assumptions of freethinkers and Hobbeseans, those philosophers who have discovered that "there is no such Passion [as love] in the human Breast," "no G——d" in the universe, and no such qualities as "Virtue or Goodness really existing in Human Nature." It then proceeds insistently to affirm the reality of all these things—love, God, virtue, and goodness—and to proclaim their unity with one another. Before concluding, the narrator pauses for a deliberate manipulative gesture directed at the audience: "Examine your Heart, my good Reader," he says, "and resolve whether you do believe these Matters with me. If you do, you may now proceed to their Exemplification in the following Pages."

We know, of course, that the narrator is Fielding's creation just as surely as—in the convention of this novel—the fictional world is the narrator's creation. But we should not be led by our own critical acuity into distrusting his voice, playful though he is at our expense sometimes. The discourse "Of Love" must be accepted as an effort to bring into sharp focus what has already been established as the central thematic issue of the novel. We have long before this time learned that Allworthy exemplifies purified Christian love and benevolence acted out in an Edenic place named Paradise Hall, that Blifil is a representation of consuming self-love, or excessive prudence. We have met Sophie as she is brought forward with a flourish (in 4.2), the fanfare provided by the sweet singing of birds. "From Love proceeds your Music," Fielding says of these "feather'd Choristers of Nature," and "to Love it returns." And we have watched Tom lavish his affections upon Molly, where (we are told) they are "not very judiciously placed" (4.6). The chapter "Of Love" actually unites the sensibilities and the judgment of the narrator with the most crucial facts of the story as it has already unfolded and as it is to develop from this point forward, while it urges the value of human love as something deified, as the means of human approach to the harmony of divine love. That, it would seem, is the point of the ironic reference to the freethinkers. Furthermore, this particular essay, even more emphatically and substantially than most of the other introductory chapters to the various books of *Tom Jones*, urges our understanding of the author's absolute knowledge of and governance over the world he has created, a world whose value he alone can define completely and whose perfected order is the product of his moral imagination. Nothing could be more conspicuously artful than such maneuvers as we find in this revealing chapter, which closes with the author's entrapment of the reader within the web of his own vision.

Each of the prefatory discourses is designed to further the reader's recognition that the novel, as practiced by this author, is an art form; the theorizing about the act of creation itself at once enforces the reader's sense of the artfulness of the story proper and commands his imaginative participation in its creation, or at least in the creation of its meaning.[13] As

Wolfgang Iser and John Preston have both observed so very tellingly, the reader is manipulated by Fielding's narrator to the point that he almost becomes part of the novel itself, one of the author's own creations.[14] We may even extend this argument further to say that Fielding's intention is to assimilate his audience as part of the completed order of his overall design. The narrator's manipulation of the reader is often ironically playful and just as often acknowledged for what it is. But it is also profoundly serious, for it proclaims the artist's responsibility to impose order upon the disordered facts of life while confronting the members of his audience with the meaning of that order, even engaging them in the process of its discovery and verification.

The mannerisms of *Tom Jones* imply a kind of authorial tyranny over the fictional world, and indeed the omniscient author convention itself has sometimes been denounced by critics of the Jamesian school because it is so blatantly domineering and manipulative. Fielding's repeated hints concerning the providential role of his narrator actually disarm the arguments of even the most contentious Jamesian partisans of the invisible author, and demand that his novel be accepted and understood in the terms of its own conventions. Nothing is accidental in this "great Creation" (10.1). The narrator, we learn very early, has set himself over his world, his characters, and his readers "for their own Good only," and furthermore, he declares, "as I am, in reality, the Founder of a new Province of Writing, so I am at liberty to make what Laws I please therein. And these Laws, my Readers, whom I consider as my Subjects, are bound to believe in and to obey" (2.1).

Fielding is often winking when he proffers such gestures, as he is here, but there is almost always a deep urgency of purpose lurking behind the jocular manner. Such remarks are really addressed directly to the contemporary assumption, voiced in scores of prefaces to works of fiction avowed and unavowed, that prose narrative ought simply to repeat the "plain truth" of life without the embellishments of art. It is in an earlier portion of this same chapter, just prior to the proclamation of his reign over the world of his novel, that Fielding alludes to Richardson as a "painful and voluminous Historian" whose manner of storytelling denies the principle of artistic construction and whose surreptitious approach to his fiction obscures the workings of the imagination. Here Fielding also renews his criticism, begun in *Shamela* and *Joseph Andrews*, of the writers of autobiographical apologies like Colley Cibber's. The juxtaposition of the narrator's playfully self-aggrandizing remarks with the sharp allusions to Richardson and the Cibberian apologists helps to define *Tom Jones* as an articulated history that is reflexive and artfully interpretive rather than gratuitously voluminous in the interest of serving some principle of circumstantial truthfulness.

The conception of the narrator in *Tom Jones* is not of a zealous tyrant unable to resist a moralizing impulse to break the reader's illusion that the made world is real—which of course it is not. As benevolent manipulator the narrator is a benign godlike overseer and even monarch of a comic world in which the resolution of all conflict must conform to his vision, since he made the conflicts as well as their resolution. One of the reasons, it seems, that Fielding introduced into his novel such a rich pattern of references to the Jacobites and their cause was to afford him a negative example which would make for implied comparisons to the perfection of his own rule *jure divino* over the world of his novel. The narrator himself suggests the appropriateness of such comparisons in chapter one of book two. The pattern of references to the Jacobites possessed undeniable topical value, and it surely heightened interest in the new novel by the author of the *Jacobite's Journal*, since it supplied fresh opportunities for political commentary that was still timely in 1749, three years after the Battle of Culloden Moor. The episode in book twelve (chap. 12), during which Tom and Partridge meet with the band of gypsies who are ruled by an absolute monarch, is certainly a political parable,[15] yet it ends in a way that may be understood also as an ironic but instructive comment on the role of the narrator in the book. "Indeed," says Fielding, the happiness of the gypsies seems so complete

> that we are aware lest some Advocate for arbitrary Power should hereafter quote the Case of those People, as an Instance of the great Advantages which attend that Government above all others.
>
> And here we will make a Concession, which would not perhaps be expected from us, That no limited Form of Government is capable of rising to the same Degree of Perfection, or of producing the same Benefits to Society, with this. Mankind has never been so happy, as when the greatest Part of the then

known World was under the Dominion of a single Master. . . .
This was the true Æra of the Golden Age, and the only
Golden Age which ever had any Existence, unless in the warm
Imaginations of the Poets, from the Expulsion from *Eden*
down to this Day.

In reality, I know but of one solid Objection to absolute
Monarchy. The only Defect in which excellent Constitution
seems to be the Difficulty of finding any Man adequate to the
Office of an absolute Monarch.

The theory of monarchy *jure divino* advocated by the Jacobites was, in
Fielding's view, the "most pernicious Doctrine, which Priestcraft had ever
the Wickedness or the Impudence to teach" (12.13). But in the comic
world of his novel, Fielding's narrator rules absolutely as creator and gov-
ernor, and a new Golden Age is established at the end of the story, when
Tom and Sophia marry and everyone is happy all round. If we believe
what we are repeatedly told by the author about his role as artist—and as
Christian moralist also—we must concur with him that in an imagined
world, ideally made, absolute rule is both possible and appropriate as the
confirmation of a symbolic design analogous to the divine design by which
good Christians might expect to succeed to a new Golden Age in the
afterlife, and to happiness in this life.[16]
Fielding's frequent calculated references to the Jacobites actually serve
the interests of his novel in many ways. They are never gratuitous. By no
means do such references constitute the only relevance of *Tom Jones* to
contemporary affairs, but we may usefully examine some of them as instances of Fielding's method of merging art and life in his story, as examples of his manner of using familiar materials to develop and underscore the value of his own art. To some extent, he was doubtless reacting
to the many sensational pseudobiographies of figures like Jenny Cameron,
Lord Lovat, and Prince Charles Edward himself that circulated in the
wake of the 'Forty-Five. These possessed all the falsifying weaknesses that
Fielding found so objectionable in contemporary biographical writing
generally. Ronald Paulson has argued that *Tom Jones* deliberately reflects
the persistent agitation over the Jacobite threat and its romantic leader
the Young Pretender so as to squelch it, to expose the whirling rumors
and active popular mythologizing it perpetuated as fraudulent, a formless

species of false history. The rumor-mongering that surrounds and afflicts Tom Jones, says Paulson, becomes a kind of false history imagined by the characters in the novel, to which Fielding as author of the whole opposes his own alternative version of true history.[17] If Paulson is correct, and his argument certainly seems plausible given the continued currency of the subject of Jacobitism and Fielding's strong feelings about it, then the popular works of fiction treating famous rebels are simply very concrete examples of such false history, and thus likely objects of Fielding's attention in the composition of his novel.

We go too far if we argue, as Anthony Kearney does, that *Tom Jones*, by pursuing the themes of imposture and usurpation, systematically allegorizes the rebellion of 1745.[18] Such an argument narrowly limits the sweep of Fielding's range of interests and simplifies the artistic complications of his novel. But there is every reason to suppose the author of *Tom Jones* quite willing to have his readers discover meaningful connections between his fiction and the real world of 1745 and 1746, and he even encourages such speculation in the interest of developing his artful design and furthering his moral purpose. In book eleven, chapters two to six, he offers an extended comic allusion to the 'Forty-Five which greatly amplifies the significance of the main characters of the novel and helps to clarify the meaning of their experience as they journey toward their fulfillment. The landlord at the inn where Sophia and Mrs. Fitzpatrick stop on their way between Upton and London is a "very sagacious Fellow" (11.2) who stupidly mistakes the heroine for Jenny Cameron and then pompously relates to her all the latest news of the Rebellion.[19] The silly officiousness of this fool is clearly designed to throw ridicule on the Stuart cause, as is the implied comparison of Sophia's character to that of the Young Pretender's Scottish mistress. But Fielding actually develops a number of complicated ironies. The comparison of Sophia and Jenny Cameron also serves to underline the purity of Fielding's heroine, and simultaneously, the association of Sophia and Tom with great figures in public life tends to elevate their status in the novel. Sophia's beauty is projected (so to speak) on a national scale, and her handsome lover is a prince of fellows, though his real claim to his inheritance is even more doubtful than the Chevalier's. The irony is enriched by the fact of Tom's role, temporary though it is, as a soldier for the Hanoverians.

We will recall that the Reverend Archibald Arbuthnot had told the story of Jenny Cameron in a lengthy volume of pseudobiographical *Memoirs* (1746). It is doubtful that Fielding knew Arbuthnot's work, but in five chapters he was able to do something more vital and interesting with the subject of the Pretender's mistress than the author of the *Memoirs* could do in some 280 pages. The episode at the inn, because it ironically places the adventures of Sophia and Tom in the context of a controversial quest for a new order on so grand a scale as the Jacobites conceived, actually anticipates the entire subsequent development of *Tom Jones*. The last one-third of Fielding's "true" history leads toward the completion of his vast design, the fulfillment of what we might call his new mythology, in the perfect establishment of a simple order brought about by the author's radical (or violent, as it were) transformation of the fictional world and founded on the principles represented in his emblematic pictures of a family of love. As the final books of the story unfold, Tom undertakes to join Mr. Nightingale and Nancy Miller in marriage and bring happiness to Mrs. Miller's "little Family of Love" (14.6). In the end, after the author has sunk his wayward hero to the depths of the chastening misery he suffers in prison, he brings him to the plateau of self-knowledge and personal prudence, rescues him, and unites him blissfully with Sophia. Theirs is to be, we are told, a future of love and fertile joy, and the new happiness they possess radiates outward to everyone so that "there is not a Neighbour, a Tenant, or a Servant," says the narrator in closing the novel, "who doth not most gratefully bless the Day when Mr. *Jones* was married to his *Sophia*" (18.13).

The ideal of the family of love is as important in *Tom Jones* as it is in *Jonathan Wild* or *Joseph Andrews*, and Fielding's pattern of allusions to the Jacobites helps to underscore its value. It is not mere happenstance that Fielding makes his crude bumpkin Squire Western a Tory, a Jacobite, and a tyrannical father. Through the character of Western he draws an analogy between the Jacobites' "pernicious Doctrine" of rule *jure divino*, by absolute authority, and the at times maniacal despotism of parents in their governance over their sons and daughters. One side of the analogy defines and illuminates the other. Tyranny is tyranny wherever it may be found, and it is always injurious to happiness. The family, like the state, is a social organism, though the two organisms are in different spheres of human action; in either sphere, when "absolute Power" is "vested in the Hands" of one who is deficient in the qualification of virtue and Christian love, the result is "likely to be attended" with a great "Degree of Evil" (12.12). It is worth noticing, by way of commenting on Fielding's political instincts as manifested in *Tom Jones*, that the Jacobites suffer more by the analogy with Western than the squire himself, whose buffoonery and country crudity actually ridicule the Stuarts and their cause. They are further reduced, through an oblique but tellingly ironic allusion, when Sophia (the Jenny Cameron of the landlord's imagination in book eleven) is seen at the end of the novel presiding over the marriage feast "like a Queen receiving Homage, or rather like a superiour Being receiving Adoration from all around her," adoration freely given and not exacted (18.13).

The way in which *Tom Jones* exploits and transforms its author's personal preoccupation with the Jacobite controversy is a measure not only of the ingenuity of its composition, but of Fielding's intense desire that the audience for his fiction should understand and respond to its validity as a carefully ordered interpretation of real life and moral experience, not a mere re-creation of the apparent surfaces of human existence.[20] The uses of Jacobitism actually help to focus the reader's sense of that order. The author of *Tom Jones* is at once god and ruler *jure divino* of the imaginary world of his creation, the sole source and the absolute instrument of its perfection. In the end, the unity of his story with his own role and vision is affirmed as complete. By his arrangement Sophia Western, always the favorite child of his imagination (16.6), now rules like a divine queen of love, the absolute monarch *jure divino* of a new Golden Age of happiness and harmony. Through her the hero of the novel also rules, because his own character is at last united with the ideal she represents. The final exaltation of Tom and Sophia is a matter of natural expectation and probability, a part of the certain order of things, in the symbolic fictional world. It is not difficult to discover the direct application of this resolution to actual life in the natural world as Fielding interprets it. His readers may not expect to enjoy so grand and complete a triumph of goodness—the comfortable doctrine of virtue rewarded in this life, we will remember, simply "is not true" (15.1). But Tom and his bride are projected not only as expressions of an abstract moral ideal; they are exemplary figures whose experience reveals the way to moral stability, tranquility, and happiness in a demonstrably troubled reality. In the providential universe for which this novel serves as analogue, the practice of Christian love and the pursuit of true wisdom bring hope of the immediate joys of harmonious living while they also assure fulfillment of the divine promise of eternal rewards in paradise. There can be no doubt that many readers in 1749 would have clearly recognized the profoundly serious message of ebullient Christian optimism dramatized in the artfully devised comic history of *Tom Jones*.

The manner of Fielding's fusion of the seemingly disparate themes of Jacobitism and Christian love in his great masterpiece is resourceful to say the least, if it is not downright magical, and the joining of these themes enforces some rich multiple meanings upon the novel's resolution, making it much more than just another routine happy ending to a rollicking comic story. By radically fictionalizing the issue of Jacobitism as an ironic source of moral truth, Fielding reveals the powers of his ordering intelligence and certifies that the prerogatives of the novelist, as artist and moralist and chronicler of human life, are not bounded by the restrictions of biographical or historical literalness.

※※※

Tom Jones is the triumphant achievement of its author's genius, and in an important way it represents the culmination of the development of the novel as a new form during the critical decade of the 1740s. Fielding's story does all the things so many other fictions attempted to do also. It excites the imagination of its audience and verifies its own truthfulness by referring to topical issues and familiar events; it punishes wickedness, rewards goodness, and in the process offers an interesting moral history of ordinary people whose private experience as Christian heroes gains public value by the way in which it reflects prevailing cultural and moral ideals. *Tom Jones* does these things and more, solidifying the dimensions of the novel as a species of imaginative literature, all in a way quite unprecedented except in Fielding's own *Joseph Andrews*.

Many years had to pass before the novel earned a literary reputation even approaching its modern exaltation as what D. H. Lawrence called "the one bright book of life." But by the end of the 1740s, the conspicuous example of Fielding's works to date had already made it abundantly clear that English literature was enriched by the emergence of a new and definable form of artful expression. Fielding's energetic advocacy in his novels, unique as they are in their self-conscious expressions of his own vision and his own sense of purpose as a writer, can only have helped to enlarge the reputations of the two other great novelistic innovators of his decade, Samuel Richardson and Tobias Smollett, by encouraging the accurate location of their works, too, in a context of art. Together these three storytellers ensured the future of the form in which they chose to work. They were the great seminal novelists of their decade, indeed of their century. But it was the author of *Joseph Andrews* and *Tom Jones* who first demanded the world's lasting acknowledgment that a work of novelistic fiction might be worthy to stand alongside such triumphs of the literary imagination as the plays of Shakespeare or the poems of Alexander Pope. As we have seen, there were many who were ready to applaud his work, and he did not have long to await the exact acknowledgment he called for, in terms as precise as he could possibly have wished. His gifted admirer and disciple Francis Coventry, in the "Epistle Dedicatory" to the third edition (1752) of his *History of Pompey the Little*, pronounced words of praise whose echo can still be heard, and not faintly, from the pages of countless scholarly articles and books: "No story that I know of," wrote Coventry, "was ever invented with more happiness, or conducted with more art and management, than that of *Tom Jones*."

Notes

Chapter I

1. D. H. Lawrence, *Selected Literary Criticism*, ed. Anthony Beal (New York: Viking Compass Books, 1966), p. 105.

2. It is one of the ironies of literary history, however, that the intellectual movements of the seventeenth century actually converged with the social currents of the early eighteenth century, enabling prose fiction to develop its narrative modes and thus to become the apparent chronicler of real life. See chapter 1 of Ian Watt, *The Rise of the Novel: Studies in Defoe, Richardson, and Fielding* (London: Chatto and Windus, 1957), for the best available discussion of this subject.

3. Francis Coventry, *The History of Pompey the Little; or, The Life and Adventures of a Lap-Dog*, 3rd ed. (London, 1752), dedication. For a full and detailed account of the reputation of eighteenth-century English fiction, see John Tinnon Taylor, *Early Opposition to the English Novel: The Popular Reaction from 1760 to 1830* (New York: King's Crown Press, 1943).

4. There seems to have been a ready market for all of the hackwork the booksellers could stimulate their hirelings to produce. Chapbook lives and *6d.* pamphlet fiction sold well across the counters of book shops, along with novels and feigned voyages, memoirs, and histories priced at *2s. 6d.* or so. The London circulating libraries, originally opposed by the trade as a threat to their vital interests, had grown from one in 1740 to at least seven by 1746, and were beginning to prove profitable as almost guaranteed customers for pulp fiction; see Alan Dugald McKillop, "English Circulating Libraries, 1725–1750," *The Library*, 4th ser. 14 (1934): 477–85.

5. The first part of *Pamela*, published in November of 1740, ran through five London editions before the end of 1741, and *Joseph Andrews* was in its third edition only fourteen months after it first appeared in February of 1742. *Clarissa* reached a fourth edition within three years of the initial publication of its first two volumes in December 1747. *Tom Jones* was in such demand that copies could not be readied quickly enough, and four editions were required before a year was out. The suc-

cess of *Roderick Random* did not equal that of *Tom Jones*, but was nonetheless very considerable; three editions saw their way through the presses between 1748 and 1750. It is true that an edition, or an impression, rarely exceeded 2,000 copies, but the sales of the major novels are still very impressive for the times.

6. Robert D. Mayo, *The English Novel in the Magazines, 1740–1815* (Evanston, Ill.: Northwestern University Press, 1962), should be consulted on the whole question of early fiction and the magazines.

7. In some important early statements, Dryden (*Essay of Dramatic Poesy*, 1668), Dennis (*Impartial Critick*, 1693), and Temple ("Of Poetry," in *Miscellanies,* 1701) drew comparisons between modern prose romance and the ancient epic. With these critics, however, long prose fiction fared badly, and the comparison proved rather damaging than otherwise. See Joseph Bunn Heidler, *The History, from 1700–1800, of English Criticism of Prose Fiction*, University of Illinois Studies in Language and Literature, vol. 12, no. 2 (Urbana: University of Illinois Press, 1928), chap. 3.

8. Although established authors were often well treated and well rewarded (Andrew Millar's behavior to Fielding was exemplary), most fiction writers were overworked and underpaid by the booksellers, who exploited their often meager talents. See Harry Ransom, "The Rewards of Authorship in the Eighteenth Century," *University of Texas Studies in English* (1938), pp. 47–66; and Arthur S. Collins, *Authorship in the Days of Johnson* (New York: Dutton, 1929), especially chaps. 1, 2, and 4.

9. Arthur Jerrold Tieje long ago identified three considerations, all deriving from popular prejudices, which motivated writers to protest their truthfulness: "the wickedness of lying, the utility of verified narrative, and the pleasure which truth affords to a reader." See "A Peculiar Phase of the Theory of Realism in Pre-Richardsonian Fiction," *PMLA* 28 (1913): 215. For a writer like Defoe, of course, the distinction between truthfulness and lying, the relationship between the verifiable and the fictional, was never so simple as Tieje's remark would suggest. For a fine discussion of Defoe's attitudes concerning this matter, see the appendix to G. A. Starr's *Defoe and Casuistry* (Princeton: Princeton University Press, 1971).

10. *Romances and Narratives by Daniel Defoe*, ed. George A. Aitken (London, 1895), 3:ix.

11. The spectrum of French works available in translation during the early years of the eighteenth century is impressive. For example, between 1700 and 1740 English buyers required more than twenty editions of Fénelon's great didactic romance, *Télémaque*. Montesquieu's spy-letter tale, the *Lettres persanes* (1721), immediately enjoyed at least four English editions of its first translation (1722). In the 1730s the eleven parts of Marivaux's sentimental epistolary novel *La Vie de Marianne* (1736–41) began to appear in England almost simultaneously with their release in France. *Marianne*'s sequential publication was still in process when *Pamela* came out in 1740, and Marivaux's fame had meanwhile been enhanced by the public response to an English rendering (in 1735–37) of his bourgeois "memoirs" of *Le Paysan parvenu* (1734–36). Likewise, translations of Prévost's novels of enslaving passion emerged in the 1730s. The various volumes of *Le Philosophe an-*

glais, ou l'histoire de Mr. Cleveland (1731–39) began English publication in 1731, and seven years later the first installment of his *Mémoires et avantures d'un homme de qualité* (1728–31) appeared in translation. LeSage's *Gil Blas* was issued in various forms at least four times between 1716 and 1735, and four more editions were called for in 1742, 1744, 1746, and 1749. In the first half of the century, editions of an English collection of Scarron's *Comical Works* appeared five times, including once in 1741.

12. See Martin C. Battestin, *The Moral Basis of Fielding's Art: A Study of Joseph Andrews* (Middletown, Conn.: Wesleyan University Press, 1959), chap. 2, for full discussion of the origins of the conception of the good man as hero. Battestin is especially convincing on the contributions of latitudinarian divines.

13. See Bernard F. Huppé, "The Gothic Hero: Chrétien's *Erec*," *The Twelfth Century: Acta* 2 (1975): 1–19; and idem, "The Concept of the Hero in the Early Middle Ages," in *Concepts of the Hero in the Middle Ages and the Renaissance*, ed. Norman T. Burns and Christopher J. Reagan (Albany: SUNY Press, 1975), pp. 1–26. See also Burton O. Kurth, *Milton and Christian Heroism: Biblical Epic Themes and Forms in Seventeenth-Century England*, University of California Publications: English Studies, no. 20 (1959); and R. A. Sayce, *The French Biblical Epic in the Seventeenth Century* (Oxford: Clarendon Press, 1955).

14. Watt, *The Rise of the Novel*, p. 244.

15. The retirement theme as it occurs in early novels receives very full discussion in two useful essays: Jeffrey L. Duncan, "The Rural Ideal in Eighteenth-Century Fiction," *Studies in English Literature, 1500–1900* 8 (1968): 517–35; and A. S. Knowles, Jr., "Defoe, Swift, and Fielding: Notes on the Retirement Theme," in *Quick Springs of Sense: Studies in the Eighteenth Century*, ed. Larry S. Champion (Athens: University of Georgia Press, 1974), pp. 121–36.

16. *Selected Letters of Samuel Richardson*, ed. John Carroll (Oxford: Clarendon Press, 1964), p. 162.

17. There are no contemporary estimates of the numbers of middle-class readers. Only one estimate exists, according to Ian Watt (*The Rise of the Novel*, p. 36), for the size of the entire eighteenth-century reading public; that one came late in the century, when Edmund Burke guessed at a total of 80,000—a small number indeed, when we consider that in the 1790s England's population exceeded six million. The whole reading public must have been much smaller prior to 1750, and though middle-class folk made up an increasingly large segment of it, they themselves could not have been very numerous. For interesting discussions of the makeup of the eighteenth-century reading audience see, besides Watt (chap. 2), Helen Sard Hughes, "The Middle-Class Reader and the English Novel," *JEGP* 25 (1926): 362–78; and chap. 2 of Richard Altick's *The English Common Reader* (Chicago: University of Chicago Press, 1957).

18. "The 'Mob' in Eighteenth-Century English Caricature," *Eighteenth-Century Studies* 12 (1978): 49. For a discussion of Walpole as a subject in early eighteenth-century prose fiction, see my article, "Portraits of a Monster: Robert Walpole and Early English Prose Fiction," *Eighteenth-Century Studies*, 14 (1981): 406–31.

19. Official reaction to the crime rate was virtually limited to the passage of laws increasing the number of capital offenses. Basil Williams reports that during the reign of George II that number rose to 160, and included such minor offenses as sheep-stealing, cutting down a cherry tree, consorting with gypsies, and petty larceny. See *The Whig Supremacy 1714–1760* (Oxford: Clarendon Press, 1939), p. 60.

20. See George's *London Life in the Eighteenth Century* (New York: Harper Torchbooks, 1965), especially chaps. 1, 2, and 5; and Plumb's *England in the Eighteenth Century* (London: Penguin Books, 1950). Plumb's descriptions of the harshness of town life are particularly graphic.

21. Defoe first used these words in the *Review*, vol. 8, no. 75 (Saturday, September 15, 1711), but repeated them in *Moll Flanders*.

22. For full discussion of these problems as they affected contemporary life see M. Dorothy George's *England in Transition: Life and Work in the Eighteenth Century* (London: Routledge, 1931); and also her *London Life in the Eighteenth Century*.

23. See Martin C. Battestin, *The Providence of Wit: Aspects of Form in Augustan Literature and the Arts* (Oxford: Clarendon Press, 1974). See also the article by Aubrey Williams, "Interpositions of Providence and the Design of Fielding's Novels," *South Atlantic Quarterly* 70 (1971): 265–86. Battestin's study in particular has been severely criticized; see, for example, C. J. Rawson's review essay called "Order and Misrule: Eighteenth-Century Literature in the 1970's," *ELH* 42 (1975): 471–505.

24. The origins of sentimental benevolence as a movement are complexly rooted in the late seventeenth and early eighteenth centuries. The very best discussion of the movement as it developed and as it affected eighteenth-century life and literature is Ronald Crane's "Suggestions toward a Genealogy of the 'Man of Feeling,'" in *The Idea of the Humanities*, ed. Wayne C. Booth (Chicago: University of Chicago Press, 1967), 1:188–213. Donald Greene's recent article entitled "Latitudinarianism and Sensibility: The Genealogy of the 'Man of Feeling' Reconsidered," *Modern Philology* 75 (1977): 159–83, attempts to discredit Crane, but is not very convincing.

25. It is true, of course, that the plight of England's disadvantaged people was still grim in the 1740s. As George points out in *London Life* (chap. 5), the poor laws, though they had improved since the turn of the century, were still repressive; and the charity schools, while they did offer the poor an education, conspired to oppress those they served by teaching them only enough to prepare them for the meanest work. But such social advances as were made were real, though tentative, and the humane spirit which promoted them was genuine.

26. Christopher Hill very perceptively treats the story of the bourgeois maiden Clarissa Harlowe in just these terms, and in addition provides the best discussion of the social conflict itself that I know. See "Clarissa Harlowe and Her Times," *Essays in Criticism* 5 (1955): 315–40.

27. John J. Richetti, in *Popular Fiction before Richardson: Narrative Patterns 1700–*

1739 (Oxford: Clarendon Press, 1969), gives a fine account of how this narrative situation (or fable) figured importantly in novels published between 1700 and 1739 and apparently made a powerful ideological appeal to readers.

Chapter II

1. See Gaylord R. Haas, "The English Novel from 1731 to 1740: A Decade Study," Ph.D. dissertation, Northwestern University, 1966, for discussion of the heroic romance in the 1730s. Thomas Philip Haviland's 1931 University of Pennsylvania Ph.D. dissertation, "The 'Roman de longue Haleine' on English Soil," is useful for its broader and more comprehensive account of the heroic romance in England, but has little to say about the second quarter of the eighteenth century.

2. A few heroic romances may have been available in circulating libraries; see McKillop, "English Circulating Libraries, 1725–1750," pp. 477–85. Joseph Collyer's list, as recorded in the *London Daily Advertiser* for November 17, 1741, included the previous decade's editions of *Cléopâtre* and *Cassandre*.

3. The title was now *Celenia and Adrastes; with the Delightful History of Hyempsal, King of Numidia*.

4. I quote from a modern photofacsimile reprint of the first English edition (1695) of Abbé Le Bossu's work (Gainesville, Fla.: Scholars' Facsimiles and Reprints, 1970), p. 15. Le Bossu agreed generally with Boileau's argument (in *Art poétique*, 1674) concerning the importance of the moral in epic poetry, but in his own *Treatise* he heavily emphasized the moral content as a major determinant of form. The comments by Boileau and Le Bossu bear in part upon an important French literary form of the latter years of the seventeenth century, the biblical epic, to which didactic romances like Fénelon's *Télémaque* are related.

5. It is interesting to note, however, that of the five new editions of *Télémaque* published in the 1740s, three appeared within a few months of Fielding's laudatory allusion to Fénelon's work in the preface to his own "prose epic," *Joseph Andrews*.

6. In fact, prior to the late 1720s only one native effort even approached an allegiance to *Télémaque*. It was Jane Barker's pious heroic romance *Exilius* (1715), which claims on its title page to have been "Written After the Manner of Telemachus." *Télémaque* did, of course, exert at least a general influence on the composition of *Joseph Andrews*. And in *Occasional Form: Henry Fielding and the Chains of Circumstance* (Baltimore: Johns Hopkins University Press, 1975), J. Paul Hunter has suggested that Fénelon's work must be counted a considerable influence in the background of *Tom Jones* (see chap. 6).

7. The respective original French titles are: *Les Mille et Une Nuits: contes arabes* (1704–17; translated 1706–17); *Histoire de la sultan de Perse et des vizirs, contes turcs* (1707; translated 1708); *Les Mille et Une Jours: contes persanes* (1710–12; translated and combined with *Turkish Tales*, 1714).

8. The finest and most famous of these is the "Vision of Mirzah," *Spectator* No. 159 (September 1, 1711). In *The Oriental Tale in England in the Eighteenth Century* (New York: Columbia University Press, 1908), Martha Pike Conant reports (p. 118) that, from the first number of the *Tatler* in 1709 to the last number of the *Freeholder* in 1716, the Addisonian periodicals featured a total of twenty-nine orientalized tales or fables.

9. Maynard Mack, in chapter 4 of his study of Pope, *The Garden and the City: Retirement and Politics in the Later Poetry of Pope, 1731–1743* (Toronto: University of Toronto Press, 1969), shows how members of the Augustan literary establishment made extensive use of oriental machinery in their frequent literary attacks on Walpole. It would appear that, by their example, native writers of oriental romance were led in the direction of political satire.

10. This situation would soon change somewhat. Among others, Hawkesworth (in the *Adventurer*, 1752–54, and particularly in his novel *Almoran and Hamet*, 1761); Johnson (*Rasselas*, 1759); Goldsmith (in the *Bee*, 1759, and in his *Citizen of the World*, 1762); Mrs. Sheridan (*Nourjahad*, 1767); and Beckford (*Vathek*, 1786) would turn their talents to the writing of orientalized fiction of a very considerable variety.

11. *Les Mille et Un Quarts d'heure, contes tartars* (1715), translated as *Tartarian Tales* (1716); *Les Aventures merveilleuses de mandarin Fum Hoam: Contes Chinois* (1725), translated as *Chinese Tales* (1725); *Les Sultanes de Guzarate, ou . . . contes moguls* (1732), translated as *Mogul Tales*, serialized in Applebee's *Original Weekly Journal* (June 2, 1733 to June 14, 1735), and published whole in 1736; and the incomplete *Les Mille et Une Heures, contes péruviens* (1733), translated as *Peruvian Tales* (1734), and "completed" by John Kelly, 1739–44. Except for the *Tartarian Tales*, which were unaccountably forgotten until 1759, all of Gueulette's works were reprinted for English readers in the 1740s.

12. Caylus's work was translated in 1745 from *Contes orientaux*, 1743. Ridicule of the oriental vogue was popular throughout its history among French authors, some of whom reached English readers (see Conant, *The Oriental Tale in England*, pp. 211–22).

13. Interestingly enough, the second and final issue of this work in 1762 (under the new title *Nutrebian Tales*) came upon the heels of the very last Jacobite stirrings in Scotland.

14. Ronald Paulson, in his book *Satire and the Novel in Eighteenth-Century England* (New Haven: Yale University Press, 1967), develops this view of the major novelists of the decade, although he does not take Richardson's posture as an antiromancer very seriously. See chapters 3, 4, and 5 of this study. See also Dieter Shulz, "'Novel,' 'Romance,' and Popular Fiction in the First Half of the Eighteenth Century," *Studies in Philology* 70 (1973): 77–91.

15. *Selected Letters of Samuel Richardson*, p. 41. I should emphasize that when the novelists of the 1730s and 1740s sneer at romance, they have in mind not the fine medieval and Renaissance works by writers like Chrétien de Troyes and Sir Philip

Sidney, which were very little known or read at the time, but more recent heroic and (sometimes) oriental romances.

16. For a good general discussion of the nature of Fielding's reaction to this mode of romance, see Arthur L. Cooke, "Henry Fielding and the Writers of Heroic Romance," *PMLA* 62 (1947): 984–94. Henry Knight Miller, in *Henry Fielding's Tom Jones and the Romance Tradition*, ELS Monograph Series, no. 6 (Victoria, B.C.: University of Victoria Press, 1976), sees Fielding's work as standing in a more positive relation to another romance tradition respectably connected to classical epic and predating the massive French heroic romances of the seventeenth century, a tradition that includes the works of such writers as Sidney, Spenser, and Ariosto. Miller is of course right, but his argument by no means diminishes the importance of Fielding's obvious interest in direct responses to recent fashions in prose narrative, including the heroic romance.

17. The only instance of orientalism in the major novels comes in book twelve (chaps. 11–12) of *Tom Jones*, when the hero and Partridge meet a band of gypsies. This episode is really a political parable attacking the Jacobites. See Martin C. Battestin, "*Tom Jones* and 'His *Egyptian* Majesty': Fielding's Parable of Government," *PMLA* 82 (1967): 68–77.

18. For a general consideration of Richardson's novels and their uses of important romance conventions see Margaret Dalziel, "Richardson and Romance," *Journal of the Australasian Universities Language and Literature Association* 33 (1970): 5–24.

19. *The Yale Edition of the Works of Samuel Johnson*, ed. Walter Jackson Bate et al., vol. 3 (New Haven: Yale University Press, 1969), pp. 19–25.

20. See Jean H. Hagstrum, *The Sister Arts: The Tradition of Literary Pictorialism and English Poetry from Dryden to Gray* (Chicago: University of Chicago Press, 1958), chap. 5, for full and excellent discussion of the concept of *la belle nature*.

21. Erwin Panofsky, *Meaning in the Visual Arts: Papers in and on Art History* (Garden City, N.Y.: Doubleday Anchor Books, 1955), p. 266.

22. Sean Shesgreen's book *Literary Portraits in the Novels of Henry Fielding* (De Kalb: Northern Illinois University Press, 1972) gives extended treatment to some of the aspects of characterization in Fielding's novels that I have been discussing.

23. Sheridan Baker, in his article "Henry Fielding's Comic Romances," *Papers of the Michigan Academy of Science, Arts, and Letters* 45 (1960): 411–19, argues that the preface to *Joseph Andrews* actually defines Fielding's work as comic romance, a mode rather different from comic prose epic. Baker sees all of Fielding's fiction as fitting in this mode; in "Fielding's *Amelia* and the Materials of Romance," *Philological Quarterly* 41 (1962): 437–49, he tries to show specifically how the author's last novel departs from the realms of epic and "private history," and follows instead the "unfactual and inquotidian tradition of romance" (p. 438). Baker's interesting but slightly extreme position in some ways anticipates the more recent claims made by Miller (see n. 16, above); it is modified by Homer Goldberg in an essay entitled "Comic Prose Epic or Comic Romance: The Argument of the Preface to *Joseph Andrews*," *Philological Quarterly* 43 (1964): 193–215. Goldberg justifies

Fielding's claim that a "comic Romance is a comic Epic-Poem in Prose"; his book, *The Art of Joseph Andrews* (Chicago: University of Chicago Press, 1969), further elaborates this argument, and develops some of its formal implications.

Chapter III

1. Goldsmith's work first appeared serially (in 1760–61) as "Chinese Letters" in John Newbery's periodical, the *Public Ledger*.

2. These are the three "characters" that Maynard Mack ascribes to the satirist. See "The Muse of Satire," *Yale Review* 41 (1951): 88–90.

3. Considerable controversy has grown up around the problem of who wrote volumes two through eight of *The Turkish Spy*. Probably Marana himself was responsible for most of the work, but additions may well have been made by both French and English writers and compilers. Defoe appears to have done a 1718 *Continuation*, which was afterward made part of the eighth volume. The latter conjecture is not supported by Defoe bibliographers, but see Joseph Tucker, "On the Authorship of *The Turkish Spy: An État Present*," *Papers of the Bibliographical Society of America* 52 (1958): 34–47, and William H. McBurney, "The Authorship of *The Turkish Spy*," *PMLA* 72 (1957): 915–35. See also Arthur J. Weitzman's introduction to the modern edition of *Letters Writ by a Turkish Spy* (London: Routledge and Kegan Paul, 1970).

4. The *Lettres persanes* first appeared in English translation in 1722, with new editions in 1730, 1731, and (almost simultaneously with the last edition of Lyttelton's book) 1736. As one bit of evidence that Montesquieu and Lyttelton remained current in the 1740s, a "fifth edition" of *The Persian Letters Continued* (1735) appeared in 1744. This is a spurious "second volume" of Lyttelton's work, offered by an anonymous Tory interested (like Lyttelton) in seeing the downfall of Walpole, but still more interested (unlike Lyttelton) in seeing the renewal of absolute monarchy in England.

5. After its moderate initial success in the late 1740s, the work ran through eight or nine more English editions during the last half of the eighteenth century, at least two of them in the 1750s; and in its native country its success was immense. See F. C. Green, *French Novelists, Manners and Ideas from the Renaissance to the Revolution* (New York: Appleton, 1929), pp. 140–42, for some details beyond those offered here.

6. Mme d'Aulnoy's work was translated as *Memoirs of the Court of England* in 1707, and it enjoyed a second edition in 1708. The popularity in England of the *Memoirs* and a number of other French works like it seems to have impelled English writers to imitation. The real genesis of this kind of writing, however, was probably in the tradition of anecdotic literature, or *anecdota*, extending all the way back into antiquity and including among its earliest manifestations the *Deipnosophistae* of Athenaeus and the *Lives* of Plutarch.

7. These would include Eliza Haywood's *Memoirs of a Certain Island Adjacent to the Kingdom of Utopia* (1725–26) and her *Secret History of the . . . Court of Caramania* (1727). Of the most successful among early native secret histories, only *Queen Zarah* was reprinted in the 1740s, and it may have owed its revival to the long-delayed publication (in 1742) of the Duchess of Marlborough's ghost-written *Account of the Conduct of the Dowager Duchess of Marlborough,, from her First Coming to Court. . . .* Several other biographical works dealing with the duchess appeared in the early 1740s, including Fielding's *Vindication* (1742).

8. The name Astrea was borrowed from an earlier purveyor of scandal, Aphra Behn; Mrs. Manley thus assumed the mantle of her predecessor. See P. B. Anderson, "Mistress Delarivière Manley's Biography," *Modern Philology* 33 (1936): 261–62.

9. Gwendolyn B. Needham's essay, "Mary de la Rivière Manley, Tory Defender," *Huntington Library Quarterly* 12 (May 1949): 253–88, makes a strong historical case for Mrs. Manley's practical effectiveness as a political satirist. On the popularity of the *New Atalantis*, see Joyce M. Horner, *The English Women Novelists and Their Connection with the Feminist Movement (1688–1797)*, Smith College Studies in Modern Languages, no. 11 (1929–30), pp. 10ff.

10. The 1740s featured at least two formidable gatherings of voyages, some of them authentic: Daniel Coxe's *Collection of Voyages and Travels. In Three Parts* (1741); John Green's *New General Collection of Voyages and Travels* (1745), published in four volumes. There were also sensational tales of pirates such as those collected in Capt. Charles Johnson's frequently reprinted *General History of the Robberies and Murders of the Most Notorious Pyrates* (1724; reprinted 1742). Pirate adventures apparently were regarded as stories of roguery on a global scale; in editions of 1734 and after, Johnson combined his work with Capt. Alexander Smith's *History of the Lives and Robberies of the Most Noted Highway-Men, Foot-Pads, House-Breakers, Shop-Lifts and Cheats of Both Sexes in and about Westminster and London* (1713).

11. On the subject of travel literature and imaginary voyages see: Philip Babcock Gove, *The Imaginary Voyage in Prose Fiction* (New York: Columbia University Press, 1941); Edward Godfrey Cox, *A Reference Guide to the Literature of Travel*, 3 vols. (Seattle: University of Washington Press, 1935–49); P. G. Adams, *Travelers and Travel-Liars, 1660–1800* (Berkeley and Los Angeles: University of California Press, 1962); R. W. Frantz, *The English Traveller and the Movement of Ideas, 1660–1732* (Lincoln: University of Nebraska Press, 1943).

12. Translated from *Les Aventures de Beauchine . . . ,* 1732.

13. See Gove, *The Imaginary Voyage*, pp. 262–64. For an interesting discussion of the circumstances of this work's initial publication, see Arundell Esdaile, "Author and Publisher in 1727: 'The English Hermit,'" *The Library*, 4th ser. 2 (1922): 185–92.

14. *Vaughan* was advertised by Osborn in 1740, and had later editions in 1754 and 1760. Chetwood was also the author of two more popular works of this kind: *The Voyages . . . of Capt. Richard Falconer* (1720; "fourth" edition, 1734); *The Voyages*

and Adventures of Captain Robert Boyle (1726; four editions before 1740, with new editions in 1741, 1744, and 1748, followed by as many as twelve more editions between 1750 and 1800).

15. "The English Novel from 1731 to 1740," p. 245.

16. See Lee M. Ellison, "Gaudentio di Lucca: A Forgotten Utopia," *PMLA* 50 (1935): 494–509.

17. The complicated Annesley case receives a thorough airing from Lewis M. Knapp and Lillian de la Torre in "Smollett, Mackercher, and the Annesley Claimant," *English Language Notes* 1 (1963–64): 28–33; and see also Lillian de la Torre, "New Light on Smollett and the Annesley Case," *Review of English Studies*, n.s. 22, no. 87 (1971): 274–81.

18. Popular fascination with the Annesley case lingered on for more than a hundred years. Scott exploited it in *Guy Mannering* (1815); and Charles Reade used it, in conjunction with the equally famous Tichborne trial of 1872, in his *Wandering Heir* (1872).

19. For an account of the real character as opposed to the fictionalized one see John Campbell Major, *The Role of Personal Memoirs in English Biography and Novel* (Philadelphia: University of Pennsylvania Press, 1935), pp. 152–59. One other work dealing with Mrs. Davies appeared in the decade: *The British Heroine; or, An Abridgement of the Life and Adventures of Mrs. Christian Davies, Commonly Call'd Mother Ross . . . by J. Wilson, Formerly a Surgeon in the Army* (1742; second edition, 1744).

20. This was Gerard Penrice's substantial *Genuine and Impartial Account of the Remarkable Life and Vicissitudes of Fortune of Charles Ratcliffe, Esq.* (1747).

21. *Ascanius* reached a second edition in 1747, and was vastly popular after 1750. See P. J. Anderson's entry in *Notes and Queries*, 12th ser. 12 (January–June 1923): 172. Anderson, by the way, suggests that the work is by Ralph Griffiths, the bookseller and founder of the *Monthly Review*, though there is no evidence to support the attribution. The work is assigned to John Burton, M.D., by Samuel Halkett and John Laing, *A Dictionary of Anonymous and Pseudonymous English Literature*, vol. 1 (Edinburgh: Oliver and Boyd, 1926). This attribution is perhaps equally doubtful, for Burton (according to the *Dictionary of National Biography*) not only had connections among the leaders of the 'Forty-Five but also was very probably a Jacobite sympathizer.

The other historical biography treating Prince Charles Edward, entitled *Young Juba; or, The History of the Young Chevalier* (1748), was by a certain M. Mitchell. *Young Juba* is no more skillfully written than *Ascanius*, though it is just as long-winded (at 296 pages, it is in fact 8 pages longer). Mitchell's work slipped into complete oblivion following the publication of its first and only edition.

22. See, for example, Herbert M. Atherton, *Political Prints in the Age of Hogarth: A Study of the Ideographic Representation of Politics* (Oxford: Clarendon Press, 1974), plate nos. 57, 58, 59, 68.

23. There were at least two other fictionalized studies of the same quite re-

markable character: *A Candid and Impartial Account of the Behaviour of Simon Lord Lovat, from the Time His Death-Warrant Was Deliver'd, to the Day of His Execution . . . by a Gentleman Who Attended His Lordship in His Last Moments* (1747); and *Memoirs of the Life of Lord Lovat* (1746), probably by Duncan Forbes.

24. This followed by only a year the publication of his translation of *Gil Blas*. Smollett knew and was probably influenced by both of LeSage's popular works during the time in which he was composing *Roderick Random*. See Lewis M. Knapp, *Tobias Smollett: Doctor of Men and Manners* (Princeton: Princeton University Press, 1949), pp. 104–5.

25. For a full discussion of Smollett's portraits of real people in the Carthagena episodes see the first chapter of George M. Kahrl's study of *Tobias Smollett: Traveler-Novelist* (Chicago: University of Chicago Press, 1945). Kahrl suspects (pp. 22–23) that Oakum may have been partly intended to suggest Adm. Charles Knowles, the victim of Smollett's celebrated attack in the *Critical Review* for May 1758; Knowles had served as captain of a ship during the expedition to Carthagena.

26. Hervey, Queen Caroline's pet minister and one of Walpole's most important allies in the House of Lords, held appointments as Vice-Chamberlain (1730) and Lord Privy Seal (1740). He used cosmetics to cover the ghostly pallor of his thin, ill face. See Martin C. Battestin, "Lord Hervey's Role in *Joseph Andrews*," *Philological Quarterly* 42 (1963): 235–39.

Chapter IV

1. Stauffer, *The Art of Biography in Eighteenth Century England* (Princeton: Princeton University Press, 1941), p. 66.

2. *Romances and Narratives by Daniel Defoe*, 3:ix.

3. Sidney J. Black's article entitled "Eighteenth-Century 'Histories' as a Fictional Mode," *Boston University Studies in English* 1 (1955): 38–44, provides an abbreviated but useful introduction to the whole question of how the popular prejudice in favor of memoir and biography was translated into a moral and artistic rationale by the major novelists of the 1740s. For a very full discussion of the ways in which one of these writers exploited contemporary fascination with history and biography see Robert M. Wallace, "Fielding's Knowledge of History and Biography," *Studies in Philology* 44 (1947): 89–107, and Leo Braudy, *Narrative Form in History and Fiction: Hume, Fielding, and Gibbon* (Princeton: Princeton University Press, 1970), especially chap. 4.

4. Richetti, *Popular Fiction before Richardson*, p. 23.

5. The Ordinaries of Newgate regularly published accounts of the crimes and deaths of famous criminals executed at the prison, and these surely helped to feed public interest in such people and their stories. On the whole question of early

eighteenth-century rogue and criminal biography see Frank W. Chandler, *The Literature of Roguery* (Boston: Houghton Mifflin, 1907), vol. 1, chap. 4.

6. Defoe's *Moll*, by the way, was reprinted in 1741, and *Roxana* had editions in 1740, 1742, and 1745.

7. The first of these two collections appeared in 1728, and kept reappearing with additions until its final edition (1735) contained over 1,300 pages. Smith's collection was originally published in 1713, but in 1734 Capt. Charles Johnson joined it with his own *General History of the Robberies and Murders of the Most Notorious Pyrates* to make a massive volume displaying roguery and criminality the world over. Tales of piracy, incidentally, were much less popular in the 1740s than they had been in earlier years. By this time English readers seem to have become obsessively interested in the criminality that immediately threatened them on the streets and in the countryside.

8. The 1740s offered such cheap pamphlet lives as the following: *The Cruel Mistress, Being the Genuine Trial of E[liza]. B[ranch]. and Her Daughter* (1740); and *The Life of Henry Simms, Alias Young Gentleman Harry* (1747).

9. "Henry Fielding's *The Female Husband*: Fact and Fiction," *PMLA* 74 (1959): 224. There is a modern edition of this pamphlet: *The Female Husband and Other Writings*, ed. Claude E. Jones (Liverpool: English Reprints Series, 1961).

10. See Ralph Straus, *The Unspeakable Curll* (London: Chapman, 1927), especially chap. 2.

11. Few of the augmented lives were so expensive or so encumbered with machinery as Curll's, but at least half a dozen works, usually priced at 6*d*. (as Fielding's was) or 1*s*., employ his tactics. Among them we may count productions with such titles as *An Authentick Account of the Life of Mr Charles Drew* (1740), or *The Case of Mr. Bartholomew Greenwood Submitted to the Publick* (1740), or *The Remarkable Case of William Bower of York, Convicted for the Robbery of Mr. Levit Harris* (1744).

12. *Betty Ireland*, at least, was nonetheless very popular. Stauffer, in the *Bibliographical Supplement* to his *Art of Biography*, reports (p. 117) that the work achieved as many as nine editions following its first. He has seen the fifth and ninth, neither of which is dated. In the Newberry Library, I have seen an 1888 reprint published in London by one S. Lee.

13. No less a figure than James Boswell himself admitted to a fascination with criminals, and one of the most poignant entries in his *London Journal* (ed. Frederick A. Pottle [New Haven: Yale University Press, 1950]) describes a hanging he had witnessed (Wednesday, May 4, 1764).

14. Starr develops this connection at some length in *Defoe and Spiritual Autobiography* (Princeton: Princeton University Press, 1965).

15. Aurélien Digeon, *The Novels of Fielding* (London: Routledge and Kegan Paul, 1925), p. 99.

16. Irwin's book, *The Making of Jonathan Wild: A Study in the Literary Method of Henry Fielding* (New York: Columbia University Press, 1941), provides a systematic account of the genesis of Fielding's work and its relationships with its literary

sources. *Jonathan Wild* was probably begun by 1738, though of course it was not published until it appeared in volume three of Fielding's *Miscellanies*, 1743. See Wilbur L. Cross, *The History of Henry Fielding* (New Haven: Yale University Press, 1918). Digeon, in *The Novels of Fielding*, p. 120, suggests that substantial portions of the book may have been drafted as early as 1737.

17. I might mention here that Irwin, in *The Making of Jonathan Wild* (p. 91), disallows the term *parody* to describe *Jonathan Wild*. Criminal biographies were invariably very short, he says, and a parody would have to approximate the length as well as other conventions of the type being ridiculed. It would be silly to quibble over this, but it is not true that criminal biographies were always short (*Gilbert Langley* runs to more than 90 finely printed pages); even if they had been, the "inflated" length of *Jonathan Wild*, a book of many purposes to be sure, would not disqualify it as calculated literary mockery of the major conventions of criminal biography. *Shamela*, we may remember, is always acknowledged a parody, though it does not at all approximate the length of *Pamela*.

18. In an interesting article of a few years ago, William J. Farrell argued convincingly that in his mockery of criminal biography Fielding actually adapted the established methods of panegyric biography to create a mock-heroic narrative. See "The Mock-Heroic Form of *Jonathan Wild*," *Modern Philology* 63 (1966): 216–26.

19. The ironic inversion upon an important contemporary moral idea of "greatness," as expressed by Richard Steele in *The Christian Hero* (1701), would have been obvious to many readers of the day. Fielding may well have taken Jonathan Wild as a likely vehicle for his parody of the genre of criminal biography because of the notoriety of the man, whose life had been written many times over, twice by Defoe, since his execution in 1725. As a thief-taker of power and skill, Wild was also a fit tool for political satire, and in the 1730s the Patriot Opposition to Walpole had made him a symbol of corrupt arbitrary power. Fielding very probably knew Defoe's biographies, and he surely knew the character of Wild as the Peachum of Gay's *Beggar's Opera* of 1728. See Irwin, *The Making of Jonathan Wild*, chap. 1, for fuller details. For a thorough, sound biographical treatment of Wild himself, see Gerald Howson, *Thief-Taker General: The Rise and Fall of Jonathan Wild* (London: Hutchinson, 1970).

20. Good nature, Fielding said in one of the *Champion* essays, is "a delight in the happiness of mankind, and a concern at their misery, with a desire, as much as possible, to procure the former, and avert the latter" (Henley Edition, 15:258). The quality of good nature is a natural endowment with which everyone may not be blessed, as Fielding explained in "An Essay on the Knowledge of the Characters of Men": people of identical background and opportunity may differ greatly from one another in such ways as could "hardly exist, unless the Distinction had some original Foundation in Nature itself. . . . This original Difference will, I think, alone account for that very early and strong Inclination to Good or Evil, which distinguishes different Dispositions in Children, in their first Infancy" (*Miscellanies*, vol. 1, ed. Henry Knight Miller [Wesleyan Edition], pp. 153–54).

21. Williams, in "Interpositions of Providence and the Design of Fielding's Novels," has argued that Fielding's Christian vision led him, in all of his comic novels, to incorporate providential intervention as a literary device and as a means of defining a formal system of rewards and punishments. In connection with Fielding's attitudes toward crime and criminals, it is especially worth recalling that he was the author of an illustrative pamphlet entitled *Examples of the Interposition of Providence in the Detection and Punishment of Murder* (1752).

22. Allan Wendt, in "The Moral Allegory of *Jonathan Wild*," *ELH* 24 (1957): 306–20, long ago demonstrated that Fielding's didactic strategy reflects principles laid down in the preface to the *Miscellanies*, displaying ethical extremes in Wild and Heartfree and suggesting a synthesis of the two (a kind of energetic goodness) as an ideal for human behavior. But in the course of his argument Wendt diminishes the activity of Heartfree much below what Fielding assigns to him. Digeon, in *The Novels of Fielding*, simply dismisses Heartfree as a "weak and theoretical figure" (p. 125).

23. Sherburn develops this subject at length in "Fielding's Social Outlook," *Philological Quarterly* 35 (1956): 1–23.

24. *Miscellanies*, 1:10.

25. Among them Lord Byron. See Digeon, *The Novels of Fielding*, p. 127.

26. *The Letters of Tobias Smollett*, ed. Lewis M. Knapp (Oxford: Clarendon Press, 1970), p. 6.

27. Paulson, *Satire and the Novel in Eighteenth-Century England*, p. 178.

28. It is worth remembering that Smollett's own translation of *Gil Blas* was published in October of 1748, only nine months after *Roderick Random*. Possibly he was working on his novel and his translation simultaneously. In any case, *Gil Blas* must have been much in his mind during those months of 1747 when he was writing *Roderick Random*.

29. The comments on *Roderick Random* and the picaresque included in this chapter repeat some of the arguments developed much more elaborately in my earlier article, "*Roderick Random:* The Picaresque Transformed," *College Literature* 6 (1979): 211–20. Critics have been debating the whole question of Smollett's adaptations from the picaresque for years. Robert Alter takes the view that *Roderick Random* starts out to be a strict picaresque novel, but aborts in the last one-third of its story; see "The Picaroon as Fortune's Plaything," in *Rogue's Progress: Studies in the Picaresque Novel* (Cambridge, Mass.: Harvard University Press, 1964). Richard Bjornson seems more sympathetic to Smollett's deliberate modifications of the picaresque; see "The Picaresque Hero as Young Nobleman: Victimization and Vindication in Smollett's *Roderick Random*," in *The Picaresque Hero in European Fiction* (Madison: University of Wisconsin Press, 1977). A number of people have recently argued, not always from the same grounds, against the appropriateness of calling *Roderick Random* a strictly picaresque novel. See, for example, Alice Green Fredman, "The Picaresque in Decline: Smollett's First Novel," in *English Writers of the Eighteenth Century*, ed. John H. Middendorf (New York: Columbia

University Press, 1971), pp. 189–207; the chapter on Smollett in Thomas R. Preston, *Not in Timon's Manner: Feeling, Misanthropy, and Satire in Eighteenth-Century England* (University: University of Alabama Press, 1975); and Paul-Gabriel Boucé, *The Novels of Tobias Smollett* (London: Longmans, 1976), chaps. 4 and 8.

30. Stevick, "Stylistic Energy in the Early Smollett," *Studies in Philology* 64 (1967): 714.

31. Alter, *Rogue's Progress*, p. 76.

32. The whole of *Roderick Random*, Smollett wrote to Alexander Carlyle in June of 1748, "was begun and finished in the Compass of Eight months, during which time several Intervals happened of one, two, three and four Weeks, wherein I did not set pen to paper, so that a little Incorrectness may be excused" (*Letters*, p. 8).

33. *Letters*, p. 98.

34. Preston, *Not in Timon's Manner*, p. 2.

35. It is important in this connection to notice that the entire movement of *Roderick Random*, from beginning to end, closely approximates a pattern aptly described by Ronald Paulson as characteristic of a great many novels of the period, and which Paulson (who, curiously, does not find the pattern in *Roderick Random*) prefers to call a "spiritual pilgrimage." The novelist's typical gesture was to

> send the hero out on his journey following a withdrawal from Eden: he may go of his own volition, as Crusoe and Clarissa and Rasselas do, denying their fathers or wanting to escape paradisal boredom; or he may be expelled as Tom Jones is. His journey then becomes an attempt to re-create—with Crusoe, literally to reconstruct—out of available materials that lost Eden; and as it turns out this was a fortunate fall in that it gives him an opportunity to make choices of his own, become a moral agent, prove and educate himself, and win for himself a "heaven" that would have been out of the question if he had remained in Eden.

See "The Pilgrimage and the Family: Structures in the Novels of Fielding and Smollett," in *Tobias Smollett: Bicentennial Essays Presented to Lewis M. Knapp*, ed. G. S. Rousseau and P.-G. Boucé (New York: Oxford University Press, 1971), p. 67.

Chapter V

1. Starr, *Defoe and Spiritual Autobiography*; Hunter, *The Reluctant Pilgrim: Defoe's Emblematic Method and Quest for Form in Robinson Crusoe* (Baltimore: Johns Hopkins University Press, 1966).

2. Nelson's *Journal*, though probably composed about 1749, may not have been published until 1810; see Stauffer, the *Bibliographical Supplement to The Art of Biography*, p. 178.

3. The quotation is from the Leeds edition of 1810, pp. 11–12.

4. See John A. Dussinger, "Richardson's Christian Vocation," *Papers in Language and Literature* 3 (1967): 3–19, for a discussion of some of the ways in which Richardson's work as a printer of numerous religious books encouraged his familiarity with contemporary homiletics and confessional literature.

5. See T. C. Duncan Eaves and Ben D. Kimpel, *Samuel Richardson: A Biography* (Oxford: Clarendon Press, 1971), p. 121.

6. *Selected Letters of Samuel Richardson*, p. 41.

7. Eaves and Kimpel, *Samuel Richardson*, p. 121.

8. The story of *Pamela*'s reception—the controversy as well as the enthusiasm—has been well and fully told. See especially Eaves and Kimpel, *Samuel Richardson*, chap. 7, and Bernard Kreissman, *Pamela-Shamela: A Study of the Criticisms, Burlesques, Parodies, and Adaptations of Richardson's Pamela* (Lincoln: University of Nebraska Press, 1960). It was of course *Pamela*, part one, that caused all the excitement and controversy; it is the novel in this original form that is my subject in these pages.

9. See Sale's article, "From *Pamela* to *Clarissa*," in *The Age of Johnson: Essays Presented to Chauncey Brewster Tinker*, ed. Frederick W. Hilles (New Haven: Yale University Press, 1949), pp. 127–38.

10. Eaves and Kimpel, *Samuel Richardson*, p. 545.

11. It is fortunately no longer necessary to apologize for Richardson's morality in *Pamela*. A good many recent scholars have revealed a genuine new sensitivity to this important dimension of his novel as it may be understood in the light of Richardson's own heritage, knowledge, and convictions. See especially Donald E. Morton, "Theme and Structure in *Pamela*," *Studies in the Novel* 3 (1971): 242–57; Stuart Wilson, "Richardson's *Pamela*: An Interpretation," *PMLA* 88 (1973): 79–91; Cynthia Wolff, *Samuel Richardson and the Eighteenth-Century Puritan Character* (Hamden, Conn.: Archon Books, 1972); Roger Sharrock, "Richardson's *Pamela*: The Gospel and the Novel," *Durham University Journal* 58 (1966): 67–74; and Michael Bell, "Pamela's Wedding and the Marriage of the Lamb," *Philological Quarterly* 49 (1970): 100–112.

12. Kearney, "Richardson's *Pamela*: the Aesthetic Case," *Review of English Literature* 7 (1966): 78–90; Brophy, *Samuel Richardson: The Triumph of Craft* (Knoxville: University of Tennessee Press, 1974); Doody, *A Natural Passion: A Study of the Novels of Samuel Richardson* (Oxford: Clarendon Press, 1974).

13. See, for example, p. 100; on p. 112, Mr. B. is described as taking great "Pains to do the Devil's Work."

14. This view of marriage was conventional among pious novelists, including Mrs. Aubin and Richardson. See Richetti, *Popular Fiction before Richardson*, pp. 256–59.

15. Even Richardson would not have argued for its moral realism, except in the context of metaphor. In a letter to his friend Frances Grainger he posed the

question, "Where shall we meet with an undepraved nature?" His answer was, "Nowhere" (*Selected Letters of Samuel Richardson*, p. 151).

16. See Doody's discussion of the novel in *A Natural Passion*.

17. *The Jacobite's Journal and Related Writings*, ed. William B. Coley (Wesleyan Edition), p. 119.

18. This famous letter is reprinted in full by Edward L. McAdam, Jr., in his article "A New Letter from Fielding," *Yale Review* 38 (1948): 300–310.

19. *Selected Letters of Samuel Richardson*, p. 83.

20. Dorothy Van Ghent, "On *Clarissa Harlowe*," in *The English Novel: Form and Function* (New York: Rinehart, 1953), p. 63. Van Ghent claims that Richardson's novel actually develops a "Clarissa-myth."

21. Quoted from Anna Seward, *Variety: A Collection of Essays* (London, 1788), in Eaves and Kimpel, *Samuel Richardson*, p. 338.

22. Eaves and Kimpel, *Samuel Richardson*, p. 287.

23. See Hill, "Clarissa Harlowe and Her Times"; and Sale, "From *Pamela* to *Clarissa*," in *The Age of Johnson*.

24. See Eaves and Kimpel, *Samuel Richardson*, p. 295.

25. Richardson's interest in the theater, and its influence on his work, has been thoroughly explored by Mark Kinhead-Weekes in *Samuel Richardson: Dramatic Novelist* (London: Methuen, 1973), and by Ira Konigsberg in *Samuel Richardson and the Dramatic Novel* (Lexington: University of Kentucky Press, 1968). John A. Dussinger, in an article called "Richardson's Tragic Muse," *Philological Quarterly* 46 (1967): 18–33, argues that Richardson wrote *Clarissa* from a specific conception of tragedy derived from Rapin and post-Restoration theory.

26. Karl Jaspers, *Tragedy Is Not Enough*, trans. Harald A. T. Reiche, Harry T. Moore, and Karl W. Deutsch (Hamden, Conn.: Archon Books, 1969), p. 41.

27. Van Ghent, "On *Clarissa Harlowe*," p. 55.

28. *Selected Letters of Samuel Richardson*, p. 83. Other readers besides myself, of course, have been ready to credit Richardson's claims that his work is a tragedy, though without remarking its transformations upon the conventions of contemporary pious biography. Besides the article by Dussinger, "Richardson's Tragic Muse," see Doody, *A Natural Passion*, pp. 99–127; William Park, "*Clarissa* As Tragedy," *Studies in English Literature, 1500–1900* 16 (1976): 461–71; and John Carroll, "Lovelace as Tragic Hero," *University of Toronto Quarterly* 42 (1972): 14–25. These discussions take different ground, but together they are very persuasive in their shared contention that the author of *Clarissa* was very deliberate in his conception and management of the tragic theme, plotting, and Christian vision of his great novel.

29. Doody, *A Natural Passion*, p. 152.

30. William J. Palmer, in an article entitled "Two Dramatists: Lovelace and Richardson in *Clarissa*," *Studies in the Novel* 5 (1973): 7–21, argues that Lovelace actually is a projection from Richardson's unconscious, and that therefore the

character and not the author is the "playwright" in control of the drama. This is a provocative and interesting suggestion, but it is just the kind of speculation about Richardson's psychological makeup by which modern criticism has occasionally diverted our attention away from the workings and the impact of the narrative itself.

Chapter VI

1. Chesterfield's letter was translated from the French by Ioan Williams, who reprinted it in his *Novel and Romance, 1700–1800: A Documentary Record* (New York: Barnes and Noble, 1970), pp. 100–101.

2. A second edition was published in 1729, and advertised again in 1740 by the bookseller Osborn.

3. The 1746 and 1747 editions (the latter published in Dublin) appeared under the altered master title *Instructive and Entertaining Novels*. Of the twelve tales collected in the original *Novelas ejemplares*, only the six dealing specifically in love and intrigue were well known in England before 1750. The remaining stories are non-amorous, sometimes quasi-picaresque narratives.

4. A Curll production entitled *Iberian Tales and Novels*, "By the Lady Donna Isabella" (1745); a volume called *Novellas Espannolas; or, Moral and Entertaining Novels* (1747).

5. George Frisbie Whicher, Mrs. Haywood's only modern biographer, reports that *Love in Excess* ran through "no less than six separate editions before its inclusion in her collected 'Secret Histories, Novels, and Poems' in 1725." See *The Life and Romances of Mrs. Eliza Haywood* (New York: Columbia University Press, 1915), p. 12.

6. In the 1740s Mrs. Haywood's own *Secret Histories, Novels, and Poems* (1725) reappeared once (in 1742), but otherwise the decade featured remarkably few new or reprinted novels of the kind she made popular in the 1720s. Among these we may include John Cleland's very skillful pornographic adaptation *Fanny Hill; or, Memoirs of a Woman of Pleasure* (1748–49).

7. *The Accomplish'd Rake* was not reprinted at all until 1756. *The Reform'd Coquet* and *Lindamira* had slightly more favored careers, and reached fifth editions in 1744 and 1745, respectively. For an important discussion of Mrs. Davys's work see William H. McBurney, "Mrs. Mary Davys: Forerunner of Fielding," *PMLA* 74 (1959): 348–55.

8. For full discussion of Mrs. Rowe's life and achievement, see Richetti, *Popular Fiction before Richardson*, pp. 239–62.

9. William H. McBurney, "Mrs. Penelope Aubin and the Early Eighteenth-Century English Novel," *Huntington Library Quarterly* 21 (1957): 256. See the entire article (pp. 245–67) for a very detailed treatment of Aubin's work. See also Richetti, *Popular Fiction before Richardson*, pp. 211–39.

10. See, for instance, Helen Sard Hughes, "Translations of the Vie de Marianne and their Relation to Contemporary English Fiction," *Modern Philology* 15 (1917): 491–512; James R. Foster, "The Abbé Prevost and the English Novel," *PMLA* 42 (1927): 443–64. See also the longer studies by Foster, *History of the Pre-Romantic Novel in England* (New York: MLA, 1949), especially chaps. 2–5; and F. C. Green, *Minuet: A Critical Survey of French and English Literary Ideas in the Eighteenth Century* (New York: Dutton, 1935).

11. For full discussion of this important aspect of Mrs. Collyer's work see Helen Sard Hughes, "An Early Romantic Novel," *JEGP* 15 (1916): 564–98.

12. See Whicher, *The Life and Romances of Mrs. Eliza Haywood*, chaps. 5–6.

13. Fielding's burlesque was published in April 1741, Mrs. Haywood's in July. Besides the almost half-a-dozen separate novels of her later years, Mrs. Haywood also produced her periodicals *The Female Spectator* (1744–46) and *The Parrot* (1747), both of which were devoted largely to fiction; a *vade mecum* for servant girls, issued in the wake of *Pamela*, called *A Present for a Servant-Maid* (1743; later editions in 1744 and 1745); and a book of narrative sketches entitled *Epistles for the Ladies* (1749, and several subsequent editions).

14. Ed. Malcolm Kelsall (London: Oxford University Press, 1969). Sarah Fielding's other works of the 1740s are less well known. One, called *Familiar Letters between the Principal Characters in David Simple* (1747), is a miscellaneous gathering of essays and short epistolary tales having little to do with the novel; its only real claim on our interest is that its preface and several of the letters (40–44) were written by Henry Fielding. One other work, *The Governess; or, The Little Female Academy* (1749, two editions; and at least five more by 1789), was actually the most popular thing Sarah Fielding ever wrote, but it is hardly relevant here since it is a group of moral fairy tales mainly for children and adolescents, cast into the form of an "educational" novel. It is among the first things of its kind, however, and as such has justified a modern edition in facsimile, with an introduction by Jill E. Grey (London: Oxford University Press, 1968).

Chapter VII

1. Robert Alter, *Fielding and the Nature of the Novel* (Cambridge, Mass.: Harvard University Press, 1968), p. 30.

2. In 1740 Cibber published his autobiography, *An Apology for the Life of Mr. Colley Cibber, Comedian*, while Middleton issued his *Life of Cicero*. These two authors, whose names are reflected unmistakably in the "Conny Keyber" of *Shamela*, Fielding regarded as outrageous maligners of truth. For the fullest and most authoritative discussion of the targets and devices of Fielding's parodic strategies, see Eric Rothstein, "The Framework of *Shamela*," *ELH* 35 (1968): 381–402. See also Hunter, *Occasional Form*, chap. 4.

3. Robert Alan Donovan, *The Shaping Vision: Imagination in the English Novel*

from Defoe to Dickens (Ithaca, N.Y.: Cornell University Press, 1966); Hunter, *Occasional Form.*

4. Donovan is particularly provocative and enlightening on this subject. But he goes too far, I think, in his argument that *Joseph Andrews* is designed entirely with the intention of systematically emphasizing Fielding's differences with Richardson in moral vision, and in his conclusion that the novel achieves its comic intensity and even its coherence and originality by the artful ingenuity of its sophisticated contrapuntal play with *Pamela.*

5. The "author-narrator of *Tom Jones*," says Martin C. Battestin in explanation of Fielding's design in that book, appears "in relation to the world of his novel as the divine Author and His Providence to the 'Book of Creation.'" The same, we may say, is true of the "author-narrator" of *Joseph Andrews*. See *The Providence of Wit*, p. 143.

6. Mark Spilka, "Comic Resolution in Fielding's *Joseph Andrews*," *College English* 15 (1953): 11–19.

7. Roger L. Cox, "The Structure of Comedy," *Thought* 50 (1975): 82.

8. Donovan, *The Shaping Vision*, p. 75.

9. According to the contemporary accounts of William Strahan, *Clarissa*—itself an unusually popular work—had sold some 3,000 copies by January of 1751, but 10,000 copies of *Tom Jones* were required within a year of its publication early in 1749. See *Selected Letters of Samuel Richardson*, p. 86 (n.76). Ronald Paulson and Thomas Lockwood, in their volume *Henry Fielding* in the Critical Heritage series (London: Routledge and Kegan Paul, 1969), provide a fairly complete record of early reactions to Fielding's work. The progress of Fielding's early reputation has, of course, been exhaustively described by Frederic T. Blanchard in *Fielding the Novelist: A Study in Historical Criticism* (New Haven: Yale University Press, 1926).

10. *Tom Jones* was begun possibly as early as 1745, and so we certainly cannot say that Fielding started out with any intention of reacting to *Clarissa*. The very real instances of his responses to Richardson's new work cannot be assigned to any particular phase of his composition, though at least some of them must have been introduced very late, since *Clarissa* itself was not complete in its published form until the fall of 1748. For a good summary account of the relatively little that we know about the stages of Fielding's composition of *Tom Jones*, see the introduction by Martin C. Battestin to the Wesleyan Edition of the novel.

11. Howard Anderson, "Answers to the Author of *Clarissa*: Theme and Narrative Technique in *Tom Jones* and *Tristram Shandy*," *Philological Quarterly* 51 (1972): 862.

12. Battestin, *The Providence of Wit*, pp. 165–66.

13. Fred Kaplan has interestingly argued that the prefatory chapters of *Tom Jones* are actually almost autonomous as a separate plot whose subject is the composition of the novel; see "Fielding's Novel about Novels: The 'Prefaces' and the 'Plot' of *Tom Jones*," *Studies in English Literature, 1500–1900* 13 (1973): 535–49. This is a provocative suggestion which, however, has the unintentional effect of frac-

turing the carefully wrought unity between Fielding's story and his own presence as author-narrator.

14. Wolfgang Iser, "The Role of the Reader in Fielding's *Joseph Andrews* and *Tom Jones*," in *The Implied Reader: Patterns of Communication in Prose Fiction from Bunyan to Beckett* (Baltimore: Johns Hopkins University Press, 1974), pp. 29–56; John Preston, "*Tom Jones* (i): Plot as Irony" and "*Tom Jones* (ii): The Pursuit of True Judgment," in *The Created Self: The Reader's Role in Eighteenth-Century Fiction* (London: Heinemann, 1970), pp. 94–132.

15. See Martin C. Battestin, "*Tom Jones* and 'His *Egyptian* Majesty': Fielding's Parable of Government," *PMLA* 82 (1967): 68–77.

16. In *The Created Self*, Preston mounts an energetic argument that we should not take Fielding's pose as ruler of his "great Creation" very seriously, or rather that we should understand it as ironic—as an attempt to "discredit the narrator, and, in the process, to make fun . . . of the pretentions of the plot" (p. 100). Preston is not the only critic to raise such issues. The trouble with his ingenious analysis is that it deflects attention away from the narrator's role as benevolent manipulator and therefore denies something absolutely essential to the comedy of *Tom Jones*.

17. Ronald Paulson, "Fielding in *Tom Jones*: The Historian, the Poet, and the Mythologist," in *Augustan Worlds: Essays in Honour of A. R. Humphreys*, ed. J. C. Hilson et al. (Leicester: Leicester University Press, 1977), pp. 175–87.

18. Anthony Kearney, "*Tom Jones* and the Forty-Five," *Ariel: A Review of International English Literature* 4 (1973): 68–78.

19. In *A Dialogue between a Gentleman of London . . . and an Honest Alderman of the Country Party* (1747) Fielding referred to the 1701 Act of Parliament which settled the disposal of the English crown once and for all. According to the act, once William, Princess Anne, and their direct issue had exhausted their line, succession was to be limited to the descendants of the Electress of Hanover, whose name was Sophia. The irony of the landlord's mistake is doubled by this fact, while the very name of Fielding's heroine serves political as well as thematic ends. See *The Jacobite's Journal and Related Writings*, p. 12.

20. For a contrary and fairly influential view of Fielding's uses of Jacobitism see Thomas Cleary, "Jacobitism in *Tom Jones*: The Basis for an Hypothesis," *Philological Quarterly* 52 (1973): 238–51. This essay points to the high frequency of allusions to the 'Forty-Five in the middle six books of Fielding's novel (as compared with the relative scarcity of explicit references in the other twelve books) and speculates that these may have been hastily added for their topical value while the author was simultaneously at work on the *Jacobite's Journal*. As a partial suggestion about the composition of *Tom Jones* the argument is interesting and useful, but it is finally somewhat misleading because it ignores the degree to which Fielding deliberately exploits the idea of Jacobitism throughout his novel, for a variety of thematic and aesthetic purposes.

Index

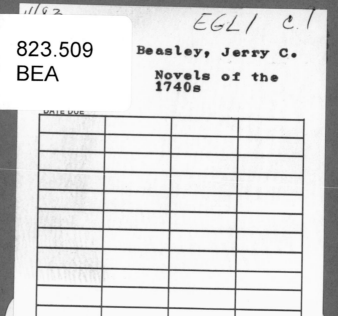